P9-BJO-028

THE STORY OF CIVILIZATION

MAN'S PAST AND PROGRESS

THE STORY OF CIVILIZATION

The International Pictorial Treasury of Knowledge

INTERNATIONAL GRAPHIC SOCIETY
ENGLEWOOD CLIFFS, NEW JERSEY

Contents

Introduction

by Professor C. M. MacInnes, C.B.E., M.A., LL.D.

In our scientific age we are so obsessed by our great technological triumphs, our inventions, and our incursions into space that we have little time left to devote to other aspects of man's life here on earth. Yet our knowledge of people and our relations with them are of far greater importance than landing on the moon. If we fail to solve the great ideological, ethnological, economic, and political problems that now confront us, our newly won mastery over natural forces, the remarkable inventive ingenuity and the daring explorations of the universe will be of little value to us. Indeed, unless there is greater understanding and sympathy between us, our very successes may turn out to be the causes of our undoing.

If such a catastrophe is to be avoided we must all try to discover how the peoples of the world can overcome the obstacles that now divide them and be induced to live together in peace. This search for a better understanding, must not be left only to the philosophers, statesmen, and priests, for it is the concern of all men everywhere.

In the past it was possible for one group to live in isolation from the other. Oceans, mountains, deserts and sometimes even superstitions kept them apart and in ignorance of each other. Thus, the Chinese could live their own lives, build up their own civilization, cut off from all other peoples whom they disdainfully regarded as "foreign devils." For centuries Japan was quite content to dwell in isolation, withdrawn from the rest of the world; Africa was the "Dark Continent" that others passed by, except when they wanted slaves; while the Americas, shut off from the rest of the world by two impassable oceans, were unknown.

Today these things are no longer possible. The ship, the cable, the railroad, the automobile, the airplane, radio, and television have put an end to such isolation and have broken down physical barriers that formerly divided people from people. Modern China is now a great world power that seeks to dominate other countries and to extend its influence everywhere. Japan has long since thrown aside its veil and now from her crowded homeland regards the most distant countries as her potential markets. Africa's period of servitude is over; it is vibrant with a new life and its peoples are determined not only to be free but to play their full part in the world of the future. The Americas, whose existence was unknown or only vaguely suspected a few centuries ago, now contain some of the most progressive, wealthy, and powerful nations on earth. A constant jostling and intermingling of the races is proceeding such as was never before seen; the lines which divide one people from another are becoming more and more blurred and it is certain that these processes will grow more marked. It is therefore obvious that the different nations and groups of the world must learn to compose the petty squabbles that now divide them. If they persist in deadly warfare they are clearly unfit to colonize the stars.

In the past it was quite natural for one people to regard all others as inferiors merely because they were different. Sometimes, indeed, they denied that these others had the right to be different and they tried to force their own culture and way of life on the nations that they conquered. There is no place, however, in the modern world for arrogance of this kind; it is not only unreasonable, it is very dangerous. Differences in culture, beliefs, and in the way of life must be accepted by us all as inevitable and, indeed, desirable, for they make for the enrichment of all mankind. The world would be unbelievably dull if all people everywhere were alike. Some peoples are richly endowed in particular ways, others in different ones, and it is to be hoped that, despite the mingling of the races, such differences will continue. Isolation, however, has gone forever, and we must look upon the world in which we live with this indisputable fact clearly in mind.

Many factors have combined to produce the differences between one people and another, such as a country's climate, its physical features, and its natural resources. Even when we accept the fact that geographical factors may cause differences between people, we have not yet gone very far towards the goal of understanding. It is necessary that we should know more about the people themselves and to do this we should know something about their history.

Henry Ford once declared: "History is bunk," an opinion, it may be said, with which not everyone will disagree. A moment's reflection, however, will show that the great man himself was talking the most arrant "bunk," to use his own inelegant terminology, when he made that remark. Thus, when Ford, or any other great industrial organization, wishes to open up a new market in a distant country, his agent tries first to discover what sort of people he will be called upon to deal with. He does not proceed very far in his investigation, however, before he decides that he must learn something about their background and who their fathers were—in other words, he studies their history.

Racial understanding and cooperation is not as easy as it may seem on the surface, for differences do exist. Often, those that are the least evident are the most significant. Even when we understand that other peoples have the same senses, affections, and passions as ourselves; that, like us, they will bleed if pricked; that they will laugh if they are tickled and die if they are poisoned, there are still many more things to be known if true understanding is to be established. Europeans, Africans, Asians, and the rest must not assume that because they have so much in common they are therefore identical, for this will lead them into serious misunderstanding and estrangement. Everyone who has had any experience of trying to bridge the gulf which separates one people from another must have found, sooner or later, that suddenly and without any apparent reason, a misconception has arisen and he has insulted his friend. To dismiss such crises as trivial or caused by unreasonable sensitivity on the part of the other person will merely make the situation worse. Sometimes these differences can be explained, in part at least, by the past history of a people—because they conquered, or had been conquered by, someone else. Here, a little learning is certainly not a dangerous thing. Indeed, on the contrary, it can be a very great advantage. Some knowledge, even of the most rudimentary nature, of the past successes and failures of other peoples, their culture and their beliefs, will help us to understand their point of view and why they regard us in a particular way. Thus, if for no other reason, the reading of history is an activity in which every sensible man and woman should engage.

To understand how great civilizations have grown to maturity and disappeared is not without value for an age that tends to be rather too satisfied with its own material achievements. A closer acquaintance with the great men of the past whose lives and work have affected succeeding ages can bring inspiration to men and women who live in this changing world. The accumulated wisdom and experience of the past is the heritage of all mankind, and the study of history can provide the key to this rich storehouse. Greater familiarity with the arts, the philosophies, and the literatures of the past will enrich our lives and widen our sympathies. If we wish to do so, we can profit by the experience, the disasters, and the triumphs of other peoples in other times and learn from them how we may battle with at least some of the problems that face us. Though history does not repeat itself, it is certain that in past ages things have happened in consequence of human frailty or virtue which are similar to what is going on today.

The plain citizen is far too occupied with the ordinary affairs of life to be able to devote as much time as he would wish to reading history, yet it is desirable, as I have tried to show, that he should have some acquaintance with this subject. Obviously he cannot possibly master the whole, long and tangled story of mankind through the ages and, indeed, few, if any, professional historians would claim to do so. Many of them, in fact, are doing their utmost to go in the opposite direction. They look upon the broad view of history with repugnance. It is superficial, they say, and bound to be inaccurate. So they spend their time trying to learn more and more about less and less. The man who knows all about what happened in a particular place on a particular day or year is acclaimed to be a great scholar, while the one who tries to see human history as a whole is dismissed as a mere dabbler. But for the majority of us it is really of very little consequence how many petticoats a long-forgotten princess, who died at the age of three, had on her second birthday. Nor does it really matter a great deal what King Harold had for breakfast the day he fell at Hastings. The specialist is essential in historical investigation, but there is also a place in Clio's temple for the historian who looks at history as a whole. The books which he writes are necessary if the ordinary citizen is to be given a general view of man's story, and this is desirable if he is to understand the point of view of other peoples and how the complex problems of his own age have arisen. Such a book, if it is to be of any use to busy people, must be free of pedantry and all the paraphernalia of self-conscious scholarship, and it must be written in a manner that the average man can understand.

This book is in some respects an exhilarating gallop through the ages and, in order that the rider may have a clearer view of the country through which he passes, it is voluminously illustrated. It is not meant for the fastidious specialist, but it is hoped that it will enable busy men and women to have a sounder comprehension of the international and interracial conflicts of our time and stimulate them to read more about other civilizations and other times in more specialized works.

How Far Back Does History Go?

No man could sit down today and write an absolutely full account of everything he did and saw yesterday. He has already forgotten countless small things. Maybe he traveled to work by bus. While on the bus he noticed a stout woman who had to fumble in a large purse for change and a small boy whose school bag kept coming undone. But the chances are that he has forgotten both of them by now, and in any case he would not dream of including them in his account of his day's activities. Again, although he read the evening paper with interest he has certainly forgotten most of the minor news items by now.

In fact, however painstaking he is, we shall get no more from him than a list of what he considers the most interesting things he has done. We shall not even get a list of the things *we* consider most interesting. For instance, if the man is a plumber he may record that he repaired two joints during the day. *We* should like to know exactly how he did it, but he has done the job so often that he has forgotten how interesting it might be to us, and so he says nothing about it.

Most people of long ago who wrote accounts of their lives and the events of their times worked in the same way. They left out everything they considered dull and simply recorded what they believed to be most important. So even the best written accounts are never complete. Fortunately we can often fill in the gaps by finding the things that the writers, and other people of their times, actually used. For instance, we read in the Bible that David drew his sword and cut off a Philistine's head, but we are not told what the sword looked like, what it was made of, or how big it was. But archaeologists have now dug up swords made in and around Palestine at the time of David, and so we have a very good idea of what it was really like.

So there are two ways of learning about the past: by reading written records and by unearthing the things that people actually made and used. Tools, weapons and buildings may last many thousands of years, and when found they may tell us something about people who lived long before writing began. But real history begins only with the first written records. From then onwards we rely on both records and remains.

The pictures opposite show how long man has existed and how far back real history goes. The strips in the middle show roughly how long the great Ice Ages lasted. The first (near the bottom) began about 600,000 years ago and ended about 550,000 years ago. The fourth (near the top) began about 118,000 years ago and did not end completely until about 10,000 B.C. Men, though not like those we know today, lived on the Earth as far back as the end of the first Ice Age, and we know a little about them from the remains of the things they made and from the remains of their own bones. We know rather more about the men who lived during and shortly after the fourth Ice Age because far more remains have been found.

But only people who lived since about 4,000 B.C. have left any written records, and it is only their history which we can really claim to know reasonably well.

The bottom left-hand picture shows the skull of a man who lived in South Africa far more than half a million years ago. The silhouette compares the skull to that of a modern man. Above it is the skull of a slightly later man who lived in Java, and at the top is a Neanderthal man, who lived in Europe about 150,000 years ago. Modern man, *Homo sapiens recens*, first appeared much later than that, and history deals mainly with his activities over only the past 6,000 years.

CENTER: *The four Ice Ages from the dawn of history until 4000 B.C. (brown line) The red line denotes, on same scale, the Christian era's duration compared with that of preceding ages.* LEFT: *Three types of early men (from bottom to top) Australopithecus africanus, Homo erectus erectus, and Neanderthal man.* RIGHT: *The Venus of Willendorf, an early work of modern man; ancient Chinese cave dwelling; map showing where prehistoric men lived (for color guide see accompanying illustrations).*

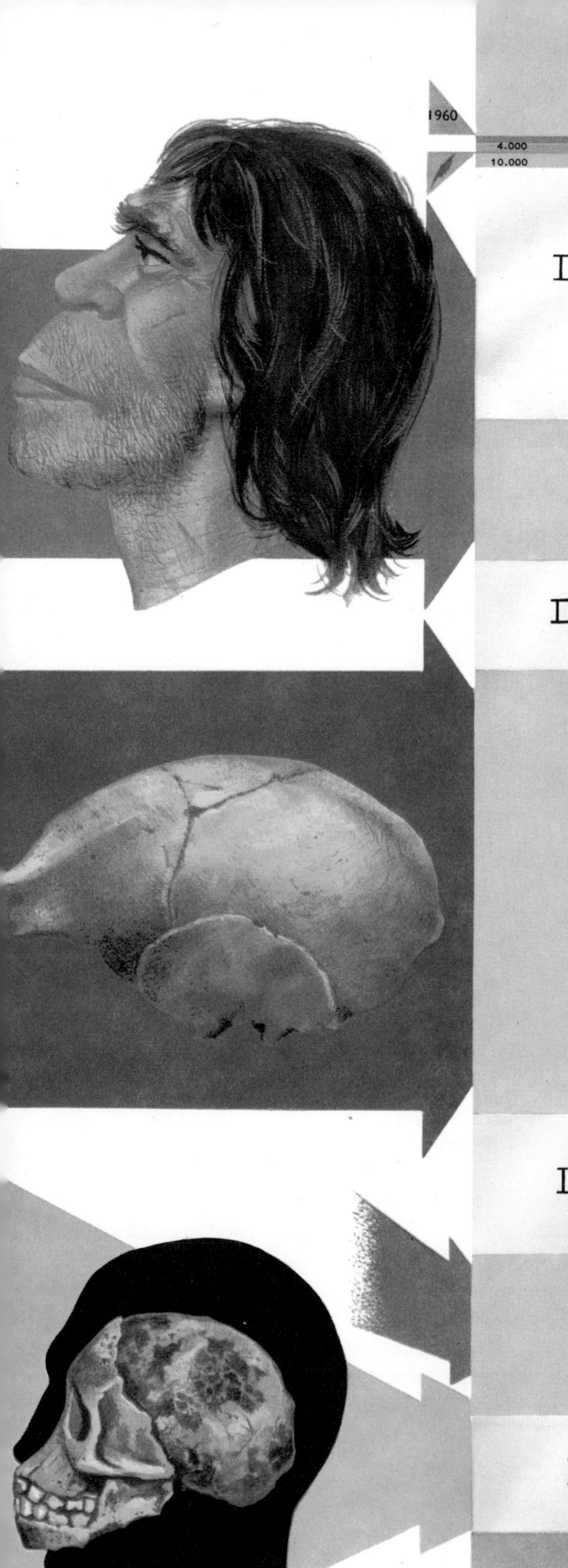

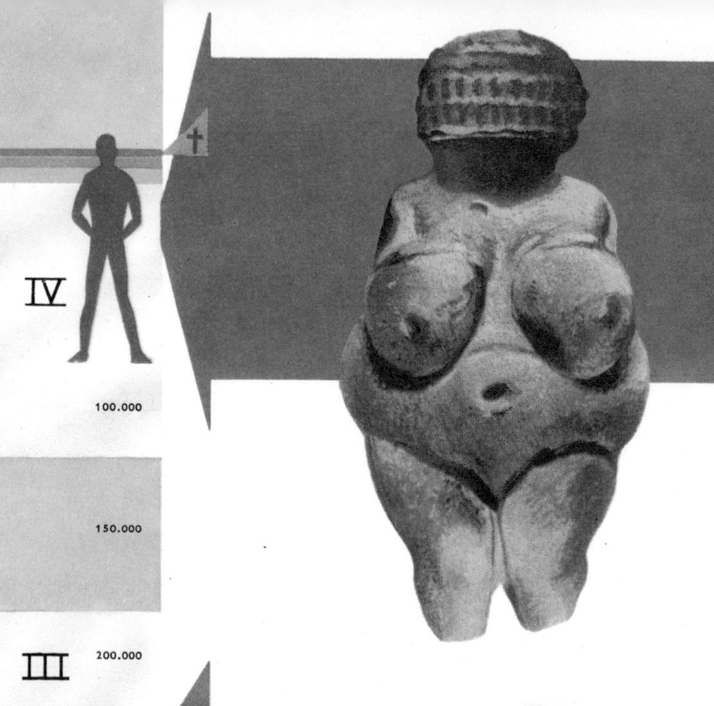

1960

4.000

10.000

IV

100.000

150.000

200.000

III

250.000

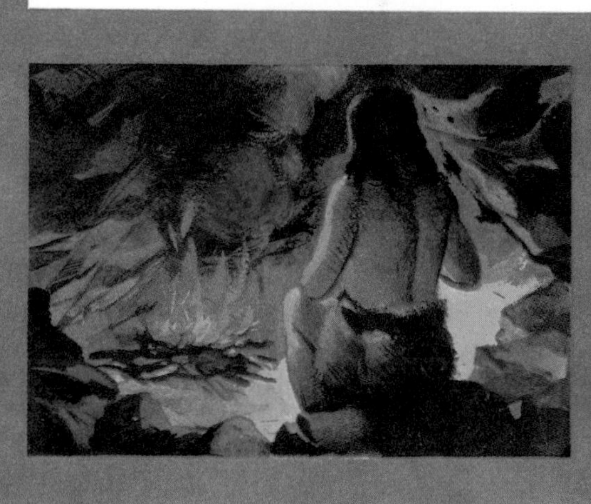

400.000

II

450.000

500.000

550.000

I

600.000

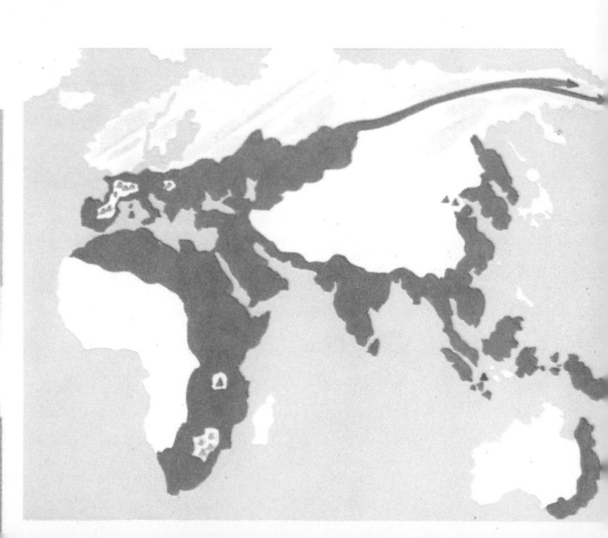

The "Land Between the Rivers"

PERHAPS the first people on Earth to keep written records were the Sumerians, who settled in the southern part of Mesopotamia, the "Land between the Rivers."

The Sumerians probably migrated to Mesopotamia from the southeast in the 5th millenium B.C. Their earliest writing was in the form of simple pictures, and each picture represented a different idea. Very slowly, over many centuries, other settlers in Mesopotamia changed this system and used each picture to stand for a sound—usually for a syllable—in their own languages. Sometimes these writings were carved on stone, but more often they were impressed on soft clay with a wedge-shaped tool, and the clay tablets were later baked hard to preserve them. Writings of this kind are called cuneiform, which simply means wedge-shaped.

The Sumerians and other early dwellers in Mesopotamia left not only written records but also whole cities which, in the course of many years, became deeply buried under sand and dust, and which archaeologists have now unearthed. Records and remains together give us a vivid picture of how these people lived. We know that their huge temples called ziggurats and shaped rather like step-pyramids, were not only centers of worship and sacrifice, but also centers of arts and crafts, and sometimes hospitals as well. We know from some of their beautiful mosaic pictures that they were able to weave cloth, harness asses, build wheeled chariots, and tend flocks and herds. We know, too, that they kept account of the years of the kings' reigns and recorded the outcome of battles.

During the three thousand years of Mesopotamia's greatness, from about 3500 B.C. on, there were, indeed, many battles and many invasions to record. The small map opposite helps us to follow some of these events. The patch of sea at the west of the map is the eastern Mediterranean (marked M), and the other patch, in the southeast, is the northern tip of the Persian Gulf (P). The Euphrates is marked E and the Tigris T.

The remaining letters on the map mark the sites of important cities of early times. Two cities which served at different times as Sumerian capitals were Ur (marked U_1) and Uruk, or Erech (U_2). Ur, once the home of Abraham, is mentioned in the Book of Genesis, where it is called Ur of the Chaldees. Erech is the place where some of the oldest picture-writing in the world was made.

In the 4th millenium B.C., Akkadian tribes from Arabia invaded the land. Centuries later, about 2600 B.C., the Akkadian king, Sargon I, founded a powerful dynasty. The Akkadians settled well to the north of the Sumerians, but in time they took control of several Sumerian cities including Lagash (L). After yet another invasion, by the Amorites, a semitic people akin to the Arabs and the Jews, one of the greatest kings of early times reigned over a great part of Mesopotamia. He was Hammurabi, the lawgiver, a man whose laws were just but harsh, a man who believed in an eye for an eye and a tooth for a tooth. He made Babylon (B) his capital city.

Babylon was invaded and sacked by Hittite invaders from Asia Minor about 1800 B.C., and for several centuries it lost much of its grandeur. From 1400 B.C. onwards the Assyrians, the men of Ashur (A), became more and more powerful and the two cities of Ashur and Nineveh (N) came into ever greater prominence. Babylon had a final burst of splendor under King Nebuchadnezzar II (604-562 B.C.), but by then other civilizations were already beginning to overshadow that of Mesopotamia.

A king of Babylon watches a sculptor making a cuneiform inscription. The frieze is a relic of Sumerian times; the statue in the corner dates from about 2000 B.C. Map shows sites of ancient cities.

N
E
A
T
B
L
U I
U 2
P
P

The Kingdom of the Pharaohs

IN early Sumerian times civilization was taking shape a thousand miles to the west, by the River Nile. At first Egypt consisted of many provinces, called nomes, each largely independent. But in time these joined together to form two main states, Lower Egypt to the north and Upper Egypt to the south. Eventually, following a war waged about 3400 B.C., the two states merged into one mighty kingdom, with its capital at Memphis.

From about 2800 B.C. to the time of Julius Caesar, no less than thirty lines of Pharaohs ruled over the land. Most of them were regarded by their people not only as kings but also as gods. Under their sway arts, crafts, building, and science flourished.

The main picture opposite shows Egyptian paintings, writings, statues, furnishings and art treasures made at different periods of Egypt's long history. Most of the things in the foreground were found in 1922, when Howard Carter opened the long-sealed tomb of the boy-Pharaoh Tutankhamen. Tutankhamen, son-in-law of one of the greatest of all the Pharaohs, Akhnaton, was not himself an important king. He reigned for only a few years and died about 1350 B.C., aged eighteen. Yet his body, marvelously embalmed, was concealed in three coffins, one inside another. The inner one, massive and tremendously heavy, was of solid gold. In the shrine beside it were statues, model ships, furniture, boxes, jewels, vases, a throne, and a scepter.

Around the walls in our picture are paintings of men and gods, and a representation of a princess. In the background is a picture of Akhnaton and his queen, Nefertiti. Akhnaton, sometimes known as Amenhotep IV, made a valiant attempt to abolish the old religion of Egypt, with its worship of many gods, and to introduce a new religion in which only one god, Aton the Sun, should be worshipped as the origin of all life. The change lasted a few years, for under the weak rule of Tutankhamen the priests brought back the old gods.

The picture-writing, or hieroglyphs, shown opposite remained a mystery to historians until 1799. Then specialists serving in Napoleon's army in Egypt found the Rosetta Stone, which carried the same inscription in Greek, hieroglyphic, and another kind of Egyptian writing. They knew Greek, and could thus begin to decipher the hieroglyphic characters. Today, from hieroglyphics written on rolls of papyrus, we know something of Egyptian progress in science. We know that astronomer-priests worked out the length of the year accurately, that they knew the times of the rising and setting of many stars throughout the seasons, and that they could forecast the vital Nile floods.

The Egyptians' mastery of architecture declares itself in the many wonderful buildings that still remain. The step-pyramid at Sakkara, designed by Imhotep during the fourth dynasty, is one of the world's first large buildings in stone. The great pyramids near Gizeh are still among the vastest of all man-made things. The tall columns of the temples at Luxor and Karnak are still wonders of world architecture.

From about 1790 to 1600 B.C., Egypt was under the heel of the Hyksos, a powerful race of nomads. Yet a century or so after, the Egyptians had driven out the Hyksos and embarked on conquests of their own, extending their sway southward into what is now the Sudan and eastward to the Euphrates. Not until 332 B.C. did Egypt's power almost completely decline. Then Alexander the Great conquered the land and set up a line of puppet kings, the Ptolemies. The last of Egypt's royal personages was Cleopatra. When she died in 31 B.C., three thousand years of Egyptian royal history ended.

TOP: *Egyptian art treasures and writings.* BELOW: *Cross-section through pyramid, map of ancient Egypt, and interior of a royal burial chamber.*

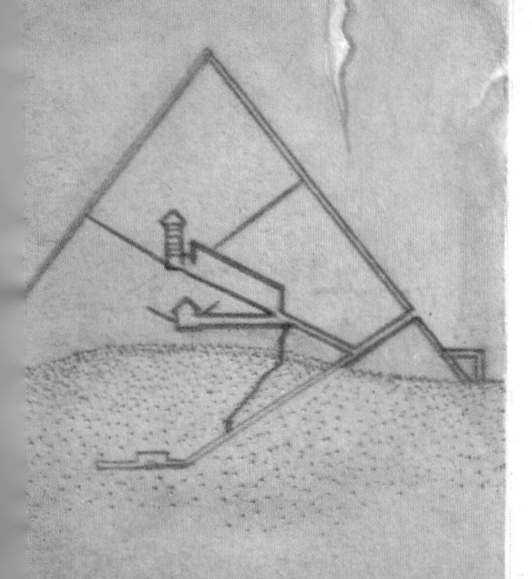

SAIS
PELUSIUM
GISEH
MEMPHIS
HELIOPOLIS
SINAI
HERMOPOLIS
AMARNA
SIUT
THIS
ABYDOS
KARNAK
THEBE
LUKSOR

Early Civilization in China

WHILE the civilizations of Mesopotamia and Egypt were still in their infancy, two others were developing in Asia. One had its beginnings around the valley of the River Indus, the other around the Hwang-Ho, or Yellow River, of northern China. Over many centuries the way of life developed near the Indus spread peacefully over the whole of India, then into Burma, Indo-China, Java and Sumatra. The civilization of the Yellow River pushed its way, mainly by conquest, over the whole vast extent of what is now China.

Modern evidence indicates that Chinese civilization, though ancient, is scarcely as old as that of Mesopotamia or of Egypt. During what is sometimes called the Golden Age of China (about 2800 to 2100 B.C.), the civilization of the Hwang-Ho was confined to a comparatively small area—roughly the area that would be covered by laying a quarter on the map opposite with its top just touching the point marked P (Peking). Much later, from about 1120 to 250 B.C., the emperors of the Chou dynasty made their headquarters in Honan, immediately to the south of the Hwang-Ho. Many of these emperors were not strong rulers, and exercised their power only with the help of religious orders and feudal lordlings. Even so, they did gradually extend the influence of Chinese civilization southward and westward. But in time the feudal vassals began to war among themselves, each attempting to gain more power and influence, and it was this struggle that brought about the downfall of the dynasty.

In 246 B.C. Ch'in-Shih-Huang-Ti, perhaps the most powerful of all the emperors of China, came to the throne. At the time of his accession he was only thirteen years of age, and he was only forty-eight when he died. But in the thirty-five years of his reign he succeeded first in quelling civil war within his domain and next in extending the boundaries of China northward into the wastes of Manchuria beyond Mukden (M), and southward as far as the Si-Kiang, within tropical latitudes.

He was said to have the voice of a jackal, the cunning of a wolf and the ferocity of a tiger. We know, too, that he was a tyrant and a despoiler. He ordered the destruction of all books to help obliterate the last traces of feudalism. He held a notorious trial which resulted in the execution of more than four hundred intellectuals. Whenever his armies conquered a city he carried off whatever art treasures were found. So well aware was he of the hatred he aroused that he took extraordinary precautions to avoid assassination. In his capital city of Hien-Yang he had more than three hundred palaces built, all joined by underground passages, so that he could move secretly from one to another without anyone knowing his whereabouts in advance.

Yet he was a man of great achievements, and not without virtues. It was he who ordered the building of the Great Wall of China as a safeguard against Mongolian invasions. When complete, this wall, marked on the map opposite, was 20 feet wide, 25 feet high and about 1500 miles long. Scattered over its great length were many thousands of massive watchtowers. Though Ch'in-Shih-Huang-Ti hated trade and did all in his power to discourage it, he used every effort to give agriculture the highest place in China's economy. He also brought about a uniform system of weights and measures throughout his Empire.

By the close of his reign the Chinese were already using several important techniques which, some soon, some later, found their way to the Western World. They already knew of the magnetic needle, which gave us our mariner's compass; they could make gunpowder and fireworks; paper-making had probably begun; and lock-gates for canals, one of the marvels of early engineering, were already in widespread use.

TOP: *Ch'in-Shih-Huang-Ti views the building of the Great Wall.* BOTTOM: *Map showing line of finished wall.* (P — *Peking;* M — *Mukden;* L — *Lan-Chou;* Y — *Yellow Sea;* J — *Sea of Japan.)*

GOBI
M
P
L

Ancient Cities of the Indus

THE picture on the previous page showed a scene set in China more than two hundred years before the time of Christ. The pictures opposite are reconstructions of scenes in Indian cities about 2000 B.C.

The people responsible for the early stages of Indian civilization, from about 2500 to 1500 B.C., were the Dravidians, short people with rounded foreheads, light to dark brown skin, slightly receding chins, and moderately full lips. The men usually wore short beards. In recent years Indian archaeologists have excavated two important cites that these people built on the banks of the River Indus. The sites of these ancient cities, Mohenjo-Daro and Harappa, are shown on the map opposite, in relation to the site of the great modern city of Karachi.

Both Mohenjo-Daro and Harappa were models of careful town-planning. The principal streets all ran in straight lines either from north to south or from east to west, and in places the main roads were thirty feet wide so that carts could pass without difficulty. The fronts of the houses were carefully lined up, and no one was allowed to have the frontage of his house projecting beyond the building line. There were no narrow side streets and no cul-de-sacs, and houses at street corners were slightly rounded to facilitate the flow of traffic. Each street had a small water-course, covered with stone, for drainage purposes.

The houses were very plain, with narrow doors, flat roofs, no ornamentation and no windows. But they were strongly built of modern-looking red bricks cemented together with dried mud, and inside they offered a high degree of comfort. Many of them had spacious bedrooms, living rooms and guest rooms, a bath, running water, a fresh water tank, and an enclosed garden.

The main building in Mohenjo-Daro, 180 feet long and 90 feet wide, housed the public swimming pool shown opposite. The pool itself was 42 feet long and 24 feet wide. Not far from the main building stood an enormous granary built with sufficient natural ventilation to prevent the grain from becoming mildewed.

Sometime before 1500 B.C. an Aryan-language speaking people—the language from which most of the languages of modern India and modern Europe have descended—found their way into northern India. They were herdsmen and shepherds, accustomed to the freedom of great rolling plains rather than to the luxury and discipline of city life, yet in time they supplanted the Dravidians as the leading people of the Indus Valley. In their early years in India they bequeathed nothing to posterity in the way of material things to compare with those made by the Dravidians.

The newcomers, however, left a legacy of a very different kind. It was they who gave India the Vedas (a great collection of hymns, prayers, and sayings of wisdom), and it was they who developed in India a deep sense of tradition and that passion for classification which led to the caste system. It was they, too, who gave the world two great religions—Hinduism, the main religion of India, and Buddhism, which is now more widespread in China than in the land where it began.

Between 516 and 327 B.C., the Indus Valley was twice invaded from the west, first by the Persians, then by the armies of Alexander the Great. But soon after the death of Alexander, in 323 B.C., the Indian general Chandragupta Maurya conquered and brought under his sway the whole of northern India. His grandson, Asoka, a man of peace and a convert to the Buddhist religion, unified almost all of what we now call India except for the southern tip of the Indian peninsula. But after his death India quickly split up once more into a large number of separate states.

TOP LEFT: *Artist's reconstruction of a city scene by the Indus about 4000 years ago.* TOP RIGHT: *Map showing sites of Mohenjo-Daro and Harappa.* BOTTOM LEFT: *Dravidian bronze statue.* BOTTOM RIGHT: *Mohenjo-Daro's public baths.*

HARAPPA
MOHENJO-DARO
KARACHI

The First Great Marine Power

THE most mysterious of all peoples of ancient times were the Phoenicians. They left very few written records and little in the way of buildings or works of art. Most of our knowledge about them has been gathered from the writings of other peoples of long ago.

Their homeland consisted of only a narrow strip of land, about 120 miles long and 20 miles wide, along the eastern coast of the Mediterranean. Yet they made their influence felt not only throughout the length and breadth of the Mediterranean, but also eastward as far as the Tigris and the Euphrates and southward along the Valley of the Nile. For they were a famous seafaring people, the first great maritime power to carry the bulk of the world's seaborne goods.

These semitic-language-speaking people appeared on the scene of history about 1400 B.C. and remained as undisputed masters of the seas for six or seven hundred years. Their ships, low and narrow, were about a hundred feet long with a draught of only five feet or so. They were propelled by heavy oars, supplemented by the power of the wind harnessed to a single large, square sail. They carried no compass and no reliable charts. Yet in these vessels Phoenician crews, setting out from Tyre and Sidon, regularly made long voyages to most of the then-known world.

From the southern shores of the Black Sea they brought back cargoes of lead, gold, and iron; from Cyprus, copper, cypress wood, and cereals; in Africa, gold and ivory, in the south of France wine, in the Tin Islands (comprising Cornwall and the Scillies in the British Isles) they secured tin, and from Danzig amber. And from all these places they seem sometimes to have carried off slaves. As time passed the Phoenicians founded colonies at strategic points throughout the Mediterranean—at Carthage, Marseilles, Cadiz, and on the islands of Sicily Sardinia, Corsica, and Malta.

Even the greatest kings of other lands were glad to call on the Phoenicians for help in any matter that required sea travel. About 970 B.C., when King Solomon determined to build his mighty temple, he knew he would need a great deal of cedar-wood logs from Lebanon, and he turned to Hiram, King of Tyre, for what he needed. The Bible records that Hiram answered: "My servants shall bring them down from Lebanon unto the sea, and I will convey them by sea in floats unto the place that thou shalt appoint me." Then, about 600 B.C., King Necho of Egypt wanted to fit out an expedition to sail around the coast of Africa. Herodotus, the Greek historian, records that the expedition, consisting of Phoenician ships manned by Phoenician seamen, completed this tremendous voyage in about three years. And all that was two thousand years before the time of Vasco da Gama, the first man of the modern era to round the Cape of Good Hope. When Xerxes, mighty king of Persia in the fifth century B.C., needed ships, he turned to Sidon for them.

For many years, until comparatively recent times, the Phoenicians were given credit for all kinds of innovations we now know they did not really make themselves. They were considered to be the first creators of glass, of coinage, and even of the alphabet. Though we no longer believe that they originated these things, we know that they made an inestimable contribution to civilization by spreading the knowledge of all those inventions.

From about 550 B.C., as the sea-faring Greeks became more and more active in the eastern Mediterranean, the power of the Phoenicians steadily declined, and they played but a small part in history after 332 B.C., when Tyre was conquered by Alexander the Great.

Big map shows Phoenician cities: B — *Byblos;* T — *Tyre;* S — *Sidon;* C — *Carthage; Dark blue shows areas covered by Phoenician journeys, and yellow shows Phoenician caravan routes. Small map shows other main routes. Bottom pictures show the alphabet known to the Phoenicians, a Phoenician ship, and part of a caravan of camels.*

C
B
S
T

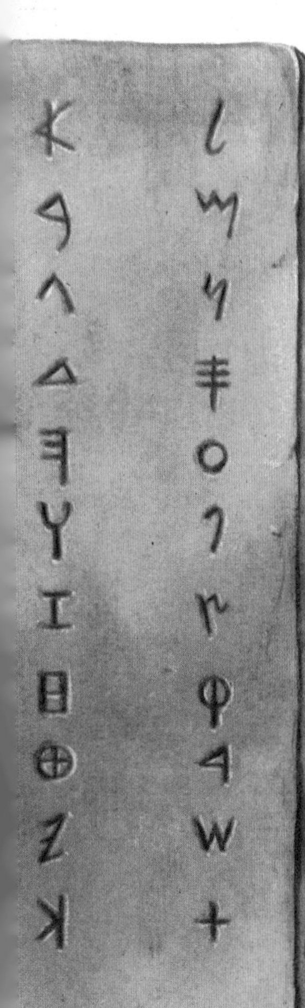

The First Gigantic Empire

TOWARDS the close of the Phoenician era of maritime power, while the Greeks were playing an increasingly important part in the Mediterranean world, a new empire was taking shape in western Asia. The building of that empire did not begin until after 600 B.C., and long before 300 B.C. the whole edifice had collapsed. Yet in that time Persia became the first really gigantic empire the world had ever known.

The story begins with King Cyrus the Great, who reigned from about 588 to 529 B.C. When Cyrus came to the Persian throne, the old kingdom of Media, to the northeast of Persia, was already weak. The armies of Cyrus quickly seized Ecbatana, the ancient capital of the Medes, and subdued the whole of Media, which stretched to the southern shores of the Caspian Sea. Later, King Croesus of Lydia (in Asia Minor), believing that the gods had promised him a great victory, made war on the Persian armies. But it was Cyrus, not Croesus, who proved the victor. By that victory, he added the Lydian capital, Sardis (S_1) and other cities of Asia Minor to his kingdom. In other campaigns Cyrus conquered the Phoenicians and the people of Babylon (B). The story of Belshazzar, last king of Babylon, is told in the Old Testament.

Cyrus not only conquered; he also knew how to hold an empire together. He seldom interfered with the rights of conquered peoples to keep to their own religion, worship their own gods, and follow their own customs.

Cambyses, son and successor of Cyrus, had not the same wisdom. After waging war on the Egyptians and seizing their capital, Memphis, he despoiled royal tombs and desecrated the mummies of the royal dead, thus stirring up hatred among the newly conquered people.

For a time there was unrest within the Empire. Then in 521 B.C. Darius, famous as the great lawgiver, obtained power. First he restored internal peace, then he too, set out on campaigns of conquest. Under Darius the Persian Empire reached its greatest extent, and the map opposite shows just how vast it was. In the east it stretched as far as the Indus (I) and in the west as far as the Danube (D); northward it reached the River Oxus (O) and Lake Aral; southward it went far along the Nile valley. At its center was the very cradle of civilization, the Rivers Tigris (T) and Euphrates (E). It commanded the eastern shores of the Mediterranean, most of the Persian Gulf (P), and the nearest fertile lands to the Red Sea (R).

It was Darius who founded a new Persian capital, Persepolis (P_2), some 200 miles southeast of the old capital, Susa (S). There he built magnificent palaces with accommodations for all his court, and houses for his guards, officials, and thousands of servants and slaves. It was Darius, too, who ordered the construction of a road about 1300 miles long, from Susa to Sardis.

Darius probably made his greatest mistake when he tried to conquer the Greek-speaking states of the Mediterranean. He underestimated their power to combine in their own defense, and he underestimated their will to win. At the battle of Marathon (M) they inflicted on him a crushing defeat.

Xerxes, son of Darius, who reigned from 485 to 464 B.C., was a great commander, but he repeated his father's mistake in underestimating the Greeks and their allies. In 480 B.C. he defeated the Spartans at Thermopylae, but the same year he suffered a disastrous defeat in the Battle of Salamis (S_2), one of the most decisive sea-battles of all time, and in the battle of Plataea (P_1) near Athens (A).

From then on the Persian Empire began to weaken, mainly because of internal uprisings. But it was still a power to be reckoned with until the armies of Alexander the Great overran it and conquered it a century and a half later.

TOP: *A Persian king receives a messenger. Bas reliefs show a row of bodyguards and people bearing tribute.* BOTTOM LEFT: *Extent of Persian Empire.* BOTTOM RIGHT: *Persian watchtower.*

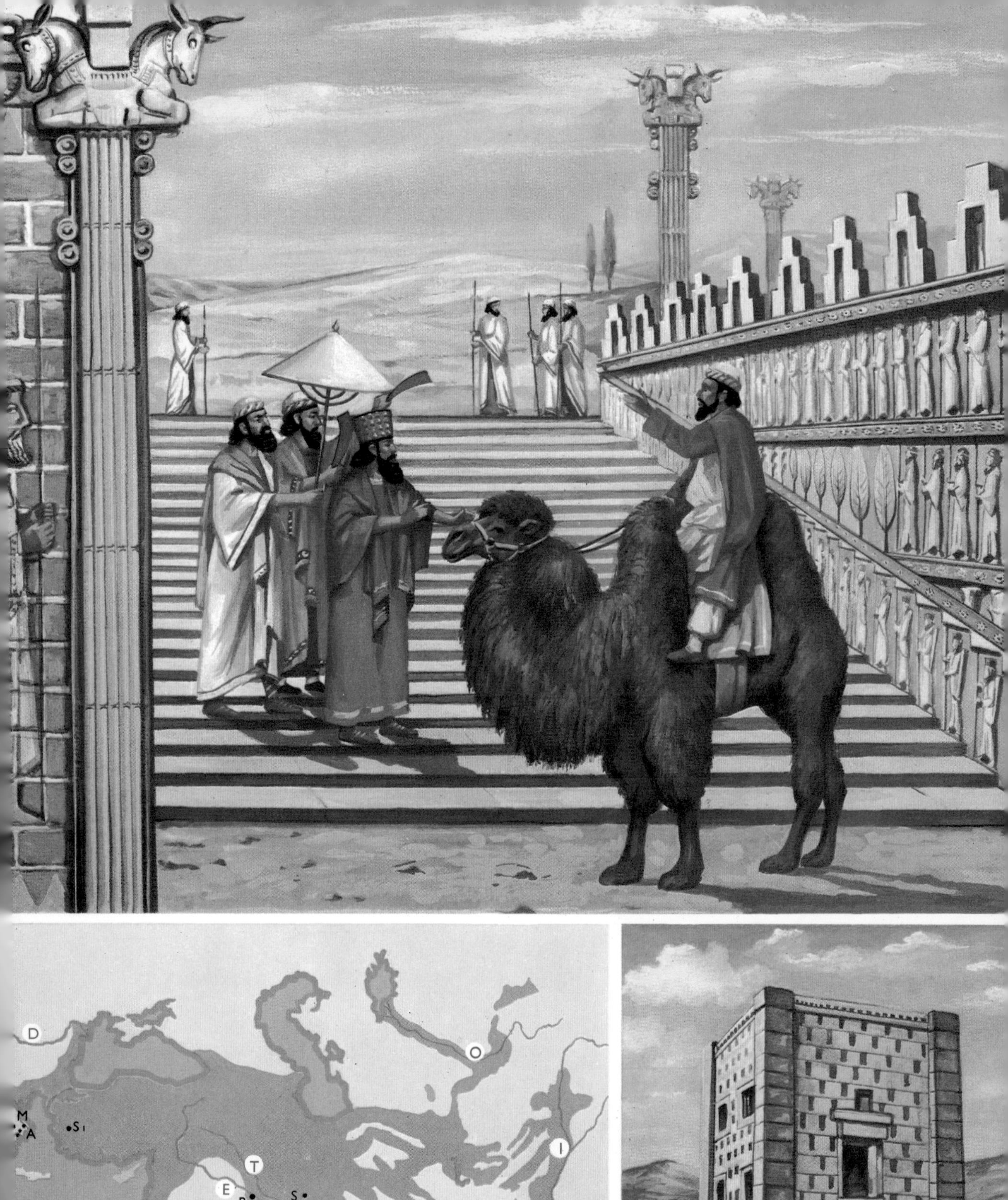

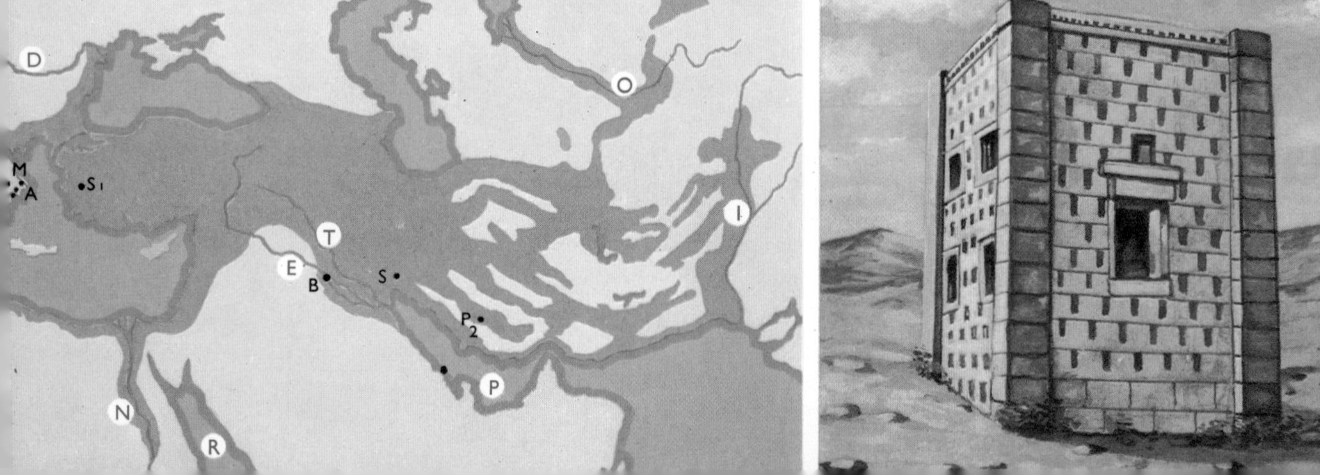

D
O
M
A
S1
T
I
E
B
S
P
2
P
N
R

Civilization in the Heart of Europe

UNTIL last century most people imagined that a thousand years before the time of Christ, while splendid civilizations flourished elsewhere, Europe was inhabited only by near-savages. Today we know that is far from the truth. Although the peoples who lived in Europe at that time left no written records, they left behind quite a number of tools and weapons, and even whole towns, which prove beyond doubt that they were civilized people, often enjoying quite a high standard of living.

In 1846 more than 2500 ancient graves were discovered at Hallstatt, near Salzburg in Austria. They dated back to periods between 1000 and 400 B.C., and they contained many surprises for the men who opened them, for they held not only bones or ashes, often in funeral urns, but also many everyday things of long ago. There were swords of bronze and of iron; there were many kinds of tools, also in bronze and iron; there were brooches of various shapes and sizes; there were drawings of animals, especially of horses and swans; and there were fragments of pottery, beautifully made and carrying intricate geometrical designs. These designs were made up mainly of oblongs, triangles, and lozenge shapes, separated by diagonal or zig-zag lines.

These discoveries enabled archaeologists to build up at least a sketchy picture of what kind of people the ancient inhabitants of Hallstatt really were. It was possible to deduce from some of their possessions, which could only have come from other lands, that they had some contact with Phoenician traders, and probably with the early Greeks. Their drawings of horses and swans seem to indicate that they knew something about the religions of other lands and may even have embraced those religions themselves; for at that time there were many religious sects around the Mediterranean that believed that a horse drew the sun's chariot across the sky by day, while a swan towed it through the river of darkness by night.

Since those finds of 1846, other discoveries have thrown more light on what we may call the Hallstatt civilization. In 1933 a whole town built about 700 B.C., apparently by men of the same civilization, was found in Poland. It was on an island in a lake to the northeast of Poznan, and it was named Biskupin.

The houses, as well as the public buildings of the town, were all stoutly built of wood. The long streets, seldom more than six feet wide, were paved with wooden blocks of identical size fitted together without the help of nails. All these streets led toward a circular road that went around the town. Beyond this road were three rows of strong ramparts, which served as the town's defenses.

Behind these defenses the inhabitants lived in strong wood-built houses covered with sloping thatched roofs. In each house an entrance nine feet wide and six feet high led into a single large hall. The eastern part of this hall, containing a stone hearth, served as living room and kitchen, and the western part as a bedroom, equipped with a wooden platform where the whole family slept. Directly opposite the open entrance, in the lightest part of the room, stood the weaving frame, where the women wove strips of cloth almost six feet wide. A flat ceiling of planks ensured plenty of storage space under the eaves of the house.

The fact that Biskupin was almost 500 miles away from Hallstatt gives us some idea of how far the Hallstatt civilization spread. Some people even believe that it spread as far as Villanova, near Bologna in Italy. But the evidence for this is by no means conclusive. Other people believe that Villanovan culture influenced that of Hallstatt and that knowledge of iron came to that region from Villanova, about 650 B.C.

Three reconstructions of scenes in Biskupin nearly 3000 years ago: the inside of a typical house; a narrow wood-paved street; and an overall view. Map shows sites of Hallstatt (H) and Biskupin (B).

B

The Gateway of Three Continents

We have seen that between 3000 B.C. and 500 B.C. many important civilizations grew to maturity in Asia, in northeast Africa, and in Europe. Though all were more cut off from each other than nations are today, there were contacts between them. Merchants carried goods along caravan routes between the Indus and Mesopotamia; a silk route grew up between China and western Asia; and troops often made incredibly long marches from one region to another. And all these contacts helped to spread ideas.

Some peoples played a particularly important part in bringing various civilizations into closer contact. We have already seen, for instance, how the Phoenicians acted as carriers of goods and ideas for much of the known world between 1400 B.C. and 600 B.C. But even earlier another nation had played a similar role. They were people who settled in Crete about 3000 B.C. and whose civilization ended violently and mysteriously about 1400 B.C.

Crete stands at the gateway of three continents. Less than a hundred miles northwest of it lies the mainland of Europe; less than two hundred miles northeast lie the western limits of Asia; less than four hundred miles to the southeast lies the river Nile which leads deep into Africa. Perhaps not surprisingly, the people who built up the ancient civilization of Crete, known as the Minoan civilization, plied a flourishing trade with all three continents. Their ships sailed west as far as Sicily, east to Cyprus and what is now Israel, north to the Dardanelles, and south to Egypt, trading in bronze tools, oils, wines, and precious vases. And Minoan remains show clearly that the short, dark-haired people of Mediterranean origin who made these things had learned much of what was best in several other civilizations.

In 1900 the British archaeologist, Sir Arthur Evans, began unearthing the Palace of Minos at Knossos, the dwelling of a long line of Cretan sea-kings. It proved to be a vast building of stone, part of which was three stories high, and was probably built and extended over a period of many years. Leading off from its many long corridors were a great number of living rooms, bedrooms, workshops, huge storage rooms for wine and oil, a council chamber, a throne room, and perhaps most surprising of all, bathrooms with excellent water supplies and drainage systems. Some scholars believe that the architects and engineers responsible for this great building borrowed some of their ideas from plans of palaces in Mesopotamia.

At different periods the people of ancient Crete used three different forms of writing. Two have not yet been deciphered, so that inscriptions in them can tell us nothing of the details of Cretan history, but it seems likely that these scripts represent a picture-writing, similar in kind though not in appearance to the hieroglyphic writing of Egypt. The third script, called Linear B, was used toward the close of Minoan civilization. It was deciphered a few years ago by a young English architect, Michael Ventris, and it proves to be a system of sound-writing in which each character stands for a different sound occurring in very early Greek.

Minoan paintings tell us something about the customs and costume of Crete more than 3500 years ago. We know that youths, and sometimes maidens, enjoyed the dangerous sport of seizing a bull by the horns and somersaulting over its back. We know, too, that women frequently wore full skirts and had wasp-waists, like the fashionable ladies of late Victorian times. The two-bladed axe, which appears so often in Minoan art, was the symbol of Crete just as the eagle is the symbol of the United States. In real life it was probably used in sacrificing animals.

A bull-leaping contest in Knossos, 3500 years ago. One youth is holding a two-bladed axe. The girl is carrying a Minoan vase.

The Cradle of the Western World

OF all the ancient civilizations, that of the Greeks has influenced the Western World more profoundly than all the rest. Yet in spite of long and careful work by archaeologists we still cannot speak with certainty about the origins of the Greeks, or as they called themselves, the Hellenes.

We know little more than that they probably descended from several peoples—Achaeans, Dorians, Ionians, and Aeolians—who settled in Greece and its surrounding islands at various times between 2000 and 1200 B.C. We also know that before Cretan civilization failed they had already built at least one flourishing city, Mycene (M_1). And that city, in its early days, evidently had strong connections with Crete, for we have already seen that one Cretan script was used to write an early form of Greek, and we know that the art of Mycene closely resembled that of Crete.

From those early beginnings until about 600 B.C. much of our knowledge of the Greeks is based on the epics of Homer, stories that are partly fact and partly fancy. Yet ever since the German archaeologist Heinrich Schliemann made the first excavations of Troy, nearly a century ago, students of history have steadily disentangled more and more fact from much that was certainly fancy. We do not have to believe the entire story of how Greek heroes, concealed in a gigantic wooden horse, were towed into the walled city of Troy and then came out to destroy its inhabitants; but we do know that Troy *was* a walled city, and that it would have been difficult for any army to conquer it without resorting to trickery.

Yet the Greece which became the cradle of the Western World was not that of Homeric times, but that of the period between about 600 and 300 B.C. By the beginning of that period the Greek-speaking peoples had already wrested mastery of the Mediterranean from the Phoenicians, and were thus in close contact with many other civilizations. They had also founded colonies in Sicily, southern Italy, Marseilles, Crete, and Cyprus as well as in many parts of Asia Minor. In many foreign ports which their ships visited they must have seen splendid examples of architecture and sculpture; they saw, learned, and surpassed the best that others had accomplished.

At the top of the facing page is an artist's reconstruction of the Acropolis, the fortified part of Athens on a high rock inaccessible on all but one side. There stood most of the main buildings of the city, including the Parthenon, erected about 447-432 B.C. under the direction of the famous Greek sculptor, Phidias. At the bottom left of the page is the beautiful statue of the goddess Pallas Athene, which Phidias placed in the Parthenon.

In sculpture and architecture the Greeks raised old art forms to new heights. But they also produced at least one art form that was entirely new—the art of writing interestingly *at length*. The Greeks had a simple alphabetic script and a good writing material, papyrus, and were thus able to write as much as they wished about whatever interested them. Fortunately almost everything interested them, and although most of what they wrote is now lost, a great deal still remains: the tragedies of Aeschylus, Sophocles, and Euripides, all written in the fifth century B.C.; the comedies of Aristophanes and the philosophical writings of Plato, written a little later; and Euclid's great works on geometry, which were written in the third century B.C.

The helmeted figure opposite is Pericles, the greatest Greek statesman of the fifth century B.C., and the map shows places of importance in the Greece of his time: A — Athens; T — Thebes; C — Corinth; O — Olympia; D_1 — Delphi; D_2 — Delos; M_1 — Mycene; M_2 — Marathon; S_1 — Sparta; S_2 — Salamis; I — Ilium (Troy).

TOP: *Reconstruction of the Acropolis at Athens.* LEFT: *Statue of Pallas Athene.* RIGHT: *Head of Pericles and, below, a reminder of the Homeric story of the wooden horse of Troy.* CENTER: *Greece at the time of Pericles.*

D1
T
M2
A
C
O
M1
S2
D2
S1

Alexander the Great

SOME Greek city states, like Athens, were democratic; others, like Sparta, were organized on aristocratic lines, and the interests of individual citizens were subordinated to the military interests of the state. Yet all these cities had two things in common: they all spoke dialects of one common language, and they all shared the same religious observances.

These cities were often ready to fight shoulder to shoulder against an enemy who threatened the things they all held dear, but when no such threat existed they were equally ready to fly at each other's throats. We saw on page 22 how they united against the Persians and inflicted crushing defeats on them at the Battle of Marathon (490 B.C.) and again at Salamis (480 B.C.). But in 431 B.C., after the threat of outside aggression was removed, bitter war broke out between Athens on one side and Sparta and Corinth on the other; and except for a short uneasy peace this struggle, the Peloponnesian War, lasted twenty-seven years.

Though this was perhaps the most bitter war between Greek cities it was not the only one; and warfare of this kind offered another country a unique opportunity for expansion. The map opposite helps to show the course of that mighty expansion.

In 400 B.C. Macedonia, with its capital at Pella (P), was a poor mountainous country, lying to the north of Greece and having no outlet to the sea. The Greeks regarded the Macedonians, who spoke a language akin to Greek, as mere barbarians. But in 359 B.C. a ruthless man of great ability, Philip II, came to the throne, and determined to extend his country's boundaries to the sea. He played on the rivalries of the Greek city states, playing one off against another to help him achieve his ambition. He poured out gold in bribes to build up fifth columns inside cities lying in his path. And where bribery or inciting rivalries would not work he employed force. Quickly he built up an army of unrivaled power, equipped with cavalry, and boasting foot soldiers carrying lances twenty feet long. On wheeling from marching position to battle formation, these men presented an almost impregnable front.

Within a few years he made himself ruler of the whole of Greece. Then, taking advantage of the Greeks' hatred of their old enemies, he organized a gigantic campaign against the Persians. But just as all was ready he was assassinated by one of his own officers, in 336 B.C.

His son who succeeded him was Alexander the Great. He was then only twenty years old, but he was a man of character and of education—a pupil of Aristotle. Alexander not only carried out his father's plan but also went far beyond it. First he destroyed the rebellious city of Thebes and next he crossed the Dardanelles with an army of 55,000 men. There, at the Granicus (G) and at Issus (I), he defeated Darius III of Persia.

Next followed sweeping victories in Syria, Phoenicia, Palestine, and Egypt, where, at the oasis of Ammon (Am) he proclaimed himself King of Africa, and ordered the building of the city of Alexandria (A_1), to the north of Memphis (M). This city was later to become the main center of Hellenistic culture. (During later conquests other cities, A_2, A_3, A_4, A_5, A_6, and A_7, were also named after him.)

When he died at Babylon (B) in 323 B.C., at the age of thirty-three, he had won a vast empire stretching from western Greece to beyond the Indus. Shortly after his death the empire was divided among four of his generals. Seleucus controlled the Asiatic part, Ptolemy controlled Egypt, Lysimachus governed Asia Minor, while Cassander ruled over Macedonia and Greece.

TOP: *Coin bearing head of Alexander, and formation of Macedonian phalanx.* CENTER: *Mosaic from Pompeii depicting Battle of Issus.* BOTTOM: *Alexander's Empire. Red letters show Nile (N), Euphrates (E), Tigris (T), Indus (I), Oxus (O), Jaxartes (J), Mediterranean (M), Red Sea (R), Persian Gulf (P), and Granicus (G). Black lines show journeys of Alexander the Great.*

G
I
M
A1
M
N
R
E
T
A7
B
A2
P
O
J
A6
A5
A4
I
A3

In Italy before the Romans

GREEK civilization did not reach its highest pitch suddenly. It doubtless owed much to the older and still-mysterious civilization of Crete.

A similar story lies behind the Romans, who eventually brought a new level of culture and new standards of living to Britain and to much of western Europe. They, too, built on foundations laid by an earlier people, the Etruscans.

The argument about where the Etruscans came from has been going on since before the time of Christ. Herodotus, who lived in the fifth century B.C., believed that they found their way into Italy from Asia Minor; Dionysius of Halicarnassus, a Greek writer who lived some four centuries later and who spent much of his life in Rome, said they were natives of Italy; other historians have declared they came from the north. And the argument remains unsettled to this day. The only certainty is that by about 800 B.C. the Etruscans began to develop a very fine civilization in that part of Italy shown opposite—between the River Arno (A) and the River Tiber (T_1).

One reason why the origins of the Etruscans remain obscure is that very little of what they wrote can now be understood. This is particularly tantalizing because they used an alphabet very similar to the early Greek alphabet, and many archaeologists know the sound-value of every letter. They can read an Etruscan inscription aloud, pronouncing it, in all probability, just as the Etruscans themselves would have pronounced it. But they simply do not know what most of the words mean. So far they know only about a hundred words, but there are hopes that they will soon know many more.

In the meantime, until their inscriptions can be fully translated, we have to judge the Etruscans mainly by what remains of their buildings and works of art. Most of these things have been found in or near the towns marked on the map opposite: Caere (C), Tarquinii (T_2), Volterra (V_1), Vetulonia (V_2), Vulci (V_3), Veii (V_4), Arezzo (A_1), and Florence (F).

The vaulted tomb, shown in the top left-hand picture, not only tells us that the builders knew how to support a heavy and complicated roof structure; it also tells us something of the respect which the Etruscans had for their dead. So does the carefully-made funeral urn (top right). The iron bracelet of the seventh century B.C., shown on the left, and the beautifully-wrought back of a bronze mirror, shown at the bottom right, tell us that Etruscan metal workers were not merely craftsmen but true artists. The bas relief showing a demon with three heads, which forms part of the façade of a church in Tuscany, hints that evil deities as well as benign ones played a part in Etruscan religious beliefs. Many statuettes in bronze and life-size statues in stone make it clear that the art of sculpture reached almost the same height among the Etruscans as among the Greeks. Delicately fashioned gold brooches and necklaces prove that the ladies of Etruria took pleasure in wearing fine jewelry.

Perhaps the most interesting of all Etruscan remains are the many fine mural paintings, for these tell us a great deal about how a long-vanished people lived and dressed. These paintings show that the Etruscans delighted in listening to music, especially to the music of pipes, that they loved dancing, feasting, and watching jugglers and circus acts.

The Etruscan figure of a she-wolf to which a much later hand added figures of Romulus and Remus, reminds us how close *in time* the Etruscans were to the Romans. The letter R on the map, marking the site of Rome, reminds us how close they were geographically.

TOP: *Etruscan tomb and a funeral urn.* CENTER: *Iron bracelet, map of Etruria, and three-headed demon in stone.* BOTTOM: *Etruscan figure of a she-wolf (Romulus and Remus were added later), and back of a bronze mirror.*

F
A
V 1
A1
Ti
V 2
V 3
T 2
V 4
C
R

Hillside Village to World City

NOT long before the time when some long-forgotten Etruscan metal-worker made the iron bracelet shown on the previous page, a small new village was built on a hill some seventeen miles from the mouth of the River Tiber. It is very doubtful whether the Etruscan craftsman had even heard of it, for it lay just outside the limits of Etruria and it was of no importance whatever. Yet in course of time that small village, Alba Longa, was to become part of one of the world's mightiest cities—Rome.

It was not until their city became important that the Romans began to feel a little ashamed of its humble origins and to invent a more romantic past for it. Then the legend grew up that the Latin twin brothers Romulus and Remus, sons of Mars and descendants of the Trojan warrior, Aeneas, had been abandoned as babies by their uncle, and brought up by a she-wolf. As men, the story went, they had begun to build the walls of Rome when a quarrel broke out between them. Remus was slain and Romulus survived to become the first King of Rome. According to tradition Rome was founded in 753 B.C., and six other kings, in turn, succeeded Romulus. First came a Sabine ruler, Numa Pompilius, then a Latin, Tullus Hostilius, then another Sabine, Ancus Marcius. These were followed by three Etruscan kings, Tarquin the Elder, Servius Tullius, and Tarquin the Proud.

Nobody can safely say that these kings (with the possible exception of Romulus) had no real existence, but we can say that they are legendary figures, in the sense that it is very hard to sift fact from fiction in the stories concerning them. Perhaps the most interesting thing about them is the alleged peoples to which they belonged, for we do know that the people we call the Romans were descended not from a pure Latin people, but from Latins, Etruscans, and Sabines—the last being a people who lived in the central Apennines, to the east of Rome.

The most noteworthy events during the period of the legendary kings are said to be the founding of the port of Ostia, near the mouth of the Tiber, under Ancus Marcius; the building of the Capitol, the Forum, and the Circus Maximus under Tarquin the Elder; and the erection of fortifications around Rome under Servius Tullius. The end of the rule of kings came in 509 B.C., when Tarquin the Proud was forced to go into exile and the Republic was proclaimed. Tarquin's downfall came partly because of the scandalous behavior of his son Sextus, and partly because he himself tried to curb the power of the patricians, or upper-class people, of Rome.

However uncertain many things may be about the early history of Rome, it is at least sure that by the time the Republic was proclaimed the city was already a powerful one. Yet, in one sense, it was a city divided against itself. For, from earliest times, there were two classes of Roman citizens, the upper-class patricians who had a monopoly of political rights, and the common plebeians who had none. The proclamation of the Republic did nothing to even up matters between them. It served, rather, to increase the powers of the patricians, because for many years it was from their ranks only that two consuls were elected annually to rule in place of the banished kings. And it took almost two centuries of fierce struggle before the plebeians gained equal rights.

Yet even while that internal struggle was going on, Rome not only met foreign invasions but also embarked on campaigns of conquest. In 390 B.C. came one of the greatest setbacks in Roman history, when the invading Gauls succeeded in capturing and sacking Rome itself. Yet by 338 B.C. the Romans had recovered to such an extent that they had conquered the whole of the Italian mainland south of the River Arno.

TOP: *A view of the Forum, the public meeting place and center of justice of ancient Rome.* BELOW: *A panoramic view of the city.*

RESTITVIT

Civil War to Peaceful Empire

By 338 B.C. Carthage had created a large colonial empire including some coastal areas of Spain and the islands of Corsica, Sardinia, and Sicily. And the Mediterranean world was scarcely large enough to contain two expanding nations like the Romans and the Carthaginians.

War broke out between them in 264 B.C. and was not finally ended until 146 B.C. During that period, the period of the three Punic Wars, there were 43 years of actual warfare, and for several of those years the troops of Carthage, whose greatest leader was Hannibal, were on the very threshold of Rome. But in the Second Punic War, Scipio Africanus Major won great victories over the Carthaginian forces both in Spain and in north Africa; and in the third war his foster-son, Scipio Aemilianus, besieged Carthage and finally leveled it to the ground.

Meanwhile Roman troops were also busy in other parts of the world, and when the Punic Wars ended, they had conquered most of Spain, Gaul, northern Italy, Macedonia, Greece, and parts of the Near East.

But at home things were not going well. Conquest had filled the countryside around Rome with an abundance of foreign slave labor, which threatened the living standards of Roman farm workers. Cheap corn was being imported from Sicily and Sardinia, and Roman agriculture was suffering as a result. Two brothers, Tiberius and Caius Gracchus, fought hard to get better conditions for the Roman peasantry and also to give all the peoples of Italy full Roman citizenship. But their efforts failed, and unrest mounted until civil war became inevitable.

Thus much of the history of Rome in the first century B.C. is the story of prolonged internal strife, and many Romans of that time whose names still remain famous took a prominent part in the struggle. Sulla fought bitterly against Marius; Pompey and Julius Caesar were enemies; Mark Antony fought against Octavius. Behind all this bitterness lay the fact that Rome was no longer just a city, but the center of a great empire. It needed a strong central government and an emperor.

In 31 B.C. Octavius defeated Mark Antony's troops at the Battle of Actium, and in 27 B.C., under the name of Augustus, he became the first real Roman Emperor, though he did not accept or use the title. Although power was firmly in his hands, he wisely maintained most of the old republican institutions. By the time his reign ended, in A.D. 14, the Empire included all France, Spain, Portugal, and Italy, almost the whole coastal strip of north Africa, Egypt, much of the Balkan peninsula, and most of Asia Minor.

In the reign of Augustus the Romans set before themselves a new ideal: not so much to conquer more territory, but to maintain peace and prosperity in the empire they had already built.

Some later emperors did, in fact, enlarge the empire: Claudius added most of Britain, Thrace, and northeast Africa; and Trajan, who ruled from A.D. 98 to 117, brought the Empire to its greatest size by adding Dacia, a large area between the Danube and the Carpathians. Then, too, not all the emperors who followed Augustus were able to maintain peace everywhere within their vast territories. But the idea of the Pax Romana, the peace of Rome, was a great and inspiring one. It brought tremendous benefits to much of the known world for several centuries, until A.D. 476 when the Empire itself, over-extended and weakened by luxury and corruption, collapsed and fell prey to foreign invaders.

TOP: *A hearing in a Roman court of justice, shortly before the time of Augustus.* BOTTOM: *Map of Roman Empire showing Claudius near Britain; Scipio Africanus in Spain; Julius Caesar in Gaul (France); Augustus near the Rhine; Trajan near the Black Sea; and Antony near Egypt. Cities: London (L), York (Y), Cologne (C_1), Rome (R), Carthage (C), Constantinople (C_2), Alexandria (A).*

N
Y
L
C1
C2
R
C
A

The People of the One God

WHERE archaeologists have found human remains and evidence of civilization, they have generally found evidence, too, of some kind of religious belief. In most, if not all, of the early religions of which we have any knowledge, men worshipped many gods: gods of the city, gods of the hearth, gods of the crops, gods of seas, gods of the elements, and so on, without number. Then, probably before 2000 B.C., a small group of people living in or near Mesopotamia became convinced that there was only one true God, creator of the heavens and of the earth, and yet a God who cared for the welfare of ordinary men. They conceived of Him as a just God, ready to protect and reward those who obeyed His laws, but swift to punish those who disobeyed. They thought of themselves as God's chosen people, chosen for service rather than for special favor.

Except for their religion, these people were hardly to be distinguished at first from the many other semitic-language peoples around them. Yet under the leadership of great patriarchs such as Abraham, Isaac, and Jacob, and under the unifying influence of their faith, they were welded into a people who, almost ever since, have played a unique part in history—the Jews. Over and over again, from the days of their captivity under the pharaohs to the time of their recent persecution under the Nazis, they have been threatened with disaster and even with extinction. But each time they have survived to play their part in the world.

The story of their first captivity really begins when, at a time of famine, Joseph invited his father together with his twelve brothers and their families to leave Palestine and settle in Egypt, where there was plenty of corn. Since Joseph, the reigning pharaoh's Jewish adviser, was the man who had ensured Egypt's corn supply, the Egyptians could have no possible objection. But over the years the Jewish settlers at Goshen, north of Amarna, increased greatly in number and later pharaohs treated them as slaves. Then, somewhere about 1300 B.C., Moses succeeded in freeing the Jews from their bondage and in leading them to the promised land of Canaan.

The map opposite shows the route that Moses followed during this epic journey that took forty years to complete. E marks Egypt, N the Nile, and A Arabia, Starting from Goshen, Moses led his people to Rameses (R), across a narrow arm of the Red Sea and then southward to Mt. Sinai (S). It was on Mt. Sinai that Moses received the Law, or the Ten Commandments, on tablets of stone. From there the long trek continued through Midian (M), then north to Kadesh (K) where the Jews made a long stay, and then to Mt. Pisgah. (P). Just before he died, from Mt. Nebo, Moses saw the land of Canaan (C), which he never reached.

On the opposite page the artist has pictured Moses holding the tablets of stone. At the top of the page is the seven-branched candlestick, symbol of the Jewish faith. Just below is a parchment scroll of the Torah, the five books of Moses.

In the promised land, the Jews probably reached their highest peak of prosperity during the reigns of David, the psalmist, and Solomon, the temple-builder. Soon after Solomon's death the land was divided into two kingdoms, Israel in the north and Judah in the south. During the eighth century B.C. Israel was destroyed by the Assyrians, and its inhabitants captured. In 586 B.C. the Babylonians invaded Judah, pillaged the temple of Solomon, and carried off many Jews into captivity. Yet in spite of these and many other disasters the Jews still remained a people to be reckoned with. A new religion—Christianity—that sprang out of the religion of the Jews was later to bring profound changes into the world of the Roman Empire.

Moses with the tablets of stone on Mt. Sinai. At the top is the seven-branched candlestick, emblem of the Jewish religion. Below is a scroll of one of the books of Moses. The map shows the route the Jews followed from Egypt to Canaan.

C
P
K
R
E
M
A
S

The Four Noble Truths

AMONG the Jewish families that the Babylonians carried into captivity in 586 B.C. there were doubtless many young children. When those children reached manhood and womanhood the seeds of another great religion were being planted far to the east. For in 563 B.C. Siddharta Gautama, founder of Buddhism, was born in northern India.

His father was king of a Hindu tribe, and it seems that Siddharta Gautama held to the Hindu creed as a youth and as a young married man. But in the India of that time he must have seen a great deal of unhappiness and poverty around him, and doubtless he often pondered what value life had when it brought such suffering.

At the age of twenty-nine he left his wife and child and began to live an entirely new life. He shaved his head, put on the saffron yellow robe of a monk, and lived as a wandering beggar, demanding nothing of life in the way of material things. Then came a time when, according to tradition, he sat under a tree, the Holy Tree of Buddha, and meditated on the meaning and purpose of life for seven times seven days. And when his meditation ended he began a great preaching campaign, a campaign that lasted for over forty years, took him to all parts of northern India, and won him many disciples.

Some of the beliefs taught by Siddharta Gautama, or Buddha (the Enlightened One), as we may now call him, seem strange to Western minds. He taught, for example, that the world is made up of many elements, not only physical but also spiritual and abstract, and that all these elements are constantly recombining in an endless variety of ways in an ever-changing world. Laws, duties, dogmas, sleep, hunger, sickness, touch, and will—all these and many others were numbered among the Buddhist elements. Then, too, Buddha taught that when a man dies his soul may pass into the body of another newly-born creature. Thus an individual may pass through the circle of birth, life, and death many times, misconduct in one life being punished in the next, and virtue in one being rewarded in the next.

But the central theme of Buddha's gentle teachings are not hard to grasp, and to this day they have a profound effect on the lives of 500 million of the people of Asia. This central theme consists of what are called the Four Noble Truths: that life does consist largely of suffering; that this suffering arises out of desire and selfishness; that suffering can be abolished only when self ceases to matter, and is lost in the One Great Self; and that this desirable state of mind, the state of *Nirvana*, can be achieved only by living an upright life of meditation and self-discipline.

Buddhism, which renounced the caste system, did not long keep its hold on India, though, as we have already seen, it was of tremendous importance there during the time of Asoka. But Buddhist missionaries soon spread the new religion to other areas of Asia, and today Buddhism is still firmly established in Indo-China, Thailand, China, Java, Korea, Mongolia, Japan, Tibet, and Nepal. It would be wrong to imagine that it is the only religion practiced in all these countries, but in each of them it is a tremendously important one. Like Christianity, it is not taught or even practiced in precisely the same way everywhere, but all its many sects still accept the Four Noble Truths, and these bring a sense of brotherhood and unity to many diverse peoples.

Relics of Buddha are still preserved in temples and pagodas in many parts of Asia. And wherever Buddhism is practiced there are still monks who live a life of meditation such as Buddha lived, possessing nothing but a simple yellow robe, a needle, a rosary of corals, a lotus flower, and a begging bowl.

A statue of Buddha and four Buddhist temples. The one at the top left is in Japan, that at the top right in Java; the next two are in Thailand (left) and India (right). Below is the famous Buddhist monastery in Lhasa, Tibet.

God and Thy Neighbor

THE religion which was to affect the Western World even more profoundly than Buddhism affected eastern Asia began in an unimportant Roman province. Its founder was not the son of a king, as Buddha was; instead, he was born into the family of a humble carpenter living in the village of Nazareth near the Sea of Galilee. Yet Christians everywhere believe that he was not only a man but also the Son of God, sent into the world by God to live, suffer, and die for the salvation of all mankind, and to rise triumphant over death and the grave, giving all men the hope of resurrection.

Written records tell us very little about the first thirty years of the life of Jesus of Nazareth, and it seems probable that they were uneventful years, spent largely, perhaps, in the carpenter's shop, in the synagogue, and by the shores of Galilee. But at the age of thirty Jesus began his great mission. For three years he taught new concepts of prayer, of duty, and of worship; he also healed the sick, restored sight to the blind, and made the lame to walk. He taught men to think of God not as a God of justice, but as a God of forgiveness and mercy; to think less about the letter of the law and more about the purity of their own motives; to seek true greatness not through self-aggrandizement but through service.

Jesus summed up his own teachings when a lawyer asked him "Which is the greatest commandment in the law?" he answered "Thou shalt love the Lord thy God with all thy heart, and with all thy soul, and with all thy mind. This is the first and great commandment. And the second is like unto it. Thou shalt love thy neighbor as thyself."

In the two thousand years that have passed since the time of Jesus, the Christian Church has many times been divided about the precise interpretation to be placed on certain of his utterances, and on the exact teachings which Christian worship should follow. But in spite of these dissensions, Christians of all times and of all sects have believed in those two fundamental commandments. They have doubtless failed at times to obey them, but they have gone on trying. And Jesus always allowed for human weaknesses for it was to Simon Peter, the disciple who failed to acknowledge Jesus in his hour of greatest need, that he said "On this rock will I build my Church."

After Jesus was crucified, statesmen of the Roman Empire doubtless thought that, like Pontius Pilate, they could wash their hands of the whole affair. But the teachings of Jesus had gripped the minds of many men, and they passed on his inspiration to others. To his followers he was the Messiah, or Christ.

Throughout the first three centuries A.D. Christianity spread rapidly in the Mediterranean world, and several Roman Emperors—especially Diocletian, who reigned from A.D. 284 to 305—sought to stamp it out by bitter persecution. But the early Christians, whether living hunted lives in the catacombs or dying martyrs' deaths in the gladiatorial ring, continued to win followers. Constantine the Great, who succeeded Diocletian, not only granted the Christians freedom of worship, but also embraced their faith himself, thus forging a close link between the Roman state and the Christian Church. In the middle of the fourth century there was a brief return to persecution under the Emperor Julian, but by the close of the century Theodosius had made Christianity the sole official religion of the whole Empire.

A century later the might of the Roman Empire, especially the western part of it, had crumbled, and its unifying effect on Europe had vanished forever. But the Christian Church lived on, and still lives on, as a community of fellowship and a mighty bond between people throughout the whole world.

The birth of Jesus in a stable at Nazareth and the Last Supper.

Allah and His Prophet

THE youngest of the great world religions was founded by an Arab, Mohammed, who lived some six centuries after the time of Christ.

When Mohammed was born in Mecca in A.D. 570, his father was already dead, and while he was still a young child his mother died too, leaving him to be brought up by an uncle. During the early years of his life he was employed in looking after camels and tending sheep. But at the age of twenty-five he married a wealthy widow, and doubtless he then became a wealthy camel-owner himself. As time passed he became responsible for organizing several caravan journeys to other countries, and as he traveled about he was horrified by the idolatry he saw all around him.

At the age of forty he forsook the life of a merchant and a caravan leader and took to living in a cave, where he declared that the Angel Gabriel visited him, and revealed to him many sacred truths, the greatest of which was that there is only one God, Allah, and that Mohammed was His prophet.

From that time onward Mohammed preached a new religion and campaigned against idolatry wherever he found it. For the next twelve years it must have seemed that the new religion was doomed to failure. Mohammed and the small handful of followers he gathered around him were bitterly persecuted on all sides. In time his wife died, and in 622 things looked so black that Mohammed himself fled to Medina, some two hundred miles north of Mecca.

Yet the year of the Hegira, or flight from Mecca, now marks the beginning of the Moslem era, for in Medina, Mohammed found followers who were ready to fight for their new faith. During the next eight years this band of followers grew into a veritable army, and in 630 Mohammed returned to Mecca as a conqueror as well as a prophet. By the time of his death, two years later, the Moslem religion had already spread over most of Arabia and to parts of Asia Minor. And for the next four centuries it continued to spread rapidly, partly because Arab influence was increasing at this time as a result of military conquest, and partly because of the appealing simplicity of the new religion.

Allah, the Arabic word for God, is essentially the same as the God of the Jews and of the Christians, and Mohammed recognized many men of earlier times, and also Jesus, as true prophets. But he regarded himself as the last and greatest prophet of all. For the rest, the obligations he imposed on his followers were simple. They must pray five times every day, with their faces turned toward Mecca; during the month of Ramadan they must fast each day between sunrise and sunset; they must give alms, not only out of charity but also as an act of piety; and they must make a pilgrimage to Mecca at least once in a lifetime. Finally, they were expected to read the *Koran*, the sacred writings that include a description of the revelations made to Mohammed by Gabriel.

As the Moslem religion spread farther and farther, it became impossible for all its adherents to make the long pilgrimage to Mecca, but to this day countless thousands still do so. The picture opposite gives an artist's impression of pilgrims at the Holy Mosque of Mecca.

By about A.D. 1000 the Moslems had conquered an empire stretching from the Indus in the east to Spain and Portugal in the west. In that Empire much of what remained of the learning of ancient Greece and Rome was united with the growing learning of Persia. And from universities which the Moslems founded at Cordova and in several other Spanish towns, this combined and revitalized learning was eventually to spread to northern and western Europe.

The Holy Mosque of Mecca is the great sanctuary of the Moslem World. At its southwestern corner is enclosed the sacred black stone. Only Moslems may enter Mecca.

Before Rome Ruled Europe

HISTORY is not made up of one long continuous story of progress. It has sometimes happened in various areas of the world that things have seemed to stand still, or even to take a backward step, for hundreds of years.

One striking example occurred in western Europe after the collapse of the Roman Empire. The Romans themselves had inherited many ideas about art, architecture, and science from older civilizations. Yet when Roman influence was withdrawn, much of western Europe quickly went back to a way of life that seemed almost untouched by the great civilized ideas of antiquity. So began the period of the Middle Ages, a period which continued until long after the Moslem Empire brought the beginnings of a revival of learning to the universities of Spain.

It is hard to understand this backward step unless we know something about the peoples whom the Romans conquered, and also about those whom they had failed to conquer, in western Europe.

Many of the peoples of Europe conquered by the Romans were essentially rural and agricultural folk, and the new Roman cities, and roads between the cities, never did hold much attraction for them. Thus when the Romans left they were simply not interested in keeping cities, roads, and public buildings in good repair. Indeed, several Roman cities in Britain, including Verulam and Caister-next-Norwich, were never re-occupied.

Among the most important peoples of western Europe in pre-Roman times were the Celts, whose migrations are shown by the arrows in the top map opposite. They seem to have originated in an area lying to the north of the Alps, and during the Bronze Age they fanned out into eastern France and Spain. Somewhere about 600 B.C. they began to occupy a large area of northern Italy and parts of Austria and Hungary. By the fourth century B.C. (and, according to some archaeologists, much earlier) they occupied a great part of the British Isles; and by the close of the third century B.C. they were established in the Balkan Peninsula and in the west of Asia Minor. The letters on the map show a few towns important in Celtic times: V — Vercellae, C — Clusium, T — Telamon, S — Sentinum, R — Rome.

Unlike the Romans, the Celts were not overwhelmingly influenced by the civilizations of Greece, Egypt, and the Near East, but they were certainly not a barbarian race. They had a highly-developed culture of their own. They made fine tools, developed their own characteristic ways of decorating metalwork and pottery, and in some areas they produced coins of excellent workmanship. They even had their own unique musical instrument, and wherever Celtic influence was strongest the bagpipes are still played.

Celtic buildings show great ingenuity in the handling of heavy materials. The most famous, Stonehenge, in South England, is shown in two of the pictures. The top picture emphasizes the size of the single columns of stone, standing over 13 feet above the ground, and the way in which other huge stones were placed horizontally over them. The small aerial view brings out the size of the surrounding moat, some 120 yards in diameter. There are similar remains at Carnac in Brittany.

In time the Roman world defeated and absorbed the Celts, except in Ireland and part of Scotland. But the Romans never defeated the Germanic peoples of Europe. The movements of these peoples, and also of the Huns who threatened the Roman Empire, are shown in the lower map. The letters there indicate the following places: A — Attila's residence, T — Tours, S — Seville, C — Carthage, W — Worms, T_1 — Toulouse, R — Rome.

Two views of Stonehenge and a musical legacy of the Celts—the bagpipes (lower right). Top map shows migrations of Celts. Bottom map shows movements of Germanic peoples and also those of the Huns towards the close of Roman times.

V
T
C
S
R
W
A
T
T
R
C

The Overthrowers of Rome

LITTLE is known about the early history of the Germanic peoples, except that they were originally settled in Scandinavia. In time many of them migrated into Germany and from there spread far out to east and west.

There were many different branches and at various times and places they had many different names. It is therefore difficult to follow their precise movements in detail even where reliable records exist. But we can say that the most important branches in the west were the Franks and the Saxons; the most important branches to the east were Goths, Burgundians, and Vandals.

At the time when the Romans were extending their power far into western Europe, we can think of all these peoples as living much the same kind of lives. All were essentially country-dwellers, who seem to have abominated cities, and few of their settlements were much bigger than small villages. The tribes of the west were mainly tillers of the soil, those of the east shepherds and herdsmen.

It was not until the Romans invaded Gaul that they came into large-scale contact with these peoples. At first Roman writers thought of them as mere barbarians. Later the historian Tacitus, who lived in the first century A.D., sentimentalized about them as if they were a noble-savage people living a life that Romans might well envy.

The truth probably lay somewhere between those two extremes. The Germanic peoples of that time certainly had none of the luxurious buildings that the Romans had, but they lived in well-built cottages not unlike those still found in parts of Scandinavia. They had no highly-developed system of law, as the Romans had, but their own laws and customs were simple, sensible, and well suited to their needs. The cultivated fields were the property of individual families, while forests and meadowland belonged to the whole community. In times of peace, justice in general was in the hands of an assembly of free men, but vengeance for private injuries was left to individuals.

The Romans, having failed to conquer these peoples, tried for many years to confine them to an area between the Rhine and the Danube. But from the end of the fourth century Germanic peoples began to infiltrate into the Roman Empire on an ever-increasing scale. Perhaps the greatest peaceful invasion was by tens of thousands of Visigoths from Transylvania. Having themselves been defeated by Huns who swept in from Asia, they appealed for shelter in Roman territory and were given it. From then on, the process of infiltration went on in almost all parts of the Empire. Often the Germanic people living in Roman territory became excellent citizens, and many even fought in defense of the Empire. But the fact is that power was steadily passing out of Roman hands and into German hands, and when Germanic tribes outside the Empire made frontal attacks on it there was not a very powerful resistance. In 439 Vandals from Spain captured Carthage, center of Rome's area of wheat supply, and they quickly built up a powerful fleet based on Carthage. In 430 the Romans had to employ Huns to defeat the Burgundian kingdom of Worms. Yet only a few years later it was mainly the great invasion of Huns, under Attila, that brought about the final collapse of Roman power.

Afterwards the Huns played no great part in the history of the Western World. Instead, the once-despised Germanic peoples became the new masters of Europe. The Visigoths ruled over most of Spain; the Franks became masters of France and most of what is now Belgium and the Rhineland; and the Ostrogoths ruled Italy and a large area to the north and east of it.

TOP: *Bronze and gold Germanic "sun-disc" on model bronze chariot now on exhibition at the National Museum, Copenhagen. It was found at Trundholm (Zealand), and dates back to before 1100 B.C.* BOTTOM: *Work on an early German farm.* CENTER: *Runic signs once used in Scandinavia.*

Clovis of France

At the time of the fall of the Roman Empire Europe must have been a very puzzling place to live in. From the middle of the fourth century A.D. the Empire had been divided into two parts, an eastern part centered in Constantinople, and a western part centered in Rome. Each part had its own emperor, and in theory they were joint rulers of the whole Roman Empire. But in practice the two halves of the Empire drifted steadily apart during the next hundred years. And in the fifth century it was the western part that suffered complete collapse. The eastern part, Byzantium, retained much of its strength and grandeur for centuries afterwards.

How did the Romans themselves feel when they saw the might of Rome steadily crumbling? They knew that their forefathers had spread a great civilization based mainly on Greek and early Roman thought and on Greek and early Roman religion. Many of them wondered whether their present troubles were a punishment for throwing over the old gods and embracing Christianity. Others wondered whether they had been trying to do the impossible in attempting to combine Christianity with pre-Christian thought.

One man gave very firm answers to these questions. He was St. Augustine.

As a young man he was a successful lecturer in rhetoric, first in Carthage, then in Rome and Milan. In later life he embraced Christianity, and in 395 became Bishop of Hippo, near Carthage, where he died thirty-five years later while Vandals were besieging the city.

In his great book, *The City of God*, St. Augustine held that no man-made city, not even Rome itself, was as important as the City of God. Even if the Roman Empire could not be preserved, he urged, it was vital that Christianity and the Church should be. He also showed that much of Greek philosophy could be accepted side-by-side with Christian teaching. He gave the citizens of the shaken Roman Empire a formula by which to live.

But power was no longer in Roman hands. The question before western Europe was whether the new masters, the Germanic peoples, could make St. Augustine's formula work. The man who solved the problem was Clovis, a Salian Frank who become first king of France, founder of the Merovingian House and Architect of France. Many of the Germanic kingdoms that sprang up as Rome declined were in disagreement with the Roman Church about one point of doctrine. They accepted a heresy called the Arian heresy, which denied the divinity of Christ, and this disagreement about religion was one factor that brought about their early collapse. Clovis became an orthodox member of the Catholic Church, and built up a kingdom stretching from the Pyrenees to the English Channel.

He became king of a small part of France in 481, when he was only fifteen. In 486 after defeating the Roman commander Syagrius at Soissons (S), he moved his capital from Tournai (T_1) to Paris (P). In 506 he defeated an Arian Germanic tribe, the Alemanns, at Zulpich (Z) near Cologne (C); and it was just after this victory that he became a Catholic, being baptized by St. Remi at Rheims. Later, all French kings were crowned there. By his last victory, over King Alaric of the Visigoths, which he won on the field of Vouillé (V) in 507, Clovis extended his kingdom south to the Pyrenees mountains between France and Spain.

Clovis was among the founders of the Salic Law, which prohibited the succession of women to the throne; this law was later to have serious effects on the history of Europe. His emblem was the golden bee, which some historians believe gave rise to the Fleur de Lys, emblem of later French kings.

LEFT: *The baptism of Clovis and a page from an illuminated copy of the Salic Law.* RIGHT: *The kingdom of Clovis, his emblem, and an example of Merovingian jewelry. On map:* P — *Paris,* S — *Soissons,* V — *Vouillé,* T — *Toulouse,* R — *Rheims,* D — *Dijon,* T_1 — *Tournai,* T_2 — *Trier,* Z — *Zulpich,* C *Cologne.*

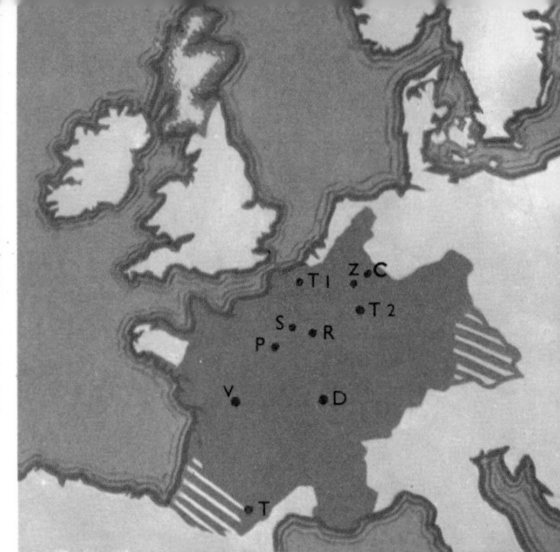

T1
Z
C
T2
S
R
P
V
D
T

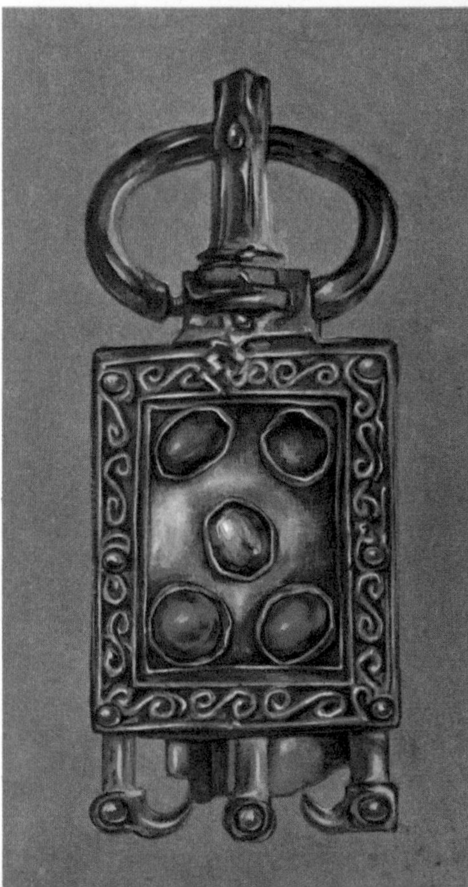

The Empire of Charlemagne

WHEN Clovis died, in 511, the kingdom he had built up soon ceased to be a unity. It was divided into four parts, each ruled over by one of his four sons: Neustria in the northwest, Austrasia in the northeast, Aquitaine in the southwest, and Burgundy in the southeast.

For generations, the monarchs of these territories engaged in constant warfare; and from the early seventh century onward most of the Merovingian kings were kings only in name. They had allowed their power to pass into the hands of court officials.

Yet the real heritage which Clovis left to the Western World was too strong to be destroyed by the laziness of his descendants. He had left behind a realization that the land which had once been Roman Gaul could be a strong and united nation, Germanic in origin but Roman in spirit.

One court chamberlain who took more power into his hands in the early eighth century was Charles Martel, among the first men in Europe to fight successfully against the invading Moslems. In 751 his son, Pepin the Short, put an end to the Merovingian dynasty and had himself proclaimed king. Pepin had two sons, Charles and Carloman, and after his death in 768 they ruled the kingdom jointly for three years. Then Carloman died and in 771 Charles became sole King of all the Franks.

He was the man whom the world was to remember as Charlemagne, Charles the Great, the most outstanding figure of the early Middle Ages.

During his reign Charlemagne fought against three main enemies: the Moslems, who had already spread their new religion as far as Spain and Portugal; the powerful Saxons, who were still pagans; and the Lombards, who invaded the domains of the Pope.

In his wars against the Moslems he tried to create a kind of buffer state stretching from the Pyrenees to the River Ebro, and in this he was never wholly successful, mainly because his rearguard, commanded by Roland, was attacked and annihilated by the Gascons. Yet he did permanently halt the advance of the Moslems.

Against the Saxons, led by Witikind, whom we should now describe as a guerrilla chief, Charlemagne fought throughout most of his reign. Thousands of the Saxon prisoners he took chose death rather than baptism, but when their leader was captured he chose to be baptized.

When, at the request of Pope Hadrian, Charlemagne fought against the Lombards who menaced Rome, he defeated them utterly and made himself the new king of Lombardy.

By 800 he had built the huge empire shown opposite, and in December of that year the Pope placed an imperial crown on his head. He was, in a new sense, a Roman Emperor of western Europe. From his capital, Aix-la-Chapelle, he governed his domains with the help of an assembly of nobles. To ensure that the nobility should govern properly under him, he set up a body of inspectors empowered to inspect their lands and estates without notice.

Though he was not himself a highly educated man he encouraged literature and the arts, built schools, and ensured that the new chapel in his capital city should be a model of ecclesiastical architecture.

In 843 Charlemagne's empire was divided between his three grandsons. The central part and the imperial crown went to Lothair, the western part to Charles the Bald, and the eastern part to Louis the German. The places shown opposite are: N — Nantes, B_2 — Bordeaux, T_1 — Tours, T_2 — Toulouse, R_1 — Rouen, P — Paris, R_2 — Rheims, A — Arles, V_1 — Vienne, B_1 — Bremen, H — Hamburg, M — Magdeburg, C_1 — Cologne, A_1 — Aix-la-Chapelle, C — Constance, R_3 — Ravenna, V_2 — Venice, R_4 — Rome.

CENTER: *Charlemagne.* TOP: *The Iron Crown of the Lombards and the Empire of Charlemagne.* BOTTOM: *The palace of Aix-la-Chapelle and Charlemagne's signature (Karolus).*

B1
M
C1
A1
R1
R2
P
N
T1
C
B2
V1
V2
R3
T2
A
R4

The Kings of the Sea

IN thinking of western Europe after the fall of Rome, we have not yet considered the British Isles or Scandinavia.

Ireland and the greater part of Scotland were never conquered by the Romans. In England, Roman influence was never as widespread as it was in Gaul; the Romans conquered it later and withdrew from it earlier. So when the Roman legions left England, it was easier there than elsewhere for Roman influence to be forgotten.

Perhaps for a time the Celts returned to their pre-Roman way of life. But we do not really know, for no reliable records of the period remain. It is not until St. Augustine of Canterbury landed in Kent that we get a clear picture once more. By that time England was no longer Celtic. It had been conquered by three Germanic peoples, the Saxons, Angles and Jutes, and it was divided into a number of petty kingdoms. The Celts now lived mainly in Ireland, western Scotland and Wales.

In Scandinavia, where Roman civilization had never penetrated, other Germanic peoples, still worshipping pagan gods, were steadily growing to nationhood. These were the Norsemen, and their seafaring men were the Viking sea kings.

By the eighth century, the Vikings, sailing in well-built ships up to 60 feet long and 15 feet wide, had explored the whole coast of Scandinavia and the Baltic, and had sailed far up many of Europe's great rivers. By carrying their ships overland from one river to another they had often succeeded in penetrating deep into Europe and Asia. They had developed river-and-land routes to places as far off as Constantinople and Baghdad. Along their trading routes they had created several small settlements, and at least two of these, Kiev and Novgorod, were later to become important cities.

Westward too, the Norsemen made long and daring journeys in quest of territory, booty, and adventure. During the ninth century they became familiar with the entire coast of Iceland; in 982 one of their leaders, Eric the Red, founded a settlement in Greenland; and a few years later his sons Leif and Thorvald reached the coast of North America.

There are several reasons why many Norsemen took to a life of voyaging, discovery, and overseas trading. First, the soil of their homeland was often poor and not capable of providing enough food for a fast-growing population. Next, a large number of men were driven into exile as a result of civil wars. But the most important reason, probably, is that the Norsemen loved adventure.

From the eighth century onward, many Norsemen realized that both adventure and wealth could be found quite near their own land. Within easy reach of all the European coast to the south and west of them, prosperous monasteries had grown up. Many of these were rich in treasure and few of them were well defended. Then, too, there were well-tilled farmlands to be taken by those who were ready to fight for them.

So the Viking raids on western Europe began. At first they were often no more than snatch-and-run raids, but in the ninth century they developed into full-scale invasions. Large areas of northern and western Scotland were taken. In France the king was forced to make terms with the invaders and to give them a large territory around the mouth of the Seine. This area was renamed Normandy, and it was from here that the Norman conquest of England was launched in 1066. In England, at the end of the ninth century, King Alfred was able to weld several petty kingdoms together in a war against the Danish Norsemen who had conquered about half the country. But in 1014, little more than a century after his death, a Danish king, Canute, ruled over England.

TOP LEFT: *Viking figurehead.* CENTER LEFT: *Stone bearing a Norse legend in runic characters.* BOTTOM LEFT: *Arab cup which Norsemen carried back to Scandinavia.* RIGHT: *Viking ship, Viking routes, and a Viking boat-sledge.*

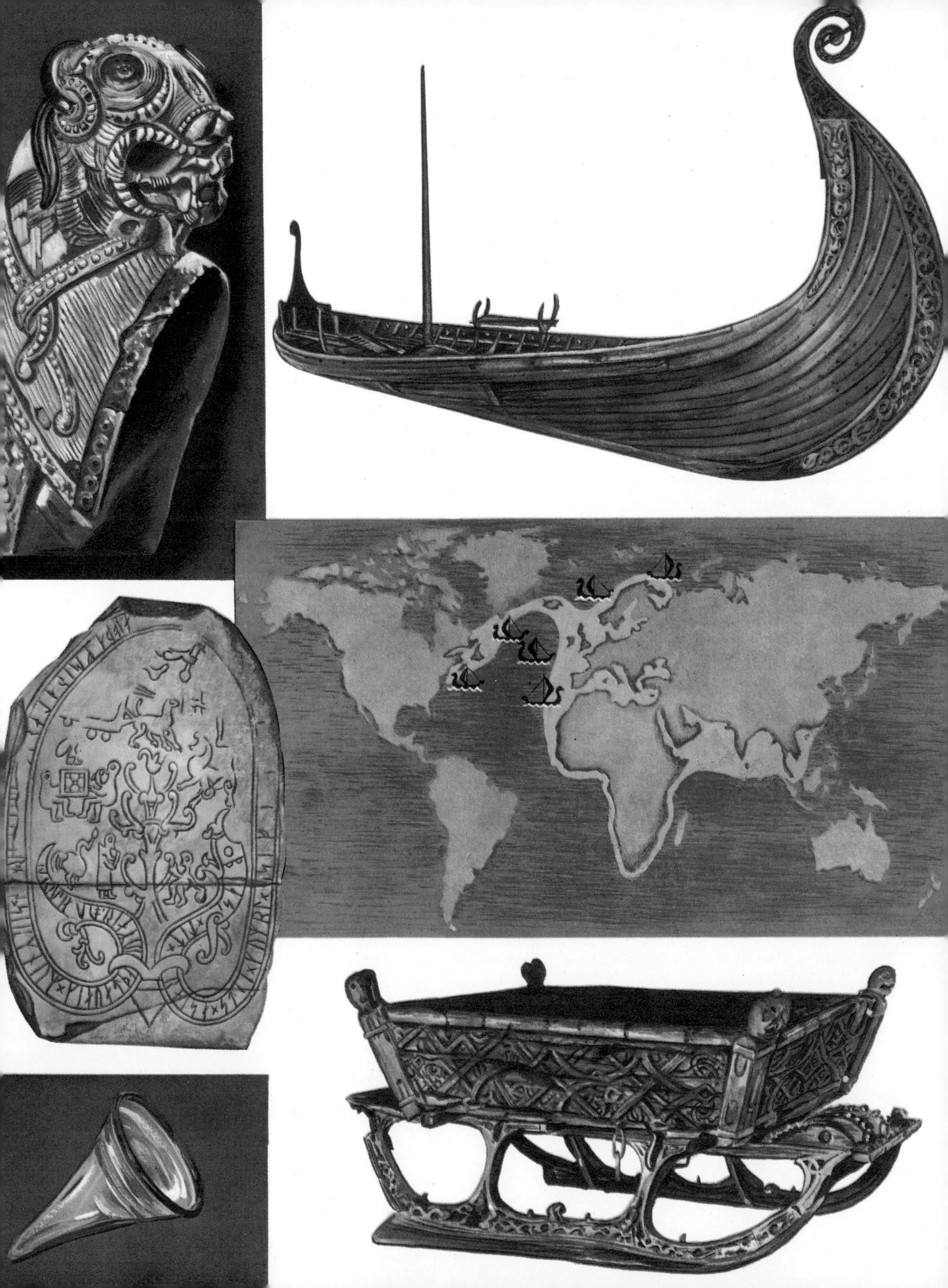

Byzantium through a Thousand Years

EASTERN Europe had no less turbulent a history than western Europe during the centuries following the fall of Rome, but there was one very big difference. The last emperor of the western Roman Empire, the weak Romulus Augustus, died in 476, and thereafter there was no continuity of imperial rule in the west. But in Constantinople, or Byzantium as it came to be called, emperors ruled for another thousand years.

There are two main reasons why the eastern part of the Roman Empire escaped collapse during the fifth century. First, its capital, Byzantium, built on the shores of the Bosporus, was far less vulnerable to attack than Rome; next its emperors engaged in a series of political maneuvers which diverted foreign invaders towards the west.

After this initial escape, the eastern Empire was often in danger from foreign invasions. Sometimes it was able to beat back the invaders and extend its boundaries; at other times foreign troops made great inroads into it. But however often its boundaries changed, Byzantium itself remained intact. It was thus able to preserve much of the thought, tradition, art, and literature of antiquity.

The Byzantine Empire reached its highest peak of power and grandeur under the Emperor Justinian, who ruled from 527 to 565—the period when western Europe came nearest to utter chaos. It would, indeed, be hard to exaggerate what Justinian did for European civilization during those years. Yet but for his wife, Theodora, that work might never have been done. In 532 there was a revolt against the young emperor, and the rebels set fire to part of the city. Justinian himself was ready to take ship and flee, but his wife was made of sterner stuff. "Flee if you wish", she told him, "but I will stay, for imperial purple will make me a splendid shroud." He stayed!

With the help of two extremely capable generals, Belisarius and Narses, he made successful war on the Persians, Vandals, and Goths, and added large areas of Spain, Italy, and northern Africa to his empire. At home he did everything possible to beautify his capital city, and was responsible for building the great Church of Saint Sophia (now a mosque) with its enormous dome, its columns of multi-colored marble, and its rich mosaics. He also became one of the world's outstanding figures in matters of law. In his great work, the *Corpus Juris Civilis*, he brought together all the Roman laws, and in the *Institutes* he gave a digest and explanation of those laws for students. Those works have had a profound effect on the laws of many European countries to this day.

After the time of Justinian the Byzantine Empire began to decline. The Lombards seized northern Italy and year by year advanced steadily southward. Only the area round Ravenna, still famous for its marvelous mosaics, long remained in Byzantine hands. In the seventh century Persian troops advanced far into the dependencies of the Empire, but the Emperor Heraclius was able to defeat them near Nineveh in 632. Yet Heraclius was less successful against Arab troops, and by the end of his reign, in 642, much of the empire had fallen into their hands.

In later times, too, Byzantium had serious troubles to face. As it lost more and more of its western territories its outlook tended to become increasingly different from that of western Europe, and in 1054 a wide breach opened between the Roman Church and the Byzantine Church—the Great Schism that gave rise to the Greek Orthodox Church. Thus during the Crusades, after the Crusaders had lost some of their zeal against the Saracens, they found excuse for turning Byzantium into a Latin kingdom for a short time, from 1204 to 1261. Even so, Byzantium regained its old character which it then retained until 1453, when it finally fell to invading Turks.

Three Byzantine mosaics from Ravenna. TOP: *The Emperor Justinian surrounded by members of his court.* BOTTOM: *Head and hand of the Empress Theodora.*

MAXIMIANVS

From Monastery to University

To keep alight the torch of learning was a far harder task in shattered western Europe than it was in undefeated Byzantium. We have to thank the monks of the Middle Ages for the fact that it was never wholly extinguished.

The founder of the first monastic order was St. Benedict, who lived from 480 to 543. He built his first monastery at Monte Cassino near Naples in 529, just after Justinian became Emperor of the Byzantine Empire.

From then onwards monasteries were rapidly established all over western Christendom, and the contribution they made to the life of their times was enormous. Often the monks brought land into cultivation that would otherwise have remained barren and neglected. Many monasteries had herb gardens where herbs believed to have medicinal properties were grown, and these gardens encouraged a new interest in botany. In an age that had no social services, monasteries often provided care for the sick and needy.

Education was also largely in the hands of the monasteries. When few could read and fewer still could write, it was the monks who taught the young and who patiently copied out manuscripts to keep alive what little learning there was. Often their manuscripts, with beautifully formed initial letters and enlivened with brightly colored miniature paintings, were works of art as well as things of utility. In the building of their religious houses, too, they encouraged a keen interest in architecture, in wood-carving, in the making of stained glass, and in mural painting. England, especially, owes a debt to the early Benedictines, for when Pope Gregory I decided to send a mission to convert England to Christianity he chose a Benedictine monk, St. Augustine, to lead it.

Like many fine institutions of all ages, the Benedictines did not always and everywhere remain uncorrupt. In 910 the monks of the newly-built Abbey of Cluny, in France, felt that discipline among many Benedictines around them had become far too lax, and they gradually developed a new and stricter order known as the Cluniacs. In the twelfth century other monks became dissatisfied with the way in which the abbots of Cluny had themselves become wealthy and corrupt, and another new order, the Cistercians, came into being. It was the Cistercians who in Britain built the beautiful abbeys at Fountains, Tintern, Melrose, and Furness. In the thirteenth century two other famous orders were founded, the Franciscans and the Dominicans, both with the purpose of going out into the highways to preach.

Centuries earlier, when the Moslems conquered Spain, they had set up great teaching centers—what we should now call universities—at Cordova, Salamanca (S), and elsewhere. Christians were not allowed to study there, but at great risk of his life, a Christian monk named Abelard of Bath disguised himself as a Moslem and studied for years at Cordova. There he translated mathematical treatises by Euclid and Alkarismi and later made them available in England.

By the twelfth century the Christian Church, and especially the monastic orders, began to found universities in Christendom, universities which were later to play a tremendous part in the revival of learning. Many are shown in the map opposite. In yellow is the old Moslem university of Cordova (C_1). The Christian universities of Bologna (B), Paris (P), and Oxford (O) in black, were all founded before 1200. All the others shown in red were founded in the thirteenth century. They are Orleans (O_1), Rome (R), Cambridge (C), Padua (P_1), Piacenza (P_2), Palencia (P_3), Vercelli (V), Vicenza (V_1), Arezzo (A), and Toulouse (T).

One of the earliest university teachers in Europe was St. Thomas Aquinas, who had earlier been a monk in the original Benedictine monastery at Monte Cassino.

TOP: *A monk copying a manuscript.* BOTTOM: *The tenth-century Abbey of Cluny, and a map showing sites of early universities.*

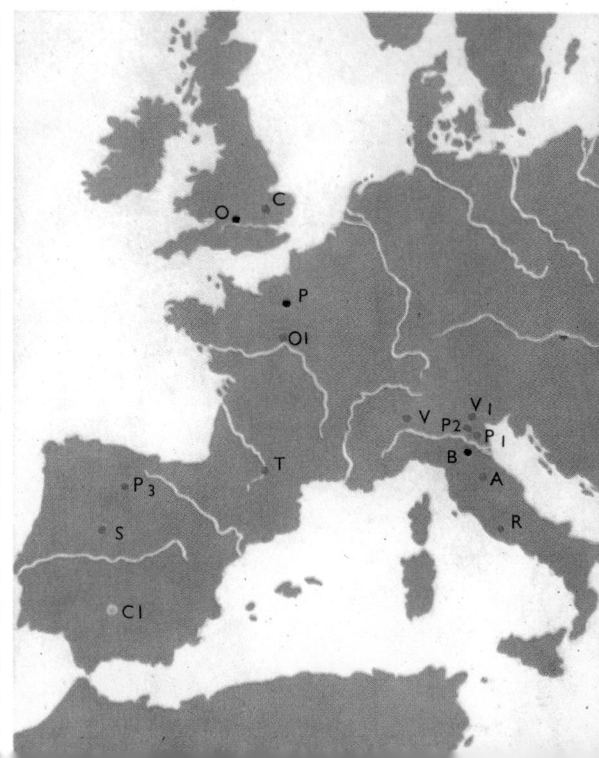
O
C
P
O1
V
V1
P2
P1
B
A
R
T
P3
S
C1

Overlord, Vassal, and Burgess

THROUGHOUT a great part of the Middle Ages, the organization of society outside the monasteries was dominated by the feudal system.

The spread of the Moslem Empire in southern Europe and the growing power of the Norsemen in the northwest had brought foreign trade to a low ebb. The circulation of money was therefore very small; and no state can be governed unless there is some way of paying for defense and the administration of justice. During the ninth century the kings of France found that the only practicable method of governing was to hand over large areas of land to various nobles who, in return, promised to provide troops and to render certain other services.

By the end of the tenth century almost the entire country was in the hands of the great nobles, and they, in turn, had parcelled out their land among lesser nobles who promised to render service to them; these lesser nobles entrusted still smaller parcels of land to the gentry, and so the process continued down the social ladder. On the lowest rung was the serf or villein—the least of the vassals. He had nothing to offer except his labor, and in return for the utmost he could give he received barely enough land to provide himself and his family with the necessities of life.

This system was not long confined to France. By the eleventh century it was established in most parts of western Europe, including England. Similar economic causes also gave rise to similar systems elsewhere. Feudalism was not uncommon in the Moslem world, and even in Japan, the Samurai, or warrior caste, were men who rendered military service in return for land. In Britain the feudal system did not break down until the late thirteenth and early fourteenth centuries; in France vestiges remained until the Revolution.

In a system that lasted so long and spread so far, we cannot expect complete uniformity, but the broad outlines were usually the same everywhere. The overlord was expected to protect his vassal and, in the ordinary course of events, not to take his land away from him. The vassal was expected to give his overlord some form of military service or manual labor and to support him in any legal struggles. He also had to contribute taxes on certain well-defined occasions: when the overlord's son became a knight in armor; when his eldest daughter married; when the overlord was captured in battle and held for ransom.

Fiefs, or grants of land, were often accompanied by a ceremony of investiture in which the overlord presented the vassal with a handful of earth, a turf, or a branch to symbolize the transfer of fields, pasture, or woodland. When an overlord made over land to a dignitary of the Church he sometimes also presented him with some symbol of spiritual power.

The main factor that brought about the decay of feudalism in the thirteenth and fourteenth centuries was a revival of trade with the East. As trade increased, towns and cities situated in places specially favorable for trading grew rapidly. In northern Italy, in the Low Countries, and near the great natural harbors of Britain villages developed into thriving towns.

Within these cities the new class of burgesses demanded the right to run their own affairs: to have lawsuits tried within their own walls, to levy rates and taxes for the upkeep of the town defenses, to regulate trade in their own way. And many cities were given royal charters conferring these rights.

In these towns serfs could find opportunities to work for a reasonable wage, and in some they could gain their freedom merely by residing inside the walls for a year and a day. Thus the whole basis of feudalism was gradually destroyed.

TOP: *Walled medieval town adjacent to the overlord's castle, outside which a tournament is in progress.* BOTTOM: *Plan of late-medieval London, showing the Thames and, at bottom right, the Tower of London.*

Church and State in Conflict

DURING the tenth and eleventh centuries there was a major conflict between the Church and the state. To understand this conflict it is necessary to consider three of the guiding ideas of the Middle Ages. First there was the idea of a Europe united in religion and united as a single political state. Next there was the idea of an uncorrupt monastic system. Last there was the feudal idea, that land could purchase military service, labor, loyalty, and almost anything.

During the tenth century the German King, Otto I, performed a great service to Europe by defeating the Magyar hordes from Asia who had ravaged areas as far apart as Austria and Andalusia. He had also made himself master of many small Germanic states and King of Italy. It was therefore natural that in 962 Pope John XII crowned him as Emperor of the Holy Roman Empire. By this act, one of the great medieval ideas, the union of a large part of Europe under one Emperor and one Church, was realized.

But Otto I and his successors had to govern the empire, and like other medieval rulers they could only pay for the means of governing by giving grants of land. They had to depend on the feudal system. And when giving land, they naturally wanted to give it to people who were at once loyal and able to govern. Among those best able to govern were bishops, who were in authority over numerous priests scattered throughout their dioceses; and some emperors felt that the best way of ensuring loyalty was to appoint bishops themselves. Thus a new form of investiture grew up. When an emperor chose a trusted man as a major vassal, he gave him a clod of earth as symbol of power over the land, and also a cross and ring as symbols of the spiritual powers of a bishop.

Here the third great medieval idea stepped in, the idea of uncorrupt monasticism. We have seen that the monks of Cluny were particularly zealous in thwarting corruption. By the early eleventh century the Cluniacs were convinced that the teaching of Christ could be practiced properly only if the Church were united under a Pope more powerful than kings and emperors. And in 1049 a Cluniac, Leo IX, became Pope. From then onward, the Popes more and more resented any infringement of their spiritual powers, and they especially resented the investiture of bishops by the emperors.

The trouble reached its height in 1075 when Pope Gregory VII declared that any priest receiving lay investiture or any layman giving investiture to a priest should be excommunicated. The Emperor, Henry IV, replied by holding an assembly at Worms, composed mainly of bishops he had nominated himself. This assembly deposed Gregory VII.

The Pope, in his turn, excommunicated the Emperor. Most of Henry IV's bishops felt they could no longer give allegiance to an excommunicated emperor, and he was compelled to seek the Pope's pardon. To do so he made a long journey in the depth of winter to Canossa, a fortress belonging to the Duchess Matilda, where the Pope was staying. He was granted forgiveness, but within a year he was again excommunicated.

This time he sought revenge. He marched against Rome and captured it, but he failed to seize Gregory VII, who later fled to Salerno.

Things were finally settled in 1122 between Pope Calixtus II and the Emperor Henry V, by the Concordat of Worms. They agreed that all Church dignitaries should henceforth be nominated by the clergy. The Emperor was to content himself with investiture by sword and scepter, symbols of earthly power; the Pope was to present the ring and cross, emblems of spiritual power.

TOP LEFT: *The Duchess Matilda and Hildebrand (later Pope Gregory VII).* TOP RIGHT: *Henry IV seeking the Pope's pardon.* CENTER: *The imperial armies of Emperor Henry IV.* BOTTOM: *Henry IV and his successor, Henry V.*

ric' quartus

The Crusades

At the time of the investiture quarrel, western Europe was steadily feeling its way toward security. The Moslems had already been expelled from Sicily and parts of Spain; in northern Europe the threat of the Norsemen was on the decline; in central Europe the power of the Magyars had been broken.

Yet there was still no western state which could compare in prestige with the Byzantine Empire of eastern Europe. Unconquered Byzantium still regarded itself as heir to the glories of ancient Greece and as rightful successor to the old Roman Empire. For centuries Byzantium acknowledged western supremacy in one respect only: it still conceded that the Pope had the highest claim to leadership of the Church. But during the eleventh century even that link was snapped, when, by the Schism of East and West, the Eastern Church completely severed its connection with Rome.

At this critical time, Byzantium was faced with one of the most serious crises in its history. Hordes of Turks from the steppes of Turkestan had long since invaded the eastern part of the Moslem Empire, made themselves virtual masters of it, and embraced the Moslem religion. In 1071 these Moslem Turks made war on Byzantium, the last great power that stood in their way in western Asia. At the battle of Manzikert they defeated the Byzantines decisively, and wrested most of Asia Minor from them. In a short time Edessa, Antioch, and Jerusalem were in their hands, and it seemed certain that their next objective was Constantinople. The Byzantine Emperor, Alexius, decided that his only hope was to appeal to Pope Urban II for help.

It would have been easy to ignore this appeal from the man who ruled the lands of the breakaway Eastern Church, and it is to the honor of western Europe that, instead, the appeal was heeded. Urban II issued a call to western Europe to fight against the Saracen invaders. The long series of Crusades which followed showed that whatever differences divided Christians, they could unite against a threat to Christianity itself.

It would be wrong to underestimate the sincerity of the early Crusaders, but it would also be wrong to ignore the fact that they fought from other motives as well. They were genuinely anxious to take the holy places from the hands of the Saracens, but they were equally anxious to seek adventure, booty, and new territories for themselves in foreign lands. They genuinely desired to establish Christianity throughout all lands around the Mediterranean, but they desired equally to drive out the Saracen pirates, and thus re-open the trade route to India.

The first popular Crusade, or War of the Cross, led by Peter the Hermit, failed completely, but in 1097 several European princes raised four armies to make a greater effort. These armies succeeded in retaking Edessa, Antioch and, in 1099, Jerusalem itself. But the glory of this victory, won by great tenacity and heroism, was tarnished by a terrible slaughter of the population. For a time a Kingdom of Jerusalem was set up, with Godfrey of Bouillon as King and Defender of the Holy Sepulchre. But this kingdom was short-lived. In 1147 the Turks again took Edessa, and this led to a second Crusade. This was an utter failure, and in 1187 Jerusalem was again in Saracen hands.

During the twelfth and thirteenth centuries there were six further Crusades, but none achieved its real objective. Indeed, in 1204 Christians from the west so far forgot their real purpose that they turned against the Byzantines and established a Latin Kingdom at Constantinople.

Yet the Crusades were not wholly unprofitable. They raised the ideas of knighthood and chivalry to new heights; they brought western men into contact with new ideas and new inventions; and they led to that revival of trade which brought about the end of the feudal system.

TOP: *Crusader galleys at the port of Rhodes.* BOTTOM: *The capture of Jerusalem as it is depicted in a miniature of the Middle Ages.*

Empires Where East Met West

AT some time between 1156 and 1162, while the Crusades were still continuing, a son was born to a petty chieftain in Mongolia. This son was the great conqueror Genghis Khan.

A typical nomad of his time, he lived nearly to middle age without ever seeing a city or learning to read and write. But, also as a nomad, he knew far more than most farmers or townsmen knew about how men and horses could live off the land while covering vast distances in rapid time. Steadily he built up a growing horde of armed horsemen and embarked on his career of conquest. By 1206 he had made himself Khan, or Emperor, of all Mongolia, with his capital at Karakorum.

Later his armies, upwards of a hundred thousand strong, swarmed across the Great Wall of China, which had kept out Mongolian invaders for fourteen centuries, and captured Peking and Korea. Southwestward his troops conquered Turkestan and captured Samarkand. Southward, they penetrated into India and Persia; and westward Genghis Khan's lieutenants undertook raids deep into Russian territory. At the time of his death, in 1227, his empire extended from the Caucasus to the coast of northern China.

As a conqueror he was utterly ruthless. In Turkestan he carried off thirty thousand people from one rebellious city as slaves, set an equal number to work on gruelling road-building projects, and beheaded the rest. Yet as a ruler he showed an unexpected degree of toleration, allowing Christians, Moslems, and Buddhists everywhere to worship in their own way.

Ogatai, Genghis Khan's son who succeeded him, became known as the Great Khan, and it was he who extended the Mongol Empire toward southern China. Kublai Khan, who succeeded Ogatai, seized the whole of China, defeated the rulers of Annam and Burma, and adapted himself wholeheartedly to Chinese civilization. It was his splendid court that Marco Polo described with such enthusiasm.

Meanwhile, at the opposite end of the Empire, Ogatai's nephew, Batou, wrought havoc in Russia and other parts of eastern Europe. His army of light horsemen sacked Moscow, Kiev, and Vladimir, laid waste Cracow and other parts of Poland, and slaughtered many of the people of Hungary.

The powerful state called the Golden Horde, which Batou founded in the southern steppes, lasted for two hundred years, until 1450. The khans of the Golden Horde allowed the former Russian principalities to continue their existence, but only on the most humiliating terms. The khans themselves nominated the rulers, set up garrisons in all the major towns, and compelled each principality to pay crippling taxes.

This long and humiliating contact with the Mongol conquerors had a tremendous effect on the Russians. Their Slav fore fathers had been little touched by the civilizations of antiquity. Traces of Greek civilization along the shores of the Black Sea had long since been erased by successive waves of invaders; and the hand of Rome had never reached the Slav lands. Now, within three centuries of their conversion to Christianity, they were subjected to strong Asiatic influences. Russia has ever since been partly European and partly Asiatic in its outlook.

The last of the great Mongol conquerors was Timur, or Tamerlane. He began his conquests in 1358, at the age of twenty-two, and before he died in 1405 he had conquered an area stretching from the Great Wall of China to Moscow. Strangely enough, it was his attack on the Golden Horde that weakened it, enabling the Russians, not long afterwards, to throw off Mongol domination.

TOP LEFT: *Genghis Khan and (below) Tamerlane.* TOP RIGHT: *A Mongolian house on wheels, as described by Marco Polo.* BOTTOM: *Map showing greatest extent of Mongol domination, red under Genghis Khan, yellow under Tamerlane.* (K_1 — *Karakorum,* P — *Peking,* S — *Samarkand,* K — *Kiev,* M — *Moscow.)*

M
K
KI
P
S

The Unification of France

AT about the time of the Crusades, and during the period of the Mongol Empires, two powerful states were steadily emerging in western Europe—France and England. France had twice been united before, first under Clovis and next under Charlemagne. It may therefore seem surprising that the process had to begin all over again. But there is a sound reason.

During the ninth and tenth centuries the Carolingian Kings of France had been compelled to introduce and extend the feudal system in order to find the means of governing. As feudalism increased some of the great vassals eventually held more land and more power than the kings.

When the last of the Carolingian kings died, in 987, the chief men of the kingdom elected the Count of the Ile de France to succeed to the throne. He was named Hugh Capet, and he was far from being the most powerful man in France. The Counts of Flanders and of Champagne, as well as the Dukes of Brittany and of Burgundy were at least as powerful; and the Dukes of Normandy, who later became Kings of England as well, were far more powerful. Yet the Capetian kings were eventually to become masters of a united France.

The first great Capetian king was Philip II, known after his death as Augustus. He reigned from 1180 to 1223, and during that time he waged war against England for more than twenty years, capturing one by one the French territories of the Norman-English kings: Normandy, Anjou, Maine, and Touraine. In 1214 he won a great victory at Bouvines over a coalition between John of England, the Emperor Otto IV, and the Count of Flanders. This victory did not add to his kingdom but it did safeguard the territories he had already won.

At home he concentrated on weakening the power of his vassals and in giving payment in return for state service to townspeople, thus building up a kind of simple civil service. He also did much to make Paris a worthy capital. He authorized the university, built the Cathedral of Notre Dame and the old Palace of the Louvre, paved streets, and improved fortifications.

The second of the great Capets was Philip II's grandson, Louis IX, who was later canonized. St. Louis came to the throne in 1226, at the age of twelve. During the forty-four years he reigned he became famous mainly for his piety. In one sense his piety was too great for the good of France, for on two occasions he took a personal part in Crusades, both of which were unsuccessful. The first kept him away from his country for several years, at a time when it needed him, and on the second one he died of the plague. Yet, in addition to building hospitals and personally nursing the sick, he still found time to reorganize the French legal system and to set up a judicial corporation to administer justice—the *Parlement* of Paris.

Philip IV, known as Philip the Fair, was St. Louis's grandson, and as unlike his grandfather as he could be. He renewed the old policy of weakening his vassals, and he succeeded in annexing certain towns formerly belonging to the Count of Flanders. So far from supporting the Church, he had a violent quarrel with Pope Boniface VIII and actually had him seized, because the Pope decreed that none of the clergy should pay taxes without Papal consent. In his zest to collect money for the state, he brought false accusations against the wealthy Order of Templars of France. Eventually their Order was dissolved and their money and lands seized by the Crown.

Yet in spite of all his defects Philip IV used the taxes he extorted (except for what the tax-farmers took) to improve the administration of his country. By the time of his death, in 1315, France was a strong state, unified under the direct government of its king.

TOP LEFT: *The old Louvre Palace.* BOTTOM LEFT: *Notre Dame.* RIGHT: *Three great kings of the House of Capet. From top to bottom, Louis IX (St. Louis), Philip II, and Philip IV.*

PHILIPVS DI GRA FRANCORVM REX

England Becomes a Great Power

ENGLAND did not become a unified kingdom until Canute seized the throne in 1014 and married Emma, widow of Ethelred the Unready, whom he had defeated.

But the Danish house was short-lived. The last of the line, Hardicanute, died in 1042, and the man chosen to succeed him was his half-brother, Edward the Confessor, son of Ethelred and Emma. King Edward was childless, and throughout his reign there was speculation about who would succeed him.

When he died, in January, 1066, the choice fell on Harold, one of the most powerful nobles in the realm. Harold had scarcely been crowned when Duke William of Normandy claimed the throne. He was indeed a nephew of Emma, King Edward's own mother, but there were other reasons for his claim. First there was his own ambition. Next there was the fact that, from 1049 onwards, the Popes were more and more zealous to extend Papal power; and William knew he could count on their support against an England that was apt to take Church matters into its own hands.

In September, 1066, he invaded England with a powerful army of archers and cavalry. In October Harold himself was killed and his army decisively defeated at the Battle of Hastings. And at Christmas William was crowned at Westminster. The main events of the Conquest are pictured in the most famous piece of needlework in the world—the Bayeux Tapestry.

It was William the Conqueror who set England on the road to becoming a great power. He introduced the French feudal system, but with a difference. The estates of the old Anglo-Saxon ruling class were handed over to Norman-French nobles, but the lesser tenants were bound to give military service not to their immediate overlords but to the king himself. The enforcement of the law was placed in the hands of officials appointed by the king. The Domesday Book, a detailed register of the possessors of land and the value of their possessions, was compiled to ensure that taxes could be levied fairly and easily.

For long after the Conquest, the affairs of England and France were closely interwoven. French became the official language of the English law courts, and over the centuries many French words passed into the common speech, helping to mold the English language.

William's successors lacked the qualities of their ancestor, and in 1154, after a domestic crisis, the Norman dynasty was replaced by Henry II, first of the Plantagenet kings. From his father, Henry II inherited Anjou and Maine; from his mother's side he inherited England and Normandy; by his marriage he obtained Guienne and Poitou in southwestern France. He thus ruled a kingdom comprising all England and much of western France. In addition, he conquered Ireland. The greatest blot on his reign was his quarrel with and assassination of Thomas Becket.

Under Henry II's successors, Richard Coeur de Lion and King John, the power of the Plantagenets declined. John not only suffered a great defeat at Bouvines, in 1214; he also aroused the hatred of his own subjects. Yet his very faults gave England one of its most prized possessions, the Magna Carta. This bound the king to respect the customs of his subjects, not to levy taxes without the consent of bishops and barons, and not to interfere with the freedom of cities.

It was under two later Plantagenet kings, Henry III (1216-1272) and Edward I (1272-1307) that the English Parliamentary system, with a House of Lords and a House of Commons, gradually took shape; and it was Edward I who conquered Wales.

TOP: *Part of the Bayeux Tapestry showing a feast on the English shore before the great battle, and a picture of William the Conqueror.* BOTTOM LEFT: *The Magna Carta of 1215.* BOTTOM RIGHT: *A meeting of the English Parliament of Edward I in 1274.*

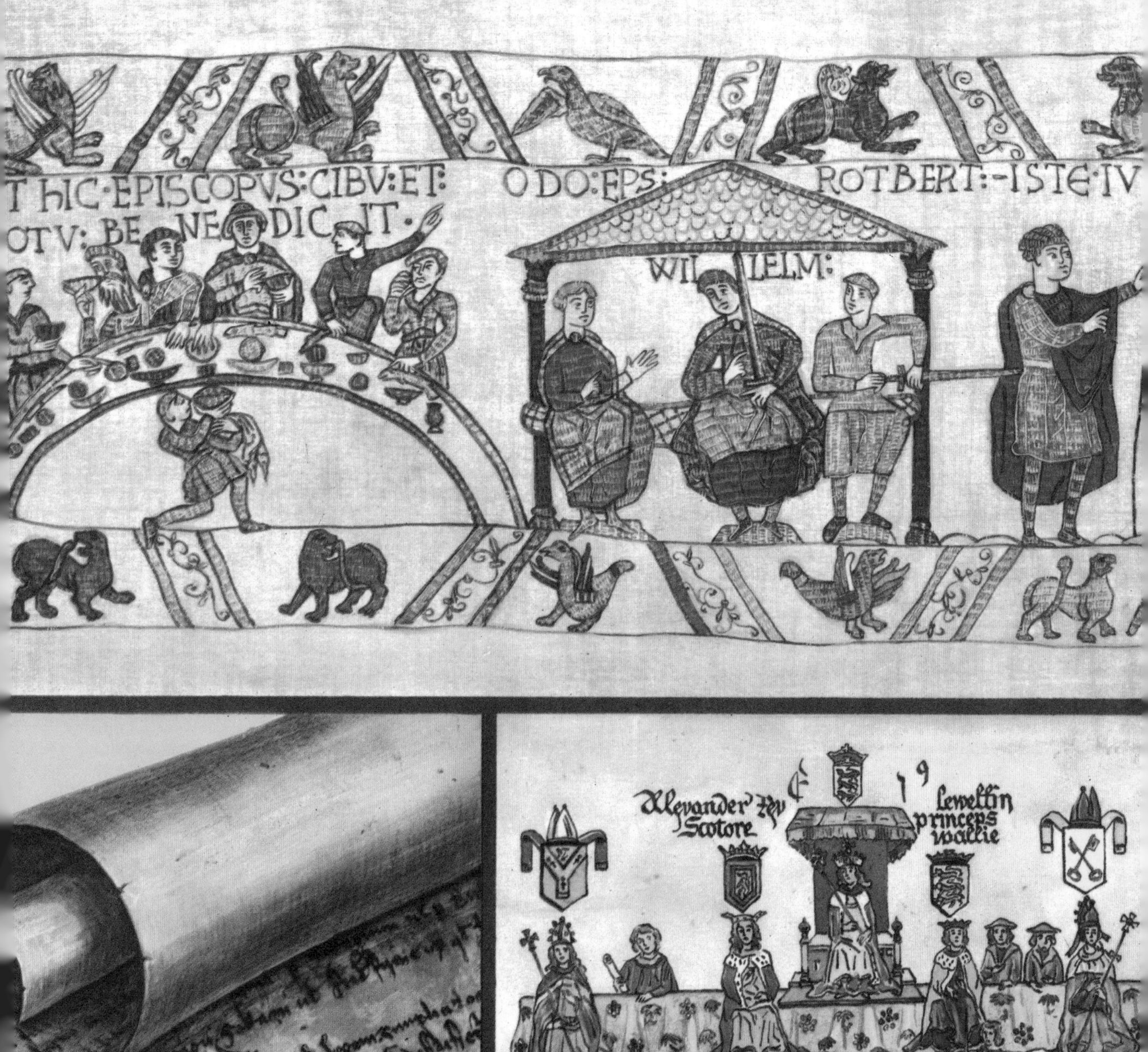
T HIC·EPISCOPUS·CIBU·ET·
OTU: BE NE DIC IT·
ODO·EPS:
ROTBERT:-ISTE·IU
WIL LELM:

Alexander Rex Scotore
Lewellin princeps wallie

The Hundred Years' War

THE Plantagenets showed a direct interest in the affairs of France, and the Kings of France naturally resented foreign interference. It needed little more than a spark to begin warfare between them.

The main thing that kept war at bay for so long was that the line of Capetian kings in France remained unbroken. But when Louis X died in 1316 he left no son, and the Salic Law of France prohibited a woman from coming to the throne. Two of Louis's brothers, Philip V and Charles IV, were crowned after him, and when Charles IV died the main Capet line ended.

The man chosen to follow him was his cousin, Philip de Valois, who became Philip VI. But later the English king, Edward III, claimed the French throne on the grounds that his mother, Isabella, was the daughter of Philip IV and a sister of the last three Capetian kings.

It is possible that Edward III might never have tried to enforce his claim except for one incident. In 1336 Count Louis of Flanders, acting under orders from Paris, declared that all Englishmen in Flanders should be arrested and cast into prison. England retaliated by stopping the export of all raw wool to Flanders and the import of all woven cloth from Flanders. If this had continued for long the trade of Flanders would have been ruined. But a Flemish merchant, Jacob van Artevelde, decided that this must not happen. In 1337 he led a revolt against Count Louis and made himself master of Flanders. Then he formed an alliance with England and prevailed on Edward III to press his claim to the French throne.

From then on England was at war with France, and apart from a number of uneasy truces the war lasted for more than a hundred years, from 1338 to 1453.

In the first stage of the war things went in England's favor. This was mainly because England had a more efficient army. Using the long bow and introducing cannons into warfare, it was more than a match for the French army which relied mainly on heavily-armored horsemen.

In 1340 the combined fleets of England and Flanders defeated the French fleet at the Battle of Sluys. Five years later Jacob van Artevelde was assassinated and the Anglo-Flemish alliance broke down, but in 1346 the Black Prince won a great victory at Crécy and ten years later, at the Battle of Poitiers, the French King, John, was captured and taken to England as a prisoner. Soon came the Peace of Brétigny (1360) by which England renounced claims to the French throne but gained Calais and a huge area of western France.

Between 1369 and 1380 the tide turned in favor of France. Under Bertrand du Guesclin, Constable of France, the French forces employed harassing tactics, exhausting the English by long marches and counter-marches. And in 1380 England had to surrender most of her French possessions except Bayonne, Bordeaux, Brest, Cherbourg and Calais.

The last period of the war began with Henry V's victory at Agincourt in 1415, which seemed to put almost the whole of France in the power of England and her Burgundian allies. But in 1429 a miracle happened. Joan of Arc, a seventeen-year-old peasant girl heard, or imagined she heard (it matters little which) voices telling her to save France. Charles VII, the uncrowned King of France, entrusted her with a small army to relieve Orleans, then besieged by the English. She succeeded and later escorted the French King to Rheims for his crowning.

From then on France rallied and inflicted defeat after defeat on the English. Joan herself was later captured by the Burgundians, sold to the English, and burned as a witch. But England's sway in France was finished. When the Hundred Years' War ended only Calais remained in English hands.

TOP: *Meeting between Edward III and Jacob van Artevelde at Ghent.* BOTTOM: *Joan of Arc sets out to liberate France.*

The Unique Story of Spain

THROUGHOUT the Middle Ages one part of western Europe, Spain and Portugal, had a very different history from all the rest.

By the beginning of the eighth century the Visigothic Kingdom of Spain was already weakened by internal quarrels, and in 711 an Arab army under the leadership of Djebl Tarik made a rapid conquest of the country. Within twenty years the Arabs had pushed beyond the Pyrenees and far into France, but in 732 they were stopped by Charles Martel, ancestor of Charlemagne.

Before the end of the century the area which the Arabs were to govern was fairly clearly defined. In the west of the Peninsula it covered all the land south of the River Douro; in the east it covered all the land to the south of the Ebro and an area almost as big as Wales to the north of it. Here the Emirs of the Ommeyad dynasty, whose capital was at Cordova, established a rule that lasted from 755 to 1031. During that time the Ommeyad Emirate of Cordova, covering much the greater part of Spain and Portugal, became the most cultivated part of all western Europe. It also became the only part which for several centuries was dominated by Moslem influences.

At this time the Moslem Empire extended from Spain to the Middle East. It included several cities such as Alexandria, which had formerly been great centers of learning in Greek times, and other cities, such as Baghdad, which were go-ahead centers of new knowledge. Thus the Moslems were able to make far greater advances in science and in practical arts than were the Christian countries of that time.

For more than two centuries Spain was in the very forefront of progress. At the great Moslem universities, mathematics, astronomy, medicine, and the science of navigation flourished. New navigational and time-keeping instruments, such as the astrolabe, were used in Spain long before they found their way to the rest of Europe. Spanish architecture took on a new and somewhat oriental look; and Spain felt the full benefit of better irrigation schemes, better trade, better craftsmanship, better standards of hygiene.

But in 1002 the Ommeyads lost one of their greatest ministers and administrators, Almansor, and from then on their power began to decline. In 1031 the last Ommeyad Emir was deposed and the country rapidly split up into a number of separate rival states, and for some four centuries there was a titanic struggle to determine who should fill the great power-gap that was left. There were several invasions of other Moslems from the south—the Moors and Berbers of North Africa—and there were determined efforts at the Christian reconquest of Spain from the north.

The first landmark in the Christian reconquest came in 1085, when Christian forces took Toledo. Then, at a time when Europe was in a state of religious fervor about the Crusades, Christians from many lands helped in the task. French, German, and Italian knights had fought at Toledo; and in 1147 English and German knights on their way to the second Crusade sailed up the Tagus, captured Lisbon, and handed it over to Alfonso Henriques, Portugal's first king.

But the Moslems were not easy foes to defeat. Each strip of territory reconquered had to be strongly defended by building and garrisoning a castle. It was in this way that part of Spain got its name, Castile, Land of Castles. Thus progress was slow, and not until 1492 was Granada, the last Moslem stronghold, reconquered. It was then that King Ferdinand of Aragon and his Queen, Isabella of Castile, became joint Christian sovereigns of a united Spain. In that very year they sponsored Columbus's first voyage of discovery.

TOP: *Interior views of the Alhambra, Granada.* BOTTOM LEFT: *A Castilian castle.* BOTTOM RIGHT: *Map showing the Douro* (D), *the Tagus* (T), *the Ebro* (E), *and Granada* (G). *The figures are Isabella, Ferdinand, and a Moslem warrior.*

D
E
O
T
G

The Ottoman Empire and Byzantium

WHILE Christendom was slowly driving the Moslems out of Spain, events were taking a very different turn at the eastern end of the Mediterranean. Ever since the early thirteenth century, when Crusaders from the west set up a Latin Kingdom in Byzantium, there was never again a full revival of power in the Byzantine Empire. From then on, only two things stood in the way of Constantinople's defeat by Moslems: its tradition of invincibility and its natural defenses. And against determined enemies they were not enough.

The threat began towards the end of the thirteenth century, when a Turkish chieftain, Othman, established his army at the northwest end of Asia Minor, where it threatened the Strait of Gallipoli, between Asia and Europe. In time he captured an important Greek town on the Sea of Marmara.

When Othman died in 1326, his son Orchan assumed the title of Sultan of the Ottomans. Early in his reign he conquered two cities of Asia Minor, Nicomedia and Nicaea. Then he concentrated for twenty years on organizing his armies. He built up a mobile cavalry, the spahis, and a highly-trained body of infantrymen, the janissaries.

Orchan's son, Murad I, who reigned from 1359 to 1389, used this model army to seize Thessalonica and Adrianople, two of the main cities of the Byzantine Empire. He also conquered part of Bulgaria and Macedonia. In 1389 a Serbian prince, Lazarus Dushan, led a combined army of Serbs, Bulgars, Bosnians, Poles, and Hungarians against the Turks. Although Dushan's army was badly defeated, Murad I was killed.

By this time Europe was thoroughly alarmed by the growing power of the Turks, and in 1396 a great crusading army set out to make war on a later Sultan, Bayazid. But Bayazid inflicted a crushing defeat on this army, and by about 1400 it seemed that nothing could now save Constantinople. Then, by an odd twist of fate, the aged Tamerlane appeared on the scene, made war on Bayazid's army and broke its power at the Battle of Angora in 1402. Bayazid himself was taken prisoner and killed, and Europe was given a breathing space of half a century.

But Europe did not take advantage of the respite. Quarrels still continued between the Eastern and the Roman Churches. The very citizens of Constantinople thought more about theological discussions than about defense.

In 1405, Tamerlane died and his empire began to crumble. The Turks at once seized the chance to rebuild their own power. Mohammed I and Murad II, the next two sultans, extended Turkish power throughout most of the Balkan Peninsula and westward as far as Hungary. But not until after 1440 did the Turks suffer any really serious opposition. Then they were strongly opposed in Albania by Scander Beg and in Hungary by John Hunyádi.

Yet by 1451, when Mohammed II became Sultan, the Turks were strong enough to decide on attacking Constantinople. The siege started on April 5th, 1453. The Golden Horn, the waterway at the right of the plan opposite, was closed by means of great iron chains. More than 200,000 troops with over a hundred cannons laid siege on the landward side of the city (top of plan), and a fleet of 250 ships prevented escape by sea. On May 29th the city's defenses were breached and the victorious Ottoman troops entered. Constantine XI, the last of the Byzantine Emperors, was killed and the glory of Byzantium was ended.

Later Sultans extended the Ottoman Empire still further. Selim I (1512-1526) conquered Syria, Egypt, and Arabia; Suleiman I (1526-1566) captured Belgrade and almost reached Vienna.

TOP: *Plan of Constantinople.* BOTTOM LEFT: *Othman, Orchan, Murad I, and Bayazid.* CENTER: *The giant, Turkish cannon that later exploded during the siege.* RIGHT: *Mohammed I, Mohammed II, Selim I, and Suleiman I.*

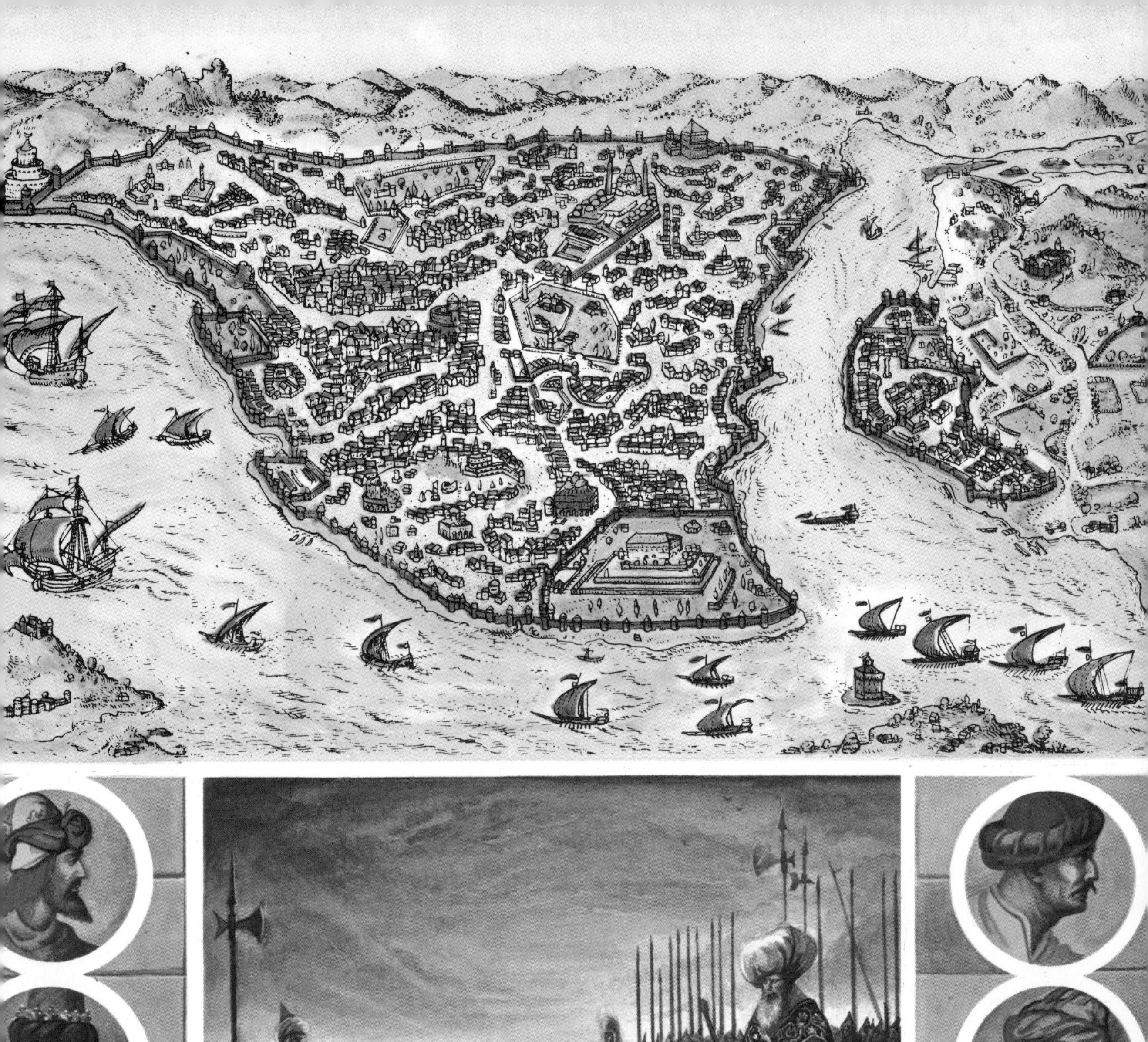

The Distant Land of Cathay

DURING the Middle Ages Spain, through its conquest by the Arabs, was made sharply aware of a thriving world beyond Europe. The people of Byzantium, too, knew only too well of the power of various Asiatic peoples to the east of them. But until the Crusades most of the people of Europe knew little about the world outside Christendom. If they had even heard of Cathay, or China, they mostly dismissed it as a far-distant place which occasionally supplied them with spices.

In fact China had already bestowed many benefits on Europe, but they had arrived by such devious routes that most people were unaware where they had originated. The silk that adorned the Roman aristocracy was first manufactured in China and brought along the ancient overland silk routes to the eastern extremities of the Roman Empire. Not until the sixth century A.D. was silk first manufactured in Europe, in the area of Constantinople. By the time of the later Crusades Sicily, Italy, Spain, and southern France all had flourishing silk industries. Paper-making, too, originated in China. Chinese prisoners, captured by Moslems during a skirmish on the fringe of the Moslem Empire, taught the art to their captors, and thereafter knowledge of the process spread slowly to all parts of Europe. Printing from wood blocks also began in China, in the eighth or ninth century A.D. At the time of the Crusades it was coming into use in Moslem lands and then it passed into western Europe.

At the close of the thirteenth century one striking event began to focus Europe's attention on China. The Venetian traveler, Marco Polo, had made the immense journey to the court of Kublai Khan, and in the Khan's service had undertaken missions to both China and India. In 1299, when he published his account of his travels, Europeans could not believe the magnificence of the China he described. Later, Dominican friars went as missionaries to China and confirmed much of what Marco Polo had written. And in the sixteenth century Europe began to make its first large-scale contacts with the fabulous land of Cathay: Jesuit missions were established there and in 1557 the Portuguese founded a colony at Macao, near Canton.

The people who traveled to China from a Europe just emerging from the Middle Ages must have been amazed by many of the ideas they saw operating there. First they saw a system of writing different from any they had ever known. In this system each written character stood for an idea, but none of the characters had any connection with the sound of a word. Thus although a man from north China and a man from South China *spoke* quite different words, they could both understand the same written characters. Equally amazing to Europeans, who were then accustomed to seeing high government posts go only to the wealthy or to those of noble birth, must have been the way China chose its civil servants. Ever since the first century B.C., Chinese civil servants had been chosen by means of competitive examinations, as American civil servants are today. The examinees were tested mainly on their knowledge of the teachings of K'ung-fu-tze, or Confucius, the great Chinese philosopher who lived in the sixth and early fifth centuries B.C.

Still more amazing to Europeans must have been China's engineering feats and her high standard of arts and crafts. China had had navigational canals linking river with river ever since the time of the Sui Dynasty (580-618 A.D.). Some of these canals could carry vessels with a capacity of more than 500 tons. In the making of pottery and porcelain, too, China was probably ahead of Europe, though Chinese porcelain did not reach its highest point of perfection until the Manchu Dynasty, which began in 1644.

TOP: *One of China's great navigational canals, built nearly 1300 years ago.* BOTTOM: *Chinese porcelain of the Manchu Dynasty.*

The Eastern Gateway of Asia

IF the Europeans of the Middle Ages knew little about China, they knew even less about Japan, the eastern gateway of Asia. In fact, Europe had no contacts with Japan until after 1500 and few large-scale contacts until last century.

The original inhabitants of the islands we now call Japan were the Ainus, a backward and somewhat mysterious people who were probably of mixed Caucasian and Indo-Germanic stock. At some time in the seventh century B.C., or even earlier, Japanese tribes arrived in the southern and central islands and began to drive the Ainus towards the northern extremities of Japan, where comparatively small numbers of them still live to this day. And in 660 B.C., according to legend, the Japanese Empire was founded.

Its founder and first emperor is said to have been Jimmu Tenno; he claimed descent from forebearers who had long held sway in heaven, and although Japan has had more than 120 emperors since that time, all of them have called themselves *tenshi*, or sons of heaven.

By virtue of this claim, a wise and strong emperor could rule absolutely and yet well; and even one who allowed every vestige of real power to fall into the hands of his ministers could still be revered by his people as a symbol of national unity. Indeed, in the late thirteenth century A.D., Yoritomo, victor of an important Japanese naval battle, did seize all real power in Japan and made himself the first shogun, or political chief. After that Japan was ruled by successive shoguns until less than a century ago; but throughout that long period the existence of the emperors helped to give the country its feeling of national unity.

Shinto, the state religion of Japan, has been strongly influenced by Buddhism and Confucianism, but it differs from both in one important respect. One of its divinities is Amaterasu, the Sun-goddess, and an ancestor of the emperor.

Certain elements in Japanese life seem to be entirely of native growth. Out of the struggle with the Ainus, and out of the system of training the Japanese warrior-class, or Samurai, there grew a distinctly Japanese code of military honor—bushido. Bushido meant loyalty to the emperor, adherence to the Shinto religion, contempt of danger and death, and honoring the pledged word. Then, too, the Japanese have evolved their own highly individual styles in art; and Japanese painting, lacquer work, and bronze work are among the finest in the world.

Yet there are many other aspects of Japanese culture that have been overwhelmingly influenced by China. The two countries had many contacts, both in peace and in war, dating back to the third century A.D., and from the beginning Japan showed a remarkable gift for absorbing new ideas.

It may well be that when the Japanese first came into contact with China they had no well-established writing of their own. But they borrowed Chinese characters and used them in a quite new way. They used each borrowed character to stand for a different syllable in their own language, and so made themselves a script that was much easier to read and write than the Chinese script. Unfortunately, they later borrowed many more Chinese characters and used them in the same way the Chinese do, thus making their script much more difficult.

In the seventh and eighth centuries A.D. Japanese cultural borrowing from China reached its height. China had adopted Buddhism from India; the Japanese adopted it from China, but modified it and blended it with their own national religious beliefs. The Japanese also borrowed certain Chinese ideas on government and on ethics, but always they molded the borrowed ideas into something new of their own.

TOP LEFT: *Yoritomo, the first shogun.* TOP RIGHT: *Seventeenth-century Japanese painting of a knight and his steed.* BOTTOM: *Samurai, members of the ancient Japanese warrior-class.*

A Duchy Becomes a Powerful State

INCREASING contacts between East and West near the close of the Middle Ages had far-reaching effects on Europe. The new knowledge which the Arabs brought to Spain did much to bring about the Renaissance. Chinese blockprinting paved the way for printing from movable type, which speeded the spread of knowledge.

During the fourteenth century another Chinese invention, gunpowder, began to affect Europe. Cannons were used at the Battle of Crécy in 1346, and just over a century later, at the Siege of Constantinople, they played a decisive part. Cannon warfare meant that an earl or a baron could no longer hope to hold his castle and its surrounding land with the help of retainers armed with bows and arrows. Thus instead of power being divided among a great many nobles, it tended to pass more and more into the hands of a few strong governments with powerful armed forces.

Until about the middle of the fourteenth century few parts of Europe except Germany, France, and England had such powerful governments. Then began a period when various small duchies and principalities began to combine to form powerful states. The first and most important was Burgundy.

At the Battle of Poitiers (1356) the youngest son of the King of France, Prince Philip, won himself the name of Philip the Bold. Later his father, King John, rewarded him by giving him the Duchy of Burgundy. At that time the comparatively small Duchy of Burgundy, with one of its main centers at Dijon, was thoroughly French in language and outlook. King John no doubt thought it would always remain so. But Philip married the heiress of Flanders, a land that then had very little sympathy with France. Later, two of Philip's children married into the house of Wittelsbach, which then ruled a large part of what is now Holland. Thus, in a comparatively short time, the Dukes of Burgundy came to control a very large area that had no inclination to be ruled by France.

Nevertheless, both Philip the Bold and his son John the Fearless who succeeded him, remained firmly French in their sympathies. Indeed, John the Fearless spent a great deal of time in Paris and played a part in French politics. But in 1419, John was assassinated and was succeeded by his son, Philip the Good.

Philip the Good, who ruled Burgundy from 1419 to 1467, adopted quite a different policy. He made an alliance with England against France during part of the great struggle of the Hundred Years' War. Then, when the tide turned in France's favor, he signed a peace treaty with her, which added important towns on the Somme to his dominions. Later, by carefully arranging marriages for his relatives, and also by force of arms, he added Flanders, Artois, and other places.

During the time of Philip the Good, Burgundy played a dominating part in western Europe. Its court was magnificent; it was the home of one of the most important of all the orders of chivalry, the Order of the Golden Fleece; and its various states all had parliaments.

Charles the Fearless, who followed Philip the Good, conceived the idea of uniting all the states under his control into a single powerful kingdom. But here he met strong armed opposition from the French King, Louis XI. In 1477 the French forces defeated his army at Nancy and Charles himself was killed. Under his daughter, Marie, the expansionist policy of Burgundy ceased, and at her death the connection between Burgundy proper and the Low Countries came to an end.

TOP: *Light area shows maximum extent of Burgundian domains. (*B_1 *marks Bruges,* B_2 *Brussels,* L *Liège,* D *Dijon,* B *Besançon.) London* (L_1) *and Paris* (P) *are also shown.* RIGHT: *Philip the Bold, John the Fearless, Philip the Good, and Charles the Fearless.* BOTTOM: *Insignia of Knights of the Golden Fleece; Marie of Burgundy; arms of Charles the Fearless.*

L1
B1
B2
L
P
D
B

Europe and the Balance of Power

IN one sense Europe was more united while it remained under the rule of many petty princes than when it came to be ruled mainly by a few powerful kings. During the Middle Ages it was not uncommon for petty princes to lay aside their bickerings and join together in some great Crusade to stem the power of the Moslems. On those occasions Europe could truly think of itself as a united Christendom.

With the growth of powerful kingdoms the idea of Christendom was gradually forgotten. Instead, each great state concerned itself first with increasing its own power and next with trying to prevent any one of its rivals from becoming more powerful than all the rest. In short, there was a prolonged struggle to maintain a balance of power.

Soon after 1500 the whole Balkan Peninsula was in the hands of the Ottoman Turks; Turkish ships controlled the eastern Mediterranean and could threaten the shores of Italy, and even of Spain, at any moment. Yet the states of Europe were scarcely concerned with the Turkish danger at all. They were far more interested in the growing rivalry between the two most powerful monarchs of Christian Europe.

Perhaps the most powerful of all was the Hapsburg Emperor, Charles V. From his father, who died when he was only six, he inherited the Netherlands. From his paternal grandfather, the Emperor Maximilian I, who died when he was nineteen, he inherited large areas of Austria and a strong claim to become the next Emperor of the Holy Roman Empire; and, indeed, he was elected in the very next year, 1520. From his mother, the feeble-minded daughter of Ferdinand and Isabella, he inherited not only Spain and parts of Italy but also Spanish possessions in America.

The only other European monarch of comparable power was the French King, Francis I (1515-1547), who had unsuccessfully contested Charles V's election as Emperor. In 1515 Francis began a military campaign in north Italy, and by gaining a victory over Swiss mercenaries at the Battle of Marignano he temporarily added Lombardy to his kingdom. Thereafter a struggle ensued between Charles V and Francis I for mastery of many of the small, divided states of Italy.

An overwhelming victory for either might have made the victor virtual master of Europe. And it was at this point that the other powers began to take sides in order to maintain the balance of power. Francis I, king of Christian France, did not hesitate to enter into an alliance with the Moslem Turks, who would thus present a threat to the coasts of Charles V's Mediterranean lands. Henry VIII of England, soon to sever the connection between the English Church and the Church of Rome, joined with the Pope, who then held large territories in central Italy, in supporting Charles V.

At first the struggle went in favor of Francis I, but later the tide turned. In 1525 Charles V won a great battle at Pavia, in which Francis I was captured and forced to relinquish some of his Italian possessions. It looked then as if Charles might emerge with too much power, and so Henry VIII and the Pope quickly went over to the side of Francis I.

Later, in 1527, Charles V's German troops stormed and pillaged Rome, thus helping to bring about the eclipse of the Italian Renaissance. Nevertheless, in 1530 the Pope himself crowned Charles as Holy Roman Emperor, thus confirming the election of 1520.

The long war between these two powerful kings achieved little except, perhaps, to weaken both. The only gainers, if there were any, were Henry VIII, the Turks, and the Popes, all of whom had tried to maintain the balance of power.

TOP: *The Battle of Marignano, from a miniature of the period.* BOTTOM: *The coronation of Charles V, after a painting by Titian.* RIGHT: *Charles V, Francis I, and Henry VIII.*

Europe and the Wider World

WHILE Europe's rulers and politicians were occupied with building nation-states, her seamen and merchants were opening up a wider world.

In the Middle Ages only a few highly educated men believed, as the later Greeks had believed, that the world was round. By the fifteenth century the revived knowledge of astronomy which the Arabs had brought to Europe had made quite a number of thinking people accept this belief.

This belief alone might not have sparked off the great voyages of discovery, but there were other favorable influences at work. In the Moslem universities of Spain many men (mainly Jews, for Christians were not allowed to study there) had learned how to make maps more accurately than ever before, and others had learned how to navigate a ship far out of sight of land. Furthermore, new navigational instruments, such as the magnetic compass and the astrolabe, had found their way to Europe. And the shipwrights of Portugal had begun to build stout sailing ships, called caravels, capable of standing up to the rough weather of the open Atlantic.

All these things helped to make ocean voyages possible, but there was another factor that made them almost essential. From the early fifteenth century until the great naval battle of Lepanto, in 1571, the Ottoman Empire dominated the Mediterranean and closed all the old sea-routes between Europe and the spice lands of the East. Genoese merchants were especially hard-hit by this closure, and they knew that their prosperity was doomed unless new routes were soon found.

The man who largely inspired the Age of Discovery was Henry the Navigator, a Portuguese prince who lived from 1395 to 1460. He opened a school of navigation at Sagres where he gathered together some of the finest map-makers, astronomers, and navigators of the age, and year after year he fitted out ships to make long voyages down the African coast and into the Atlantic as far as Madeira, the Canary Islands, and the Cape Verde Islands. After Prince Henry's death, Portuguese seamen made even more daring voyages. In 1487 Bartholomew Diaz reached the southern tip of Africa, and ten years later Vasco da Gama, still in his twenties, rounded Africa and crossed the Indian Ocean to Calicut, in southern India. Within the next few years Portuguese pioneers had established settlements in Goa, at Macao in China, and in the Malaccas; they had also claimed Brazil.

Yet the credit for making the first voyage to America since Viking times goes to a Genoese captain in the service of Spain—Christopher Columbus. His aim was to reach eastern Asia by sailing westward, and as a poor man, he sought financial backing for his expedition from several European sovereigns. He finally got it from Ferdinand and Isabella of Spain in 1492, the year they recaptured Granada. The cost of fitting out Columbus's three small ships was negligible but the reward was colossal. Columbus, to his dying day, believed that his westward voyage really had taken him to India. In fact he had discovered a new continent—the New World, as people soon began to call it. And from America (which probably got its name from a later explorer, Amerigo Vespucci) fantastic quantities of gold flowed into the coffers of Spain for many years.

In time, the Old World and the New began to share their products. The Old World came to know of potatoes, tobacco, quinine, and corn. The New World began to grow sugar and cotton and to rear domesticated animals. But colonization brought evils as well as good. Perhaps the greatest was slavery. Arab traders had for centuries past snatched Negro slaves from Africa. From the time of Henry the Navigator until the early nineteenth century Europeans joined in the slave trade and eventually almost monopolized it.

TOP LEFT: *Henry the Navigator.* TOP RIGHT: *A cotton plantation.* CENTER: *Some products that crossed the Atlantic: gold, cotton, rice, sugar, coffee, tobacco.* BOTTOM: *Arabs capturing Negroes for European slave traders.*

Mayas, Aztecs, and Spaniards

THE colossal task of exploring the coasts of the New World took time. It was not until 1513 that Balboa became the first European to set eyes on the Pacific Ocean. And it was not until 1519 that Ferdinand Magellan's expedition rounded the southern tip of the American mainland and crossed the Pacific in the first voyage around the world.

In the same year came one of the most dramatic episodes in the whole story of the colonization of the Americas. Hernando Cortez, during an earlier stay in the West Indies, had heard tales about Mexico, a land of fabulous wealth populated by a well-organized warrior people. In 1519, leading an army consisting of only five hundred men and sixteen horses, he set out to conquer it.

He did indeed find Mexico to be a land of fabulous wealth. Not only did it abound with gold and silver, but it was also rich in vegetation and richer even in architecture—architecture of a kind utterly new to Europeans. But it was a land populated by many civilized American-Indian peoples, of which the most powerful were the Aztecs.

Cortez was able to conquer the land only by an amazing combination of courage, craft and cruelty. By craft he made alliances with some of the smaller tribes who were jealous of Aztec power, and thus added some seven thousand Indians to his original small army; further, he encouraged the Aztec Emperor, Montezuma II, to welcome him as a friend, yet soon afterwards deposed him. His courage showed itself when, to prevent his own followers from deserting him and sailing home, he burned his ships to make retreat impossible. Cruelty manifested itself more, perhaps, in his lieutenants than in himself. One of them, Pedro de Alvarado, caused six hundred Aztec nobles to be slaughtered so that he could secure their riches.

Within about two years Cortez had conquered the whole of Mexico from Honduras in the southeast to the Gulf of California in the northwest. And with his conquest came the eclipse of the native civilizations of Central America. Very few Spaniards of that time were interested in leaving records of native customs and achievements, and much of what we now know about the early American civilizations we have learned from the work of modern archaeologists.

It is highly probable that the original inhabitants of America found their way there from Asia between 10,000 and 20,000 years ago, traveling by way of Siberia and Alaska, which are less than fifty miles apart and which may then have been joined by an isthmus. From then onwards they had no contact with the peoples of the Old World and their progress toward civilization evolved in a quite different way. None of these peoples ever learned to make wheels and none of them, except for the Incas of Peru who made use of llamas, ever domesticated animals.

Yet some of them reached a very high standard of civilization. The Mayan civilization, in Guatemala and Yucatan, flourished between about 300 and 900 A.D. The Mayas had worked out the length of the year as 365 days. They used a number system which had a zero sign, so that any number, however large, could be written with only nineteen different signs and a zero. The Mayas were also magnificent builders, as the ruins of many great temples, such as that at Chichen-Itza, still testify.

The Toltecs who occupied the Mexican plateau before 1300 A.D., built many large step-pyramids and also made excellent pottery. The Aztecs, who later conquered them, excelled in feather work and in shaping tools and ornaments of copper, gold, and silver. They owed their dominating position in the fourteenth and fifteenth centuries to their flair for organizing many towns and cities into a federation of small independent states. Their civilization was marred by the great number of human sacrifices entailed by their religion.

TOP LEFT: *Hernando Cortez.* TOP RIGHT: *Map of Montezuma's capital, Tenochtitlán, site of present Mexico City.* CENTER: *Scene in Mexico before the arrival of the Spaniards.* BOTTOM: *Mayan frescoes.*

The Empire of Sons of the Sun

WITHIN a few years of the conquest of Mexico, the Spaniards came into contact with another ancient American civilization, that of Peru.

By about 7000 B.C. some of the Neolithic peoples who reached America from Asia had made their way down the narrow Isthmus of Panama and into South America as far as Peru. By about 1500 B.C. many of their descendants had learned to grow crops and had settled down as farmers. From then on they gradually built up a unique civilization which reached its height between 500 and 1500 A.D.

Early in the thirteenth century one group of tribes, called the Incas, began to gain ascendancy over all the rest. They regarded their ruler, whom they called the Sapa Inca, as a god—Intip Cori, or Son of the Sun. Always, when a Sapa Inca died, one of his sons succeeded him and all his sons, together with their descendants, formed a special aristocracy called the royal ayllu.

In making warrior raids on other tribes the Incas were at first no different from their neighbors. But in 1438 an outstanding man, Pachacuti, was crowned. To him war was not merely a matter of making raids; it was a means of permanently extending the territory under Inca rule. One of his first victories was over the Chanca people who had previously threatened Cuzco, the Inca capital. After that, other victories followed, and in twenty years Pachacuti ruled all the land between Lake Junin and Lake Titicaca. Pachacuti's son, Topa Inca, continued the conquests, fighting his way northward as far as Quito and Manto. So the Incas went on extending their power, and by about 1520 they ruled the greatest Empire that ever existed in the Americas before the white men came.

The rule of the Sapa Incas was generally a benevolent one. It is true that only the royal ayllu held positions of responsibility and authority, and only they received the best education available. But the ordinary people had a degree of security rivaling that offered by a modern welfare state. Arable land was allocated among the various tribes and clans in proportion to their numbers, so that everyone was assured of a sufficiency of food. All the people were classified into some twelve groups, and all were found work appropriate to their age, sex, and abilities. Men called on to take part in military campaigns, to build roads, or to serve as professional runners carrying important messages, were supported out of public funds; and while they were absent from home their lands were tilled for them.

Scattered throughout the Inca Empire were magnificent temples, some built from large slabs of stone carried from many miles away. Inca metal workers used not only copper, gold, and silver but also the tougher metal, bronze. For keeping records of numbers, accountants used an arrangement of strings of different colors and knotted in different ways, called quipus. Farmers knew the art of terracing hillsides, which helped to prevent soil erosion; and unlike other native American peoples, they used domestic animals—llamas.

One weakness of the Inca Empire was that there was no fixed way of deciding which of the Sapa Inca's sons should succeed him. In 1532 two sons, Atahualpa and Huascar, were disputing the right to succeed their father. At that moment the Spanish conqueror, Pizarro, arrived with a force of less than two hundred men. He claimed to be a friendly ambassador from the King of Spain. Then, by massacring court officials, he seized Atahualpa. After accepting a colossal amount of gold for his release, he had him executed. By this and many other acts of violence and treachery did Pizarro and his associates establish Spanish power in Peru and bring the Inca Empire to an end.

An Inca aristocrat in ceremonial costume. The Spaniards called these men Orejones, or Big-ears, because of their ear-plugs. In the background are terraced farmlands, llamas, and a sun temple. Map shows greatest extent of Inca Empire.

PASTO
QUITO
CHINCHASUYO
CUZCO
ANTISUYO
CUNTI SUYO
COLLAS
TIAHUANACO
ARICA
CHARCAS
TUCMA
COLLASUYO
CODAYADO
VALPARAISO

Dividing the World, Sharing the Spoils

It is not hard to see why fifteenth-century Spain and Portugal took the lead in exploring and colonizing. During the long period of Moslem occupation they had learned more about navigation, map-making and astronomy than any other part of Europe. And when they finally drove the Moslems out, they emerged as two of the most powerful and united countries in Europe.

What is surprising is that the rest of Europe allowed the Spaniards and the Portuguese to monopolize the advantages of exploration and discovery for so many years. Everyone knew of the gold and silver that flowed into Spain each year from the Americas, and everyone knew of the rich harvest the Portuguese reaped from the spice trade and from the import of oranges from southeast Asia before orange-growing was well established in Europe. Yet it was many years before other countries obtained similar advantages.

Perhaps the main reason lies in a single act of statesmanship by Alexander VI, the man who became Pope just when Columbus first set foot in the New World. At that time only Spain and Portugal were active in discovering new lands. There was a real danger that rivalry between them might lead to war, and war between two neighboring Christian countries only recently freed from Moslem rule would have been a tragedy. The Pope acted as arbitrator between them, and by the Treaty of Tordesillas in 1494 he divided the world into two spheres of influence, one to be exploited only by Spain and the other only by Portugal. The dividing line ran from the southern tip of Greenland to the mouth of the Amazon. Everything to the west of it was for Spain, everything to the east for Portugal.

It was once fashionable to laugh at the Pope for dividing a largely-unexplored world between two comparatively small countries. But Alexander VI was also Rodrigo Borgia, a man born near Valencia in Spain while the Moslems still held a strong foothold there; and his act may well have prevented a disastrous war between Spain and Portugal. Further, it prevented several other countries from clashing with Spain and Portugal in a scramble for new colonies.

Some of the effects of Tordesillas have lasted to this day. When Brazil was discovered, in 1500, the Pope's dividing line made it Portuguese; all the rest of America, to the west of that line, was Spanish. Even today almost the whole mainland of America south of the U.S. border is a Spanish-speaking area; the only big exception is Brazil, which speaks Portuguese.

The Treaty of Tordesillas also meant that other European countries came late into the scramble for American possessions, when only North America was still almost wholly unexplored. Today almost all of North America is English-speaking, except for the Canadian province of Quebec, where French is the main language.

Although other governments long continued to show outward respect for the Pope's division of the world, there came a time when they turned a blind eye to the activities of seamen who decided to share the spoils of discovery with Spain. From the mid-sixteenth century onward buccaneers like Francis Drake, Martin Frobisher, Walter Raleigh, Jean Bart, and Piet Hein knew that their own governments were only too happy to let them raid Spanish settlements and rob Spanish galleons. Indeed, when Spain complained to Elizabeth I about English acts of piracy, she answered firmly that the Spaniards had brought the trouble on themselves by monopolizing American trade. Very significantly she added that "she did not acknowledge the Spaniards to have any title by donation of the Bishop of Rome." By that time the decrees of the Popes meant little to England.

TOP: *Pope Alexander VI, and the line with which he divided the world between Spain and Portugal.* BOTTOM LEFT: *Galleons that carried treasure from the New World to Spain in battle with buccaneers.* RIGHT: *Drake, Raleigh, and Jean Bart, men who harried the Spaniards.*

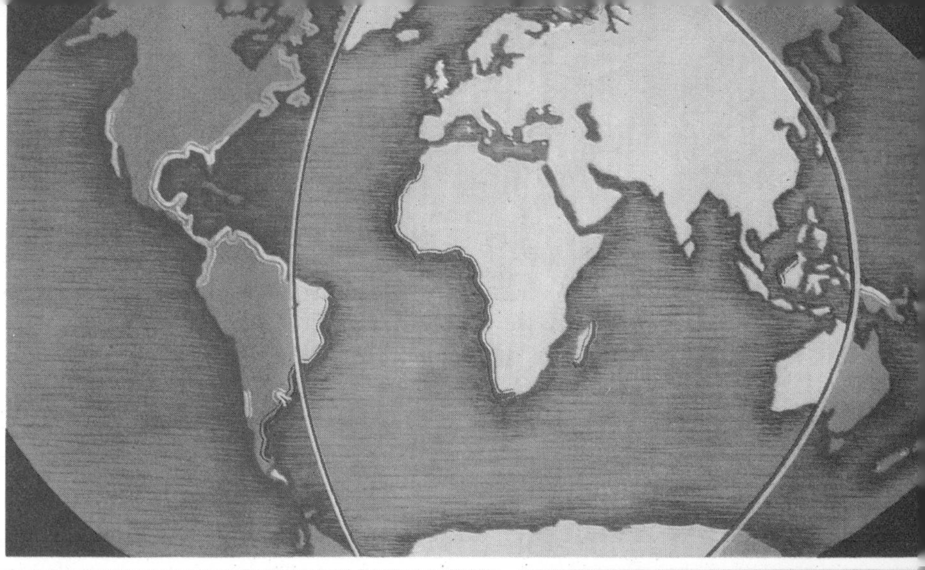

The Rise of the Protestants

WHEN we think of the power the Popes had exercised during the Middle Ages, it is at first sight astonishing that so many countries came to set that power at nought during the sixteenth century.

The Church had always had members who saw its faults and sought to put them right from within. But what happened during the Reformation of the sixteenth century was quite different. Here was an attempt at reform at all costs, even if it meant breaking away from Rome.

It is not possible here to outline all the reasons for this change, but we can see a few of them. From 1309 to 1378 the Popes had resided in Avignon. There they had become almost puppets of the Kings of France, thus shaking the confidence of other countries in their integrity. From 1378 to 1417 there had been two or more rival Popes, which again weakened Papal authority. In many parts of Europe, too, the Church had grown too wealthy for its own good or for the good of the people it served: many priests lived idle, lax lives, and had ceased to have any passionate belief in the doctrines they preached.

In the fourteenth century John Wycliffe, the man whose name is associated with the first complete translation of the Bible into English, preached not only against the wealth and worldliness of the Church but also against one of its important doctrines, the doctrine that the bread and wine of the sacrament are changed into the very body and blood of Christ. In England Wycliffe escaped condemnation for heresy, but in 1415 John Huss, a Czech preacher, was burned at the stake for preaching exactly the same ideas in Bohemia.

The first break with Rome came through a German priest, Martin Luther. Luther was at one time a monk himself and he remained a Roman Catholic until he was thirty-three. Then in 1517, disgusted with the sale of indulgences and having worked out new and unorthodox doctrines of his own, he challenged a friar named John Tetzel to a debate on his ideas which he had expressed in his famous 95 theses. As a result the Pope excommunicated him and issued a bull condemning his views. Luther replied by burning the document. From then on his break with Rome was complete. Under the protection of the Elector of Saxony he spent much of his later life in organizing the Reformed Church in Germany, and soon much of Germany, Austria, Scandinavia, and Holland had become Protestant and Lutheran.

In England, Henry VIII wrote a book arguing against Luther's views, and the Pope bestowed on him the title of Defender of the Faith. A few years later, when the king wanted to divorce Catherine of Aragon, the Pope refused to annul the marriage. Henry VIII thereupon broke with Rome, constituted himself head of a separate Anglican Church, dissolved the monasteries, and used much of their wealth for his own purposes. But he still retained his title, Defender of the Faith.

In Switzerland, the French theologian John Calvin led a very intense opposition to the Roman Church and its doctrines, and Calvinism quickly gained ground in Switzerland, France and, with the help of John Knox, in Scotland.

But the Church of Rome was not defeated by these defections from its ranks. It began a great counter-Reformation of its own. New religious orders were formed to preach Catholic doctrines and to fight for a revival of Catholic influence. The most notable was the Society of Jesus, founded by a great Spaniard, Ignatius Loyola, in 1540. Within a few years Jesuit missionaries had begun preaching and civilizing missions in many parts of the world. The work of Loyola, and the fact that there was now a succession of outstanding Popes, enabled the Church of Rome in time to regain much of the ground it had lost.

Around the crucifix are four leading figures in the religious upheavals of the sixteenth century. TOP: *Henry VIII and Martin Luther.* BOTTOM: *John Calvin and St Ignatius Loyola.*

Poland and Bohemia

THE awakening of initiative, enterprise, and intellectual effort which marked Europe's emergence from the Middle Ages began mainly in Spain, Italy, and Portugal. But by the time of the Reformation several countries of central and northern Europe were rapidly catching up with them.

Prominent among the countries moving to the forefront of progress were Poland and Bohemia. From the time of its foundation in the tenth century, Poland had been a Catholic state, and had shared in the civilization of western Christendom. For many years its main problem was to safeguard itself against repeated attacks from its northeasterly neighbors, the Lithuanians, who were powerful and still pagan. Then, early in the thirteenth century, Poland was attacked by the Mongols who seized Silesia and ravished Cracow, one of Poland's chief cities. At the battle of Liegnitz in 1241 an army of Poles and Germans was almost annihilated, but it did succeed in stemming the further advance of the Mongols.

When we consider Poland's long effort to hold onto its religion, to ward off powerful enemies, and to maintain itself as a kingdom, it is no wonder that one of its most famous medieval buildings, the Wawel at Cracow, was not only a cathedral and a palace but also a fortress.

By the mid-fourteenth century Poland had emerged as a powerful state and an important outpost of western Christendom. Casimir the Great, who ruled from 1333 to 1370, distinguished himself among all other European monarchs by offering asylum to the Jews who were then suffering bitter persecution in other parts of Europe. It was he, too, who built Poland's first university, at Cracow. Not long after his death, the ruling houses of Poland and a now-Christian Lithuania were united by marriage, and Poland became an important power in central Europe.

Poland reached the height of its power in the fifteenth and sixteenth centuries, and it was then that one of her greatest sons lived. Nicholaus Koppernigk, or Copernicus, was born at Thorn on the River Vistula in 1473. As a young man he studied first at Cracow then in Italy. On returning to his native land he worked out his famous theory that all the planets, including our own Earth, revolve round the sun. This revolutionary idea was later to have a marked effect not only on astronomy but also on religious questions. Copernicus withheld his ideas from publication until just before his death because he foresaw the trouble they might foment.

The Czechs and Slovaks, descendants of Slav tribes who had settled between the Dnieper and the Elbe two thousand years earlier, formed the independent kingdom of Bohemia in the tenth century A.D. Its principal city, Prague, soon became one of the main commercial markets of central Europe. In 1306 the original royal house of Bohemia, the Přemyslids, died out, and the new monarchs who came to the throne were of the House of Luxemburg. They were members of a noble family from near the borders of France and Germany, famous for its brilliance and love of adventure ever since the early Crusades.

Perhaps the greatest of the Luxemburg monarchs was Charles IV. Although he was also Holy Roman Emperor, he devoted almost all his energies to strengthening and beautifying Bohemia. Under his rule Bohemia's borders were extended from the Danube almost to the Baltic, and soon Prague became one of Europe's finest cities with imposing buildings such as the Hradčany, the Cathedral of St. Vitus, and Charles Bridge.

It was in Prague, soon after 1600, that Kepler followed up the work of Copernicus by discovering the laws of planetary motion.

TOP: *The old Wawel at Cracow.* BOTTOM: *Prague, with the Hradčany Palace, Cathedral of St. Vitus, and Charles Bridge.* CENTER: *Map of central Europe, showing Prague* (P_1), *Breslau* (B), *Warsaw* (W) *and Cracow* (C). *Also marked are London* (L), *Paris* (P), *Stockholm* (S), *and Moscow* (M). LEFT: *Copernicus.* RIGHT: *Charles IV.*

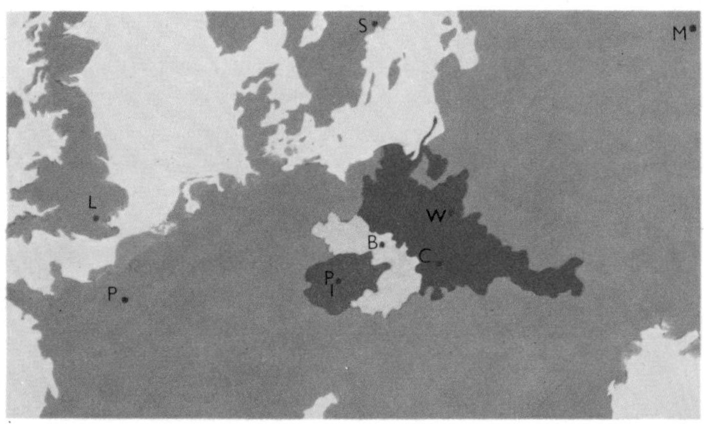
S
M
L
W
B
C
P
P
I

England Under Elizabeth I

DURING the Reformation both Poland and Bohemia became Protestant. In Poland, Jesuits slowly reconverted the country to Catholicism. In Bohemia, Protestantism was only stamped out by Catholic persecution under the Hapsburgs.

In England things took a very different course. Henry VIII broke with Rome not because he was imbued with Protestant ideals but mainly for personal and political reasons. After the break he was capable of executing Lutherans for heresy as well as Catholics for treason. His aim was to steer a middle course.

At that time most Englishmen were more concerned with maintaining the Tudor dynasty than with theological matters. But nevertheless there were some who hoped to guide the Anglican Church back to Rome and others, the reformers, who hoped to make it more like the Protestant Churches of continental Europe. During the reign of Edward VI (1547-53) the reformers largely had their way, but then, when Queen Mary came to the throne, the position was reversed. Brought up as a staunch Catholic, she reunited the English Church with Rome and put to death many leading Protestant reformers. Her persecution of the Protestants, and the fact that she married the Catholic Philip II of Spain, brought a powerful reaction against her policy.

When Mary died childless in 1558, her successor, Elizabeth I, was faced with the task of rebuilding the Church of England in a form acceptable to a large majority of her subjects. Only in that way could she hope to keep England strong and united. Had she married Philip II, who sought her hand, England might well have become Catholic again, and a mere satellite of Spain. Had she married any Protestant prince, the reformers might well have gained control of the Anglican Church, and England might have been embroiled in religious wars. Instead, she remained unmarried.

For nearly thirty years Elizabeth and her cautious advisers refused to be drawn into continental wars as champions of the Protestant cause, but they were constantly aware that the Catholic powers, especially Spain, were plotting either for England's return to Rome or for her downfall. Thus although the English government did not make open war on Spain, it privately encouraged men like Hawkins and Drake to make armed attacks on Spanish ships in an attempt to break Spain's monopoly of trade with the New World.

Philip II was not only goaded by these attacks, but he also felt it to be his duty to bring England back to the Catholic faith. And for this purpose he constantly encouraged Elizabeth's rival and next of kin, the Catholic Mary Queen of Scots. Mary, widow of Francis II of France, had later married Darnley who murdered her secretary Rizzio; then she married Bothwell who murdered Darnley. This last act caused an insurrection in Scotland, and Mary fled to England where she plotted to usurp Elizabeth's throne. She was imprisoned for nineteen years before Elizabeth reluctantly signed her death warrant in 1587. And it was this that finally decided Philip to launch a great Armada against England in the summer of the following year.

But ever since the reign of Henry VIII, who built royal dockyards, founded a school for pilots, and supervised the construction of a royal fleet, England's sea power had been steadily growing. In July, 1588, the smaller but faster English ships, under the command of Lord Howard, destroyed or routed many of the 130 galleons carrying 20,000 Spanish soldiers; many others were destroyed by storms. Though the war with Spain continued for some years this battle really broke Spain's sea power and proved England to be the leading maritime country in the world.

TOP: *Elizabeth I, Mary Queen of Scots, and Philip II of Spain.* BOTTOM: *English ships attacking Spanish galleons of the "Invincible Armada" in the English Channel in 1588.*

The Thirty Years' War

AT about the time England and Spain were at war there were several armed clashes between Catholics and Protestants in Europe. In 1608 the Protestants formed a Protestant Union, under the leadership of the Elector-Palatinate, and on the other side, the Catholics formed the Catholic League, led by Maximilian of Bavaria. War seemed inevitable.

In 1617 Ferdinand of Styria, a man educated by the Jesuits and already known for his persecution of Protestants, became king of Bohemia and Hungary. Soon he was to be elected Holy Roman Emperor. This was a tremendous blow to the Protestants of Bohemia. The utmost privilege they had ever gained from earlier Emperors was a Charter of Toleration, sometimes called the Letter of Majesty, granted them in 1609. This gave them the bare right to practice the Calvinist religion and to build temples. But in spite of the charter, the Emperor Matthias had allowed the Bishop of Prague to pull down their temple at Klostergrab. What would happen when Ferdinand became king and Holy Roman Emperor?

When a decree was issued forbidding Protestants to hold assemblies, they replied by throwing two Catholic ministers and a secretary from a window of the Hradčany Palace, an act which became known as the Defenestration of Prague. They refused to acknowledge Ferdinand and offered the throne of Bohemia to the Elector-Palatinate, Frederick V, known in England as Palsgrave. He accepted the offer though he knew it would involve him in war with Ferdinand. Palsgrave's luck did not hold for long. In November, 1620, he was defeated at the White Hill, near Prague, by the forces of the Catholic League, led by Maximilian of Bavaria.

He then fled the country, leaving the Bohemian Protestants to their fate. Not only did Ferdinand take harsh and repressive measures to exterminate Protestantism in Bohemia, but he also deprived the wealthier Protestants of their estates which he distributed among German and Czech Catholics. German became the official language and the Crown of Bohemia became part of the Hapsburg inheritance.

His greatest mistake was to ban Palsgrave from the Empire and give the Palatine territories to Maximilian, the victor of White Hill. The people of those lands were strongly Protestant and were not prepared to accept the Catholic Maximilian as their ruler. They called on a Lutheran king, Christian IV of Denmark, to help them. At this stage Wallenstein, a prince of Friedland and a somewhat mysterious adventurer, raised an army at his own expense and fought for Ferdinand against King Christian. He fought and won, forcing Denmark to withdraw from the struggle. But he then proceeded to pillage Protestants and Catholics alike, until the Emperor was persuaded to dismiss him.

All these moves had made the Emperor the strongest figure in Europe. France was now fearful of him, and in 1631 Cardinal Richelieu, France's powerful minister, agreed that France would finance a Swedish military expedition to restore Protestant fortunes. The idea fitted in perfectly with the ambitions of the brilliant Swedish king, Gustavus Adolphus. He wanted to make the Baltic a Swedish sea, to thwart Ferdinand's plans to place a Catholic on the Swedish throne in his stead, and to fight for Protestantism.

His highly mobile, well-equipped army took part in many battles—at Magdeburg, Breitenfeld, Lützen and elsewhere. The long war dragged on until 1648, but by the time of Breitenfeld (1631) the results were scarcely in doubt. Sweden emerged as the main power in northern Europe; Germany was devastated and its progress held up for more than a century; France was strong enough to claim and get most of Alsace-Lorraine; and the Catholic counter-Reformation was halted.

TOP: *Gustavus Adolphus, and the Siege of Magdeburg.* BOTTOM: *The Defenestration of Prague.* RIGHT: *Wallenstein and Cardinal Richelieu.*

The Great Reign of Louis XIV

UNLIKE most countries that took part in the Thirty Years' War, France emerged from it stronger than she entered it. By the Treaty of Westphalia, signed in 1648, she gained much of Alsace-Lorraine. The many small states of Germany, weakened by long years of fighting, were no longer a threat to her. Instead, they served as a buffer between a powerful Austria and a powerful France.

From this it might be expected that the French king would be the most influential figure in Europe. But in 1648 Louis XIV of France, who had already occupied the throne for five years, was as yet a mere boy of ten. The people who held real power were his mother, Anne of Austria, and Cardinal Mazarin, who had succeeded Richelieu as chief minister. In order to pay for France's expensive wars Mazarin imposed heavy and unpopular taxes. These so aroused the wrath of French lawyers and many of the French nobility that in the very year of the Peace of Westphalia they resorted to civil war.

This first "Fronde" insurrection lasted until 1649. Then, after a brief breathing space, there came a second one, in 1652 and 1653. In these risings, Condé, a brilliant young soldier who had earlier gained a great victory over the Spanish at the Battle of Rocroi (1643), played a prominent part. In 1652 he even entered Paris at the head of an army recruited from Spain. It was probably this act that made most Frenchmen realize that Condé was playing a game far too dangerous for his country's good, and which helped to bring about the collapse of the rising. Another factor which quelled the rising was that Anne of Austria was able to enlist the services of Marshal Turenne, a soldier even more able than Condé, on her side.

The Frondes made a tremendous impression upon the boy-king, Louis XIV. He had seen the nobles of his own country in league with foreign enemies; he had seen his mother hounded from Paris; he had seen the throne on the verge of collapse. He determined that when he came to manhood he would take the reins of government into his own hands. To his way of thinking the state and the king must henceforth be completely identified, a thought which he expressed in the famous words, "L'état, c'est moi."

His reign lasted, all told, for seventy-two years, from 1643 to 1715. From the middle 1660s onwards he was, indeed, absolute master of France, exercising enormous influence not only in internal politics and foreign policy but also in fashions, literature, and art. His emblem was the blazing sun, from which he was often called Le Roi Soleil, the Sun King. And he took as his motto *Nec pluribus impar*, no unequal match for many.

At Versailles, eight miles from his capital, he set 30,000 men to work to build a palace equal to his dignity, a palace set in a park of more than 20,000 acres abounding in game. Crack troops, 10,000 strong, constituted his household brigade. So high did he raise himself above the nobility—the nobility whose fickleness he had witnessed as a child—that the greatest men of France, men such as Marshal Condé and Marshal Turenne, deemed it an honor to serve him in even a menial capacity.

Yet Louis XIV cared for the dignity of France, too. Early in his reign, with the aid of his faithful assistant Colbert, he restored France's finances, promoted better trade, modernized roads, and encouraged colonization. With the help of men such as Louvois and Vauban, the great military engineer and fortress-builder, he made the French army the most efficient of his time. Until almost the end of the sixteenth century France enlarged its territories under his rule. Only in 1697 did it lose some of these gains.

TOP: *Louis XIV at Versailles, with Louvois, Colbert, and Vauban. In the background are musketeers.* BELOW: *Plans of two kinds of Vauban fortifications, and Louis XIV's emblem and motto.*

NEC PLVRIBVS IMPAR
1674

The Golden Age of The Netherlands

DURING the seventeenth century a new power vied with France and England for the leading place in western Europe—the country we now call the Netherlands.

In the sixteenth century the Netherlands, where cities such as Antwerp and Amsterdam were rapidly becoming main centres of world trade, formed a very valuable source of revenue to Philip II of Spain. But Philip, as a devout Catholic, was just as interested in the religion of the Netherlands as he was in its trade and prosperity. While he himself was in Spain he left the affairs of the country in the hands of Margaret, Duchess of Parma, and three Catholic advisers who were under instructions to take stern measures against Protestantism. Then in 1564 he made a decree that the entire population of the Netherlands should accept Catholic doctrines. William of Orange and Egmont drew up a petition begging the king to revoke this decree but instead, Philip sent a strong army to the Netherlands to enforce it.

Egmont was captured and beheaded, but William of Orange, who was declared an outlaw, escaped to Germany and raised an army to fight the Spaniards. Meanwhile, Protestant Dutch seamen and pirates, with the active support of England's Queen Elizabeth, harried and plundered Spanish coastal strongholds.

The struggle was long and severe, and it was aggravated by the fact that the Catholic population of the southern provinces could not long make common cause with the Protestant population of the northern provinces. In 1584 William of Orange was assassinated, but still the fight went on. Eventually, in 1588, the seven northern provinces of Holland, Zeeland, Utrecht, Gelderland, Overijssi, Groningen, and Friesland declared themselves to be a united republic. The declaration, made at the town of Delft, famous for its beautiful porcelain, meant that the northern provinces had separated not only from Spain but also from the southern provinces (now Belgium).

It was not until 1609 that Spain recognized the independence of the United Provinces, but in the meantime the new state had begun to make headway. Each province had its own government for its home affairs, and in addition there was a federal government for all of them—the States General, which was composed of representatives from all the provinces. There was also a Stadtholder, or governor, who commanded the armed forces and exercised many of the powers of a president. Since Holland was by far the largest and wealthiest province it soon became customary to choose a representative from Holland—a member of the House of Orange—for that position.

The United Provinces, or Holland as we may now say, was only about the size of New Jersey, yet during the seventeenth century it became one of the most influential countries in the world. By 1700 its merchant fleet had a tonnage far greater than the tonnage of the French and English merchant fleets combined. After the founding of the Dutch East India Company and the Dutch West India Company, Holland conquered a large overseas empire. The names of great Dutch seamen like Martin Tromp, and his son, Cornelis van Tromp, Michael De Ruyter, and Piet Heijn, were known in every sea and ocean.

During this golden age of Holland the Dutch school of painting attained its zenith with the work of Rembrandt, Franz Hals, and Jan Vermeer. Spinoza, a Dutch lens-polisher, became known as one of the world's outstanding philosophers. And in that age of piracy at least one great Dutchman, Hugo Grotius, was a notable man of law. His book, *Concerning the Law of War and Peace*, is still a foundation-stone of international law.

TOP: *William of Orange; map of United Provinces showing Leyden, Amsterdam, and Utrecht; Seal of the States General.* CENTER: *Amsterdam headquarters of Dutch East India Company.* BOTTOM: *Hugo Grotius; Piet Heijn; a Delft plate.*

A
L
U
SIGILLVM
ORDINVM
BELGII

Britain in Stuart Times

WHILE Holland's influence in international affairs increased, Britain's declined. It was not until 1603 that the term Great Britain was first officially used, for in that year, when Elizabeth I died, she was succeeded by James VI of Scotland, son of Mary Queen of Scots and Darnley. James now became James I of England and King of Great Britain.

From the moment when this first Stuart king came to the English throne, two great problems paralyzed English politics. The first was whether power should be wielded by the Crown or by Parliament. The second was whether or not the Anglican Church should become more puritanical and govern itself without bishops.

The English people had a very old Parliamentary tradition, and while they were prepared to let the Tudor monarchs override Parliament in times of national danger, they were not prepared to let an untried king do so. James I and many bishops, on the other hand, claimed that a king ruled by Divine Right, and that all power therefore resided in him.

So far as the Church was concerned, the whole idea of a separation from Rome was still new in Elizabethan times. Under their beloved Virgin Queen, most people were prepared to accept a religion that was neither Catholic nor Puritan. But towards the end of Elizabeth's reign the counter-Reformation had gained strength. Many Englishmen now felt the time had come to copy those Protestant Churches which had dispensed with bishops and with all Catholic ritual.

Here again, James I had very different ideas. He felt that if the bishops were robbed of their authority, so might he be too. "No bishops, no king", he declared.

Charles I, who succeeded James I in 1625, shared his father's opinions. And it was this deep division between the views of the king and the views of many of his subjects that led to the Great Rebellion. In 1640, when Charles I tried to force the Presbyterian Scottish Lowlanders to use the Anglican Prayer Book, they promptly raised an army against him. Then in 1642, when the Long Parliament declared that there must be no taxation without Parliamentary consent, and called for the abolition of bishops, Charles decided to arrest five Members. When he tried to do so he found they had fled. A week later he himself had to flee from the wrath of the London mobs.

The war between Puritan Roundheads and Loyalist Cavaliers which followed these events ended in a Puritan victory, and Oliver Cromwell became virtual military dictator of England. The moderate Parliamentarians were prepared to negotiate with the king, but Cromwell and his extremists were satisfied only when Charles I was beheaded in 1649. Cromwell enhanced his prestige but not his popularity by his ruthless crushing of the Irish Rebellion and by his victory over the Scots at Dunbar in 1650.

Perhaps the chief contribution Cromwell made to England's welfare was his Navigation Act. This forced English shipyards to build more ships, thus helping to restore England's sea power. This Act was one cause of England's two brief naval wars with Holland (1652-54 and 1664-67).

In 1660, two years after Cromwell's death, the monarchy was restored and Charles II came to the throne. It was in his reign that the Test Act of 1673 was passed, compelling all people holding office to take the sacrament, according to the rites of the Church of England, at least once a year. But Charles II's successor, James II, who reigned from 1685 to 1688, was a convert to Roman Catholicism and it was this that led to the Glorious (and bloodless) Revolution and to his abdication. The throne then passed to the Dutch William III, grandson of the great William of Orange, and to his wife Mary, daughter of Charles I.

TOP: *Charles I, Cromwell, and William III.* BOTTOM: *William III, on becoming King of England, lands at Brixham. (After a painting in St. James's Palace.)*

Wars Waged for an Empire

By about 1650 the chief powers in western Europe were Britain, Holland, and France. In central Europe only Austria could compare with them in might, and in southern Europe only Spain.

Spain's power was waning but the Spanish Empire was the biggest and richest in the world, comprising Sicily, Sardinia, Naples, Milan, the Balearic Islands, the Spanish Netherlands, and the greater part of South America. It is no wonder that rivalry for the Spanish throne eventually involved all the European powers in war.

While Louis XIV, France's Sun King, was young it seemed probable that when Philip IV of Spain died his heir would be his daughter, Maria Theresa. No doubt when Louis married her he thought he might one day be able to put forward a strong claim to the Spanish throne. But when his father-in-law remarried and became the father of a male heir (later Charles II of Spain), Louis became impatient. In 1667, two years after Philip IV died and Charles II came to the throne of Spain, he made war on the Spanish Netherlands and seized part of it. In 1672, in alliance with England's King Charles II, he also made war on the Dutch republic. But all that France gained was a few towns on her northeastern border, together with the Franche-Comté.

After 1688, when France also sent troops into Germany, many countries became alarmed by Louis XIV's aggressiveness. The result was the formation of a Grand Alliance against him. This alliance eventually included Austria, Spain, Sweden, Britain, and Holland, as well as several small states. For nine years the Grand Alliance waged war on France, and by the Treaty of Ryswick, which ended the war in 1697, Louis had to give up many of his earlier territorial gains.

But Ryswick was only a breathing space. Charles II, the last Hapsburg King of Spain, childless, imbecile and in poor health, could not live much longer, and all Europe was concerned about who should succeed him. In 1700, when Charles died, it was found that he had bequeathed his Empire to Philip, Duke of Anjou, Louis XIV's grandson, on condition that if he did not accept it *in its entirety* it should go instead to a Hapsburg—Charles, Archduke of Austria. Up to then Louis XIV had agreed with England and Holland that the Spanish Empire ought to be divided between the two men. Now he realized it was all or nothing, he changed his opinion and decided to support his grandson's claim to all of it.

Most European powers, still absorbed by the idea of maintaining the balance of power, were appalled at such a vast prize falling into French hands, and it would have taken little provocation to goad them into war over the Spanish Succession. Louis XIV now provided more than they needed. He threw an army into the Spanish Netherlands, seized Dutch towns, and boasted that the Pyrenees no longer existed.

At once all the members of the Grand Alliance, with the exception of Spain, were ranged against him. Britain and the other allies were well served by such soldiers as the Duke of Marlborough and Prince Eugène of Savoy, and at first all the big victories—Ramillies, Oudenarde, Malplaquet—went to them. But in time the tide turned. Marlborough fell into disfavor with Queen Anne and was recalled, and Charles of Hapsburg quarreled with his allies. Now the victories began to go to France, and finally the exhausted adversaries negotiated a settlement.

By the Treaty of Utrecht (1713), Philip, the Frenchman, became King Philip V of Spain and its overseas colonies. Charles, now the Emperor Charles VI, received Milan, Naples, Sicily, and the Spanish Netherlands. England received Gibraltar, Minorca, Newfoundland, and Nova Scotia.

TOP LEFT: *Map of Europe in 1713.* TOP RIGHT: *The Duke of Marlborough and Prince Eugène of Savoy.* BOTTOM: *Marlborough and Eugène at the Battle of Oudenarde.*

The Growing Power of Russia

In the early seventeenth century the history of Europe was changed by the emergence of Holland. A hundred years later Russia also became an important factor in European affairs.

In the Middle Ages, the rulers of Moscow had been chief tax collectors for the Golden Horde, and this unenviable task gradually gave them ascendancy over almost all the other Russian states. Thus in time the Grand Dukes of Moscow began to call themselves Grand Dukes of all the Russias. It was Ivan III (1462-1505) who first really justified the title. By 1480 he had united most Russian states under his own rule. Then, after refusing to pay tribute to the Khans, he finally broke their power, made Russia independent, and began to extend its boundaries.

After the fall of Constantinople he married a niece of the last Byzantine Emperor, Sophia, who had escaped to Italy. She brought with her to Russia a number of painters and architects, and it is this that explains the Byzantine influence seen in many Russian buildings, such as the Kremlin at Moscow. But Ivan's marriage with Sophia had even greater effects on Russia. Russia had always followed the Orthodox Church—the branch of the Christian Church that originated in Constantinople. Ivan had always regarded Constantinople as the successor to Rome, and the Byzantine Emperors as heirs to the Caesars. Now he thought of Moscow as "the third Rome" and of himself as heir to the Caesars.

In 1547 when Ivan IV, later known as Ivan the Terrible, became ruler of Russia, he insisted on being crowned as Tsar—another word for Caesar. During his reign, which lasted until 1584, he concentrated on weakening the remaining power of the Russian dukes and boyars (petty princes), forcing them to provide troops for Russia. He waged successful wars against Sweden, Poland, and Lithuania to give Russia its first foothold on the Baltic coast, and with his encouragement Russian adventurers penetrated deep into the almost empty vastness of Siberia, winning new lands for the Tsar.

After Ivan's death Russia suffered a period of great unrest for nearly thirty years. During this period there were great peasant uprisings, there were also several claimants to the Russian throne, and Swedish and Polish armies invaded the country. Eventually, in 1613, the first Tsar of the House of Romanov, Michael, was crowned. During his reign and that of his son Alexei (1645-1676), Russia extended its rule to the Pacific coast of Siberia, waged war against the Turks, and united with Little Russia.

But Russia first made its great impact on western Europe under Peter the Great (1682-1725). In 1696 he made war against the Turks to regain Azov. His failure convinced him that Russia must modernize itself and improve its technology. For two years this giant of a man labored as an ordinary working man in Germany, Holland, and Britain, learning all he could about western ways and especially about ships and ship-building. On returning to Russia he reorganized his armies, created a new administration, built schools and factories, ordered his subjects to shave their beards, and startled all Russia by founding a new capital at St. Petersburg (now Leningrad). During a war with Sweden, which lasted through most of his reign, he at first suffered many defeats. But in 1709 he won a great victory over Charles XII of Sweden at Poltava. From then on the war went in his favor. In 1721, when it ended, Russia gained a commanding position in the eastern Baltic.

TOP: *Map illustrating the expansion of Russia. The area shaded khaki had been acquired by 1689; the red area by 1721; the white area by 1795; and the grey area by 1815. (*SP — *St. Petersburg,* K — *Kiev,* P — *Poltava.) The two figures are Charles XII of Sweden and Peter the Great.* RIGHT: *Ivan the Terrible and the Cathedral of St. Basil, within the Kremlin, Moscow.* BOTTOM: *The exterior of the Kremlin or Citadel, Moscow; its ancient walls and towers enclose palaces, churches and cathedrals.*

S P
K
P

The Making of a Kingdom

IN the seventeenth and eighteenth centuries yet another new kingdom was welded together, this time from the most unpromising materials.

The Hohenzollerns were one of the most able ruling families of Europe, but the territories over which they held sway were small and scattered. In 1640 one of the ablest of them, Frederick William, became Elector of Brandenburg. Besides Brandenburg, with its capital at Berlin, he was also master of the Duchy of Prussia and of the small duchies of Ravensburg, Mark, and Cleves, which lay far to the west, in the Rhineland. Prussia was deeply embedded in Polish territory, and was a fief of the Polish crown, and all the rest of Frederick William's lands were within the boundaries of the Holy Roman Empire.

Yet out of these scattered and somewhat sparsely populated lands Frederick William determined to build a strong modern state. He modernized his armies, laid the foundations of a civil service, and introduced new methods of taxation. Above all he encouraged people driven from their own countries by religious persecution, whether Huguenots, Lutherans, or Catholics, to settle in his domains. In 1660 he succeeded in gaining complete sovereignty for the Duchy of Prussia, and in 1675, during the war in Holland, he won a victory over the Swedes at Fehrbellin, which brought his name prominently before other European countries.

During the War of the Spanish Succession, the Emperor agreed that Frederick, the son of the Great Elector, should be crowned King of Prussia. Frederick I reigned only until the end of the war, and during his reign Prussian troops distinguished themselves in many battles.

Then in 1713, at the time of the Treaty of Utrecht, Frederick William I came to the throne. It has been said of him that he was generous with nothing except thrashings. But his methods were harsh mainly in the cause of strengthening his country. Soon after his coronation he sold his best horses, his state coaches, and his precious stones. Within a few months he had spent much of the money in forming two battalions of grenadiers. Before he died, in 1740, his army was among the best in Europe.

His son, Frederick the Great, who reigned from 1740 to 1786, constantly used the army to extend Prussia's boundaries and enhance its prestige. Very soon after his accession he made war against Austria, and during the war of the Austrian Succession (1740-1748) he annexed Silesia, a large province rich in mineral wealth. Then followed eight years of peace during which he wrote some verses criticizing three of Europe's most powerful women: Madame de Pompadour (favorite of Louis XV of France), the Empress Elizabeth of Russia, and Maria Theresa, Empress of Austria.

From 1756 to 1763 Frederick II was at war with all the three countries he had thus offended—the Seven Years' War. His only ally was Britain, where Pitt the Elder was then in power. At first Frederick had successes against all his enemies, but eventually he was defeated by the Russians who occupied Berlin. But Frederick II was a man of many parts. He loved music, philosophy, and theology. A great admirer of French culture, he had built his palace of Sans Souci at Potsdam on the model of Versailles. He was also something of a poet, and because the Tsar Peter III admired him for this, the Tsar evacuated Russian troops from Berlin. Finally, Prussia was allowed to keep Silesia, and emerged from the Seven Years' War as a recognized great power.

At the close of the eighteenth century, after Prussia, Austria, and Russia joined in partitioning Poland, Prussian domains occupied a sizable area of central Europe.

TOP: *The Palace of Sans Souci at Potsdam.* BOTTOM: *Eighteenth-century Europe. The arrows indicate which countries fought against Prussia. On Prussia is Frederick II; on Britain, Pitt the Elder; on France, Madame de Pompadour; on Austria, Maria Theresa; on Russia, the Tsarina Elizabeth; and on Turkey, a Turk.*

Russia under Catherine the Great

At the time of the partitioning of Poland a woman, Catherine the Great, occupied the Russian throne. Indeed, apart from a break of only a few months, Tsarinas ruled Russia from 1741 to 1796.

After Peter the Great died in 1725 he was succeeded, in turn, by his widow, his grandson, and his niece. The first of these, Catherine I, reigned for only sixteen months. The next, Peter II, came to the throne in 1727 at the age of twelve and reigned for three years, a period during which Russia turned its back on westernization for a time and re-established Moscow as its capital. The third, Anne, with the help of her German favorite, Biren, reigned by terrorism from 1730 to 1740.

Then, after a year of unrest with several rivals for the throne, Elizabeth became Tsarina and gave Russia a period of more settled government. She founded agricultural banks, created a university at Moscow, and contributed much to the beautifying of St. Petersburg. The reign of her predecessor, Anne, had been marked by a strong German influence on Russian affairs. Now it was French influence that prevailed. The Tsarina and her court favored French teachers and bought their clothes and even their furniture from Paris. So far from admiring Germany, Elizabeth's main concern during the last years of her reign was to bring about the downfall of Frederick the Great of Prussia, and, as we saw on page 112, Russia came near to achieving that objective at the close of the Seven Years' War.

What saved Prussia was the fact that Elizabeth died in 1762 and was succeeded by Peter III, a passionate admirer of Frederick the Great. It was he who, when the war was almost ended, withdrew Russian troops from Berlin. But Peter III reigned only a few months before he was murdered, and the throne passed to his widow, Catherine II.

Though German by birth and French by education, Catherine II became more Russian than the Russians. In home affairs her prime concern was to strengthen her control over all the many regional governments submitting directly to the Imperial Council. In all these governments the nobility was responsible for administration, justice, and finance, and to ensure that the nobles should be loyal to the throne, Catherine distributed enormous grants of land among them—land complete with serfs to work it. Thus serfdom became widespread, even in southern Russia where it formerly had little hold. This was one of the causes of a five years peasants' revolt.

In fertile territories that had previously not been properly exploited because of the sparse population, and in regions newly conquered by Russia, Catherine pursued a policy of immigration. In this her favorite, Potemkin, played a leading part. It has been estimated that when he began the colonization of a large area of southern Russia its population was only 200,000. By the time of his death it had risen to 800,000. Catherine would have liked progress to be even faster, and Potemkin sometimes had to trick her into believing that things were moving at an impossible speed. When the Tsarina visited the newly colonized areas, Potemkin is said to have brought in hundreds of serfs and compelled them to build sham villages like that in the picture, where false façades hid uncompleted buildings or even ruins. Potemkin's villages were a fair symbol not only of Russia but also of all Europe in the eighteenth century.

It was Catherine the Great who, between 1792 and 1795, played the leading part in the partitioning of Poland between Russia, Prussia, and Austria, an event that was to erase Poland from the map of Europe for more than a century. She also took the Crimea and other lands bordering on the Black Sea from the Turks.

TOP LEFT: *Catherine the Great and Potemkin.* TOP RIGHT: *Map showing growth of Russia's boundaries under Catherine.* BOTTOM: *Potemkin's sham village being visited by Catherine.*

A Land Isolated from the West

We can think about the main events in Europe during the early Middle Ages without looking very far afield. The story is confined almost entirely to the lands around the Mediterranean and those of northwest Europe. In the later Middle Ages we must also take account of the westward surge of the Moslems, and of the invasions of eastern Europe by Mongol hordes from central Asia.

From the close of the fifteenth century onward the horizon broadened rapidly. Spanish seamen were then opening up a far wider world. Within a few years the civilizations of the Mayas, the Aztecs, and the Incas were all things of the past, and the laws, language, and religion of Spain were gaining a firm foothold in the New World. Portuguese seamen rounded the Cape of Good Hope, established a direct sea-route to India, traded with the East Indies, and in the middle of the sixteenth century, founded a colony at Macao in China.

Within a few decades other European powers were in quest of new lands and new trading opportunities. The Frenchman, Jacques Cartier, sailed to Newfoundland and far up the St. Lawrence River; Drake of England rounded Cape Horn and voyaged up the west coast of the Americas as far north as Vancouver Island; the Dutchman, Willem Barents, visited Spitsbergen and Novaya Zemlya in the Arctic. Even Russia, not yet in close contact with western Europe, began to push outwards, and by the close of the sixteenth century the explorer and adventurer, Yermak, extended Russian power far eastward into Siberia.

Thus we cannot think of the history of Europe after that time without thinking of the world as a whole, for almost the whole world was coming either under European dominion or under strong European influence. The War of the Spanish Succession was not waged only for Spain's European possessions, but also for control of her vast overseas empire. So far as England and France were concerned, the Seven Years' War was not so much a European struggle as a struggle for supremacy in North America and India.

But for many years one country of the Far East, Japan, succeeded in isolating itself almost completely from the West. At first it seemed that Japan, like almost everywhere else in eastern Asia at that time, would open her doors to Europeans. Indeed, from 1549 to 1551 Francis Xavier, one of the original members of the Society of Jesus, led a Catholic mission to Japan. Later, in the opening years of the seventeenth century, it looked as if a flourishing trade might develop between Europe and Japan. The English East India Company, founded in 1600, and the Dutch East India Company, founded two years later, both sent ships there until they reached an agreement by which the Dutch concentrated on the Far East trade and Britain on trade with India.

Then, owing to political changes inside Japan, the situation suddenly altered. Between 1573 and 1615 Japan was mainly under the control of three men. The first, Nobunga, was a champion of Catholicism and a friend of foreigners. But after his death, control passed to his lieutenant, Hideyoshi, who had very different views and who banished foreigners. Next in power was Iyeasu, also an anti-foreigner, whose descendants were to be shoguns until after the middle of the nineteenth century. Under Iyeasu and his immediate successor Japan was closed entirely to Spanish and Portuguese ships, and the most severe restrictions were placed on Dutch ships. Vessels visiting the port of Nagasaki were deprived of their cannon, munitions, and rudder, and their crews were forbidden to go ashore.

In this way Japan began its long period of isolation. Not until the nineteenth century was its history again linked with that of Europe.

TOP LEFT: *The Shogun Hideyoshi.* TOP CENTER: *Map of Japan.* TOP RIGHT: *The Shogun Iyeasu.* BOTTOM: *This European ship visiting Nagasaki was compelled to hand over its cannon, ammunition, and rudder. A passport for Dutch ships, in Japanese, is shown upper right.*

The Struggle for India and Canada

WHILE Europe made little headway in Japan it was rapidly coming to dominate other parts of the world, and in several areas there were bitter struggles for supremacy.

For France, and more especially for Britain, the Seven Years' War was mainly a war to decide which should control India and Canada. France helped her European allies, Russia and Austria, by sending an enormous army to fight against the Prussians. Britain, on the other hand, gave little help to her European ally, Prussia, and threw all her strength into the colonial war.

India at this time was a densely populated Empire with a civilization comparable to western culture in all but technical matters. But it was also an Empire that was beginning to crumble. Between 1658 and 1707 the ruler of India was the Great Mogul Aurangzeb. A fanatical Moslem, he greatly extended his Indian Empire but also weakened it by persecuting the Hindus. After his death power fell more and more into the hands of local rajahs, few of whom were strong enough to withstand pressure from European colonists.

Up to then Britain, as represented by the London East India Company, and France, as represented by a Company founded by Colbert in 1664, had had to be content with a few fortified trading posts near the coast. The main British posts were at Bombay, Calcutta, and Madras. The main French posts were at Chandernagore, north of Calcutta, and Pondicherry, south of Madras. By 1744 Joseph Dupleix, the French governor of Pondicherry, had realized that India's strength was crumbling. When war broke out between France and Britain, he occupied Madras and seized a large coastal area of southeast India. But in 1748, when peace was restored, France returned Madras to Britain. Nevertheless French prestige now stood very high, and by skilful diplomacy Dupleix was later able to extend French influence in southern India.

In 1751, however, the young English soldier Robert Clive seized Arcot, the capital of the Carnatic in southern India. French prestige suffered a severe blow, Dupleix was recalled, and his successors proved to be less capable men. Thereafter, during the Seven Years' War, Clive gained many victories for Britain, notably those at Calcutta and Plassey. Before the war ended Britain was master of the whole of Bengal Province.

In North America the situation was simpler. The British colonies there were strung out in a long line along the Atlantic coast. Their populations were increasing and the time was clearly coming when their people would want to push westward beyond the Mississippi River and possibly northward beyond the St. Lawrence and the Great Lakes. But the French already held many settlements along the St. Lawrence and had thus laid the foundations of a Canadian colony. In 1682 they had also acquired the vast territory of Louisiana which sprawled far out to both east and west of the Mississippi.

The British colonists, with the support of the mother country, were determined to break through the fence of French territory, and the Seven Years' War supplied a suitable opportunity. They entered into what is known as the French and Indian War.

Because France was employing so much of its army in Europe, its American possessions were not as strongly defended as they should have been. In 1758 the British colonists were able to capture Fort Duquesne on the Ohio River in French Louisiana. A year later General Wolfe laid siege to Quebec, France's chief Canadian stronghold. The French, who had been commanded by General Montcalm, were forced to capitulate after Wolfe's troops had scaled the Heights of Abraham. Both Wolfe and Montcalm lost their lives in the battle. Thus in North America as well as in India supremacy passed into British hands.

TOP LEFT: *Map of North America, with Montcalm (top) and Wolfe (bottom).* TOP RIGHT: *Map of India, with Clive (top) and Dupleix (bottom).* BOTTOM: *Fighting in North America during the Seven Years' War.*

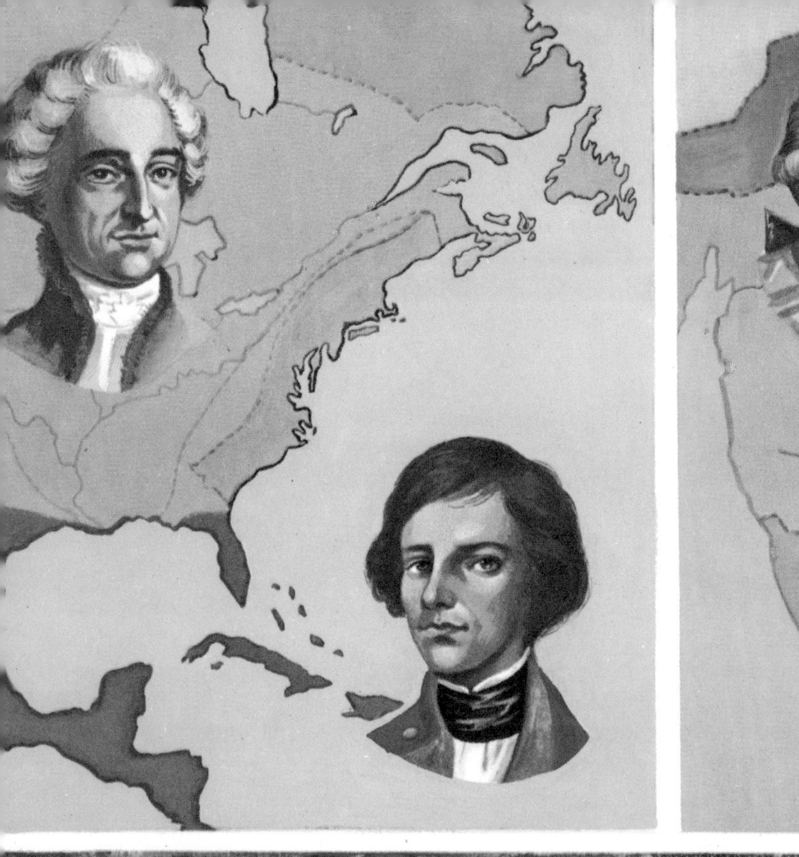

The American Revolution

BRITAIN had long placed restrictions on the trading of her American colonies in order to benefit traders at home. But from about 1715 onwards these restrictions were not rigidly enforced. Many American colonists indulged in smuggling, and Britain turned a blind eye. Nevertheless, the colonists objected to the principle of trade restriction, and bore it only because they needed British troops and British ships to protect them from possible aggression by France.

After France's defeat in Canada, there was nothing to fear, and the colonists objected more strongly than ever to the restrictions. On the other hand, Britain had waged a long and expensive war largely for the colonists' benefit, and felt that they ought to pay something towards its cost. Grenville, Britain's Prime Minister, invited them to make a voluntary contribution to the British Treasury. When none was forthcoming he took two drastic steps. First he gave orders that the British navy must end smuggling in America; next he brought in his Stamp Act, which required all legal documents in the colonies to bear a revenue stamp.

Now the colonists had a real grievance. They were being asked to pay taxes and yet they had no representatives in Britain's parliament. The cry of "No taxation without representation" which they immediately raised was the prelude to revolt. They refused to buy British goods, wrecked government offices, and burned many of the offending stamps. For several years after that Britain imposed and rescinded various levies, taxes, and customs duties, but the damage was already done.

Late in 1773 three British ships from India loaded with tea, which then carried a tax, were at anchor in Boston harbor. Disguised as American Indians, a number of Boston colonists boarded the ships and pitched their cargo into the water. Britain decided on strong retaliation. Early in 1774 the charter of Massachusetts was suspended, the port of Boston was closed, large numbers of troops were quartered in and around the town, and it was decreed that citizens of Massachusetts could be tried in Britain or in Nova Scotia.

At once all the other colonies except Georgia rallied to the side of Massachusetts. They sent delegates to the Congress of Philadelphia and issued a Declaration of Rights, demanding that Britain should withdraw the Penal Acts against Massachusetts. On the 18th of April, 1775, British troops searching for arms at Lexington, near Boston, were fired on by aroused colonists. The armed rising had begun. Soon the colonies called a second Congress, but this time they issued not a Declaration of Rights but a Declaration of Independence (July 4th, 1776). Among the famous men who helped to frame this declaration were Benjamin Franklin, Thomas Jefferson, John Adams, Robert R. Livingstone, and Roger Sherman.

It still took much time and effort to make American independence an established fact. At first the colonial troops, under Washington, suffered many reverses from the British forces, which often consisted of German professional soldiers under seasoned British officers. But after every reverse Washington rallied his troops and fought again. Meanwhile Franklin went to France and succeeded in bringing back many notable volunteers, including the Marquis de Lafayette and the Polish hero Kosciusko, to fight under Washington. Later, too, France made an official alliance with the Americans.

In 1781 Washington, with the help of a French fleet, was able to trap the last considerable body of British troops in Yorktown, on a narrow peninsula in Virginia. On October 19th the British, under Cornwallis, were compelled to surrender. From that moment the independence of the United States of America was a reality, though Britain did not acknowledge the fact until 1783.

TOP: *Map of newly-formed United States. (See also page 133.) On the left is Franklin, on the right Jefferson and John Adams.* BOTTOM: *Washington and Lafayette on the battlefield.*

MASS.
N.H.
B
MASS.
NEW YORK
CONN.
R.I.
PENNSYLVANIA
N.J
P
MD.
DEL
VIRGINIA
NORTH CAROLINA
SOUTH CAROLINA
GEORGIA

Liberty, Equality, and Fraternity

THE American colonists had revolted because of grievances, but the grievances of ordinary Frenchmen at this period were far more severe. The peasants still had to render services to their lords though their lords had long since ceased to offer them any sort of protection. French industry had fallen far behind British industry, and French agriculture, run on feudal lines, could scarcely meet the needs of the population. The kings of France had waged many ruinously expensive wars and had little to show for it except the overthrow of French power in India and Canada.

French philosophers had already seen the need for sweeping change. Voltaire had ridiculed a corrupt Church and clergy; Rousseau had put forward revolutionary ideas on the relationship between state and citizens. All that was needed to start a revolt was the right opportunity.

This came in May, 1789, when the French States-General was called together for the first time since 1613 to devise some way of saving France from the bankruptcy towards which her extravagant wars had led her. The States-General consisted of representatives of the "three estates," Nobility, Clergy, and Commons. It was soon clear that the first two would never agree with the Commons on the need for reform in French affairs, so in June the Commons declared themselves to be the National Assembly and agreed not to disperse before giving France a new constitution.

Alarmed by this turn of events, Louis XVI dismissed Necker, one of those responsible for reformist ideas on finance. The people of Paris saw this as a threat to all their hopes of reform, and on July 14th, 1789, a crowd stormed the Bastille, the prison to which so many ordinary people had been committed by the nobility without trial.

Even among people who strongly sympathized with reform by constitutional means, there were many who now feared that a wave of anarchy might sweep over France. And, indeed, as time passed the revolutionaries did divide up into moderates and extremists. Mirabeau, leader of the Third Estate of the States-General, tried to turn France into a constitutional monarchy like Britain. But in other quarters there was already talk of a republic. In Paris there was a communal administration under a mayor, and the townspeople had created the National Guard under Lafayette. Everywhere the new tricolor flag was beginning to wave.

In 1791 Mirabeau died, and the rulers of Europe feared that the French monarchy now stood little chance of surviving. Austria and Prussia declared their intention of intervening if Louis XVI were not restored to full power. From then on the French saw the Revolution in danger. They decided to take the initiative and offer armed assistance to any other peoples who wished to obtain freedom. They were ready to carry "Liberté, Fraternité, et Egalité" to other lands even if it meant war.

After this the Jacobins, or extremists, began to gain power from the more moderate Girondists. In 1792 the National Assembly forced Louis to declare war on Austria, and soon both Austria and Prussia were fighting the French. Though the French defeated them at Valmy and Jemappes the Revolution was clearly at bay.

The extremists Robespierre, Danton, and Marat now made themselves supreme and inaugurated the Reign of Terror. Early in 1793 the King, who had been virtually a prisoner since his attempted escape from Paris two years earlier, was put to the guillotine. A few months later Marie Antoinette, daughter of Maria Theresa of Austria, shared the same fate. Then for nearly two years the guillotine daily took a toll of aristocrats and others suspected of being out of sympathy with the Revolution.

Not until 1795 was the Terror finally ended, a revised constitution set up, and affairs placed in the hands of a small group called the Directory.

TOP: *Louis XVI, Mirabeau, and Robespierre.* BOTTOM, *The storming of the Bastille, July 14, 1789.*

Napoleon

In 1793 Britain was at war with France, and a British fleet was blockading the French fleet in Toulon harbor in order to help French Royalists who held the town. But Britain was unable to prevent a brilliant Republican artillery officer, Bonaparte, from recapturing Toulon.

Two years later Napoleon was in Paris just when it looked as if the Republic might come to a sudden end. Austria and Prussia had gained successes against France and people were becoming dissatisfied with the way the Directory was running the country. Once more the cry "Vive le Roi" was heard in Paris as reactionary crowds began to gather. The Directory entrusted the task of subduing them to Napoleon. A typical artilleryman, he sent for big guns and cleared the streets with one brief cannonade. Napoleon was at once made General of the Interior, and a year later was given command of the French forces in Italy.

In Italy he gained victories over the Sardinians and Austrians and for a time established himself in princely splendor in a castle near Milan. Then, after a brief campaign in Egypt, he returned to France where, under a new constitution, he became First Consul with autocratic power. In 1802 he was made Consul for life. Two years later he was proclaimed Emperor.

The picture opposite (after a painting in the Louvre in Paris) shows his Coronation. The new Emperor allowed himself to be blessed by the Pope while seated but placed the crown on his own head and then himself crowned the Empress Josephine.

From then onward the story of Napoleon is one of strong despotic government at home and almost continuous military campaigns abroad. At the great battles of Austerlitz (1805) and Jena (1806) he broke the opposition of Prussia. For several years England lived under the constant threat of a French invasion. At Eylau and Friedland (1807) Napoleon's army inflicted great defeats on the Russians. By 1810 both Holland and Belgium had been incorporated into France, and almost all Europe was either dependent on France or in alliance with her.

It was then that Napoleon divorced Josephine and married Marie Louise, daughter of the Emperor of Austria. A son born to them the following year was proclaimed King of Rome.

But even then events were already conspiring to bring about Napoleon's downfall. In southwest Europe, where the people had revolted against Napoleon's brother Joseph who had been placed on the Spanish throne, British forces under Sir Arthur Wellesley had already won victories over the French at Vimeiro and Albuera. Victories at Salamanca and Vitoria were soon to follow. Ever since Nelson's victory at Trafalgar in 1805, Britain had steadily worn down the French navy.

Then in 1812, Napoleon set out with half a million men to march on Moscow. The Russians retreated, pursuing a scorched-earth policy. On a September day, twenty-four hours after the exhausted French troops reached their goal, Moscow was set ablaze. With no means of living there through the bitter winter they were forced to return, and only two in five survived the retreat.

In 1813 unseasoned French troops suffered a crushing defeat by the Russians, Austrians, and Prussians at Leipzig. The following year France was invaded from all sides by her many enemies. Napoleon, compelled to abdicate, was banished to Elba and the Treaty of Paris was signed.

Yet Napoleon had left France one enduring legacy—the famous *Code Napoléon*, which brought together the traditions of Roman law and Church law, ordinances of the old monarchy, and the principles of the Revolution.

TOP LEFT: *Map showing sites of some of Napoleon's triumphs and disasters:* T — *Toulon,* P — *Paris,* M_1 — *Milan,* C — *Cairo,* J — *Jena,* A — *Austerlitz,* E — *Eylau,* F — *Friedland,* R — *Rome,* TV — *Torres Vedras,* V — *Vimeiro,* A_1 — *Albuera,* S — *Salamanca,* V_1 — *Vitoria,* M — *Moscow,* B_1 — *Beresina,* T_1 — *Trafalgar,* W — *Waterloo.* TOP RIGHT: *The* Code Napoléon. BOTTOM: *Napoleon's Coronation.*

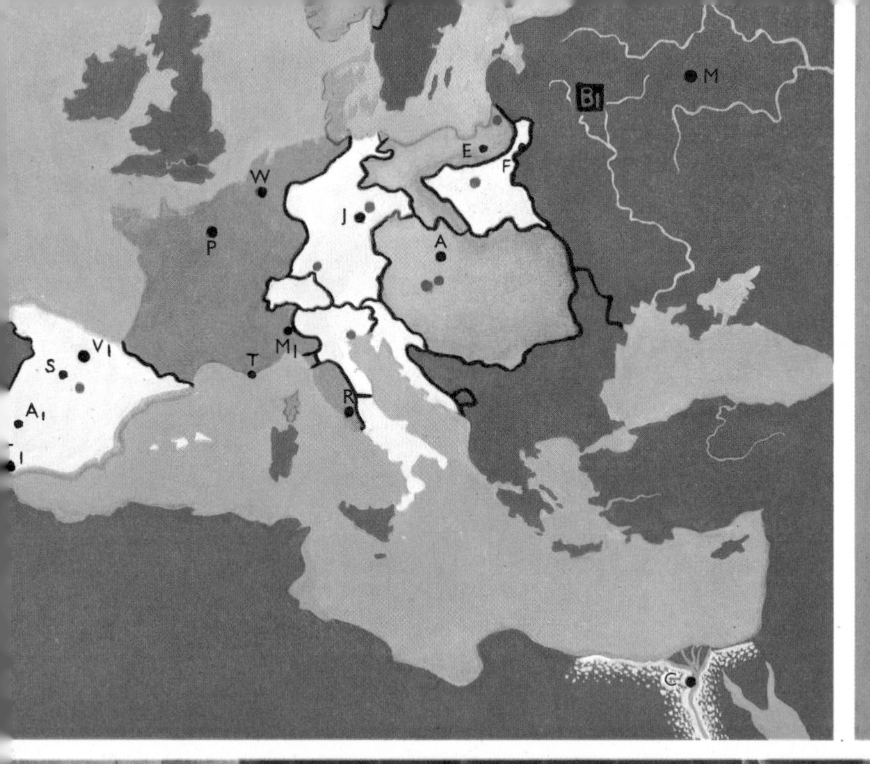

M
B1
E
F
W
J
P
A
VI
S
M1
T
R
A1
C

Reshaping Europe on Old Lines

NAPOLEON'S abdication put an end to over twenty years of warfare but raised the tremendous problem of reshaping Europe.

The Treaty of Paris did little more than settle the immediate future of France. More than anything else the rulers of Europe feared that France's democratic ideas, which had never been wholly lost sight of even when France became an Empire, might again sweep the whole continent. The obvious way of preventing this seemed to be to restore the monarchy.

Louis XVIII, a brother of Louis XVI, was placed on the French throne. France had to surrender the territories she had conquered, but she was not called upon to pay any indemnity, nor was she asked to restore the art treasures which Napoleon's troops had taken from so many lands.

The more complicated problem of resettling the rest of Europe was left to the Congress of Vienna, which met in the autumn of 1814. There, kings and emperors, statesmen and aristocrats discussed this terribly complex problem in an atmosphere of gaiety and dissipation. To them the occasion was one for rejoicing rather than for hard thinking. They felt that the absurd idea that ordinary people should have some say in how they should be governed had been banished when Napoleon was banished. The clock could now be turned back to the time when only birth and wealth counted. Therefore they could eat, drink, and be merry and, above all, dance.

The three men who dominated the Congress were the Austrian Metternich, later known as "the Master of Europe," Talleyrand, the wily French statesman who in the past had sworn allegiance to several different regimes, and Castlereagh, the Irish peer who represented Britain. Talleyrand and Metternich supported legitimacy: they urged that the way to settle how any country should be ruled was to find the heir to the last legitimate ruler and hand it over to him, irrespective of what its inhabitants thought. It was agreed that France was dangerously strong, and that buffer states should be created along her frontiers.

Before the deliberations and dances of Vienna ended news came that Napoleon had escaped from Elba and landed in France. The armies under Marshal Ney sent to stop him, made common cause with the "Little Emperor," and on March 20th he made a triumphal entry into the Tuileries. But the rulers of Europe, assembled at Vienna, had already made a new and powerful alliance against him. On June 18th, 1815, his army, marching toward Brussels, was defeated by an army of British, Belgian, Dutch, and German troops under Wellington, powerfully aided by a Prussian army under Blücher. Again Napoleon had to abdicate, and this time he was banished to the island of St. Helena for the rest of his life.

This remarkable episode had little effect on treaty-making at Vienna, except that France was now compelled to pay a large indemnity, submit to an army of occupation, and restore her looted art treasures. For the rest, Austria received Lombardy, Venetia, and the Tyrol; Prussia regained her Rhineland territories and her original share of Poland, besides gaining northern Saxony; Russia gained Finland from Sweden, and the Duchy of Warsaw became a constitutional kingdom under the Tsar; Norway was taken from Denmark and given to Sweden; Holland and Belgium were united (for fifteen years only, as it turned out) under one sovereign; Germany consisted of a loose federation of thirty-nine states with Austria as president; Swiss independence was guaranteed; and in Spain, Tuscany, Sardinia, and the Papal States of Italy the old dynasties were restored. Britain gained colonies and valuable trading and naval posts, including Malta, the Cape of Good Hope, Mauritius, and Ceylon.

TOP: *Congress of Vienna.* (*Talleyrand seated second from right; Metternich standing near left; Wellington standing extreme left*). BOTTOM LEFT: *Europe in 1815.* BOTTOM RIGHT: *Abdication of Napoleon at Fontainebleau.*

Rise of Nationalism

AFTER the Settlement of Vienna, the rulers of Europe were anxious to prevent the recurrence of devastating wars. With this end in view, Russia, Prussia, Austria, and Britain agreed to meet at intervals in an attempt to settle disputes peacefully. France joined the association in 1818, and it then became known as the Quintuple Alliance.

Quite separate was the Holy Alliance, formed at the instigation of Tsar Alexander I. The original members (the sovereigns of Russia, Austria, and Prussia) jointly declared their intention to rule according to Christian principles and announced their support of absolutism.

At meetings of the Quintuple Alliance held at Troppau, Laibach, and Verona, dissension arose between the great powers. Britain disliked the reactionary policies of the Russian, Austrian, and Prussian rulers. Castlereagh and his successor, George Canning, refused to support intervention against foreign revolutions, which they regarded as domestic problems for the states concerned.

For twenty years after Waterloo the rise of nationalism and democracy dominated European history. In Germany nationalist aspirations quickly showed themselves. Some people wanted union under Prussia while others favored Austrian leadership. A third group sought a stronger tie between the thirty-nine petty states. As early as 1817 student societies in many German universities united to form a single confederation for the whole of Germany. Two years later, when a German student shot a reactionary writer, Metternich seized the opportunity to dissolve the student confederation and to impose a tight censorship of the press.

Spain had already been granted a constitution in 1812, but when the Bourbon King Ferdinand VII came to power in 1814, he ruled as an absolute monarch. In 1820 naval officers at Cadiz raised a revolt against him, and only the intervention of a French army sent into Spain by Austria, Russia, and Prussia was able to keep him on his throne. It was not until early in the reign of Isabella II (1833-1868), that Spain became, even in name, a constitutional monarchy.

Meanwhile the people of the Kingdom of Naples soon followed Spain's example. They rebelled against their king, Ferdinand II (an uncle of the King of Spain), and secured a more liberal constitution. A year later, in Piedmont and Sardinia, a liberal rising forced King Victor Emmanuel I to abdicate in favor of his son Charles Albert, who granted the kingdom a constitution. But in Italy, too, Austria restored absolute authority and the new constitutions were annulled.

Almost simultaneous revolutionary movements in northwest Europe were more successful. In 1830 a rising in France forced the abdication of Charles X and installed Louis Philippe, the Citizen King and a one-time member of the old Revolutionary army, on the throne. In the same year, as a result of a revolution, Belgium broke away from Holland, drew up a very liberal constitution, and elected Prince Leopold of Saxe-Coburg as its king. Belgian neutrality and independence were guaranteed by the Treaty of London, 1839.

In Greece, too, nationalism became a great liberating force. In 1821, the Greeks rose against their Turkish masters. Here was a case of a Christian people revolting against Moslem overlords, and volunteers from all the Holy Alliance countries, as well as men such as Lord Byron from Britain, fought side by side with the Greeks. In 1827, at the Battle of Navarino, a British fleet, aided by the French and Russians, sank an Egyptian fleet supporting the Turks. By 1829 Greece had gained her independence.

Two years later a Polish nationalist rising against the Russians met with a very different answer. Tsarist troops crushed it ruthlessly. Rebel property was confiscated, there were mass deportations to Siberia, and thousands of patriots, including the composer Chopin, were forced to go into exile.

TOP: *Map of Europe with dates of nationalist risings. On Spain is a naval officer; on Belgium, King Leopold; on Poland, Chopin; on Greece, Byron; and on Germany, a student.* BOTTOM: *Fighting in Brussels in 1830.*

1830-31
1830-31
1830
1821
1831
1820
1812-20-34
1821-29

A Continent Gains Independence

IN Latin America, as in Europe, nationalism came to the fore after Waterloo.

The colors on the map opposite denote how the rule of Central and South America was divided at the beginning of the nineteenth century. Areas shown blue were Spanish possessions; those shown violet were Portuguese. Of the remaining areas, some were originally colonized by other European states while the rest (yellow) were not yet occupied at all by white people.

In the Spanish possessions the population was very mixed and lacking in unity. First there were Spaniards born in Spain. These, with the Viceroy as their leading member, held the reins of government and controlled most of the industries. Next, and counting for little among the Spaniards, came the Creoles, people of Spanish descent but bred and born in the New World. Then came the *mestizos*, of mixed Spanish and Indian descent, who were hardly considered at all. Finally, there were the Indians and the black slaves.

Without these social divisions revolts might have come earlier, for Spain had long governed her American possessions almost exclusively for the benefit of the mother country. She had forbidden the development of industries or plantations that might compete with Spanish products, placed tight restrictions on trade, and concentrated on squeezing money from her colonies.

In 1810, after Spain and Portugal were occupied by Napoleon, several revolutions occurred—in Mexico under the leadership of Father Hidalgo y Costillo and Father Morelos, and in Venezuela under Francisco Miranda. Argentina had also declared itself independent. After Ferdinand VII was restored to the Spanish throne these rebellions were suppressed with a brutality that served only to spark off other risings.

Supported by England, Simón Bolívar, a member of the Creole aristocracy of Caracas, left Jamaica in 1817 and landed in Venezuela, which he was able to conquer together with Colombia and Ecuador (1819-1821). When Ferdinand VII, supported by the Holy Alliance, tried to send reinforcements to South America from Cadiz, his troops mutinied, and the South American people seized this opportunity to extend their gains. Bolívar, assisted by Antonio José de Sucre, set out for Peru, and José de San Martín, a Creole officer in the Spanish army, made his way to Chile from Argentina in order to join him. Between them they broke the last Spanish resistance in 1821.

Meanwhile Chile, whose most famous liberator was Bernardo O'Higgins, had succeeded in obtaining independence in 1818. In 1821 Mexico had broken away from Spain, and in 1822 Brazil, under José Bonifacio de Andrada e Sylva, proclaimed its independence from Portugal. There, Don Pedro, the elder son of the King of Portugal, became the new head of the state.

In 1823, when the Holy Alliance contemplated intervening in the struggles, the American President, James Monroe, anunciated his famous doctrine of "America for Americans," declaring that the United States would not tolerate the interference of any European country anywhere in the New World except where they already held power (as in Canada). To this day the Monroe Doctrine is still a cornerstone of American foreign policy.

The efforts made soon after the Wars of Liberation to bring about a union of all the Latin American states came to nothing. Today South America consists of no less than ten separate sovereign states excluding British, French, and Dutch Guiana. Even the small area of Central America between the Mexican border and Colombia is split up into six distinct countries.

Latin America and some of the men who played a leading part in its struggles for independence. LEFT: *Father Hidalgo y Costillo, Bernardo O'Higgins, and Antonio José de Sucre.* RIGHT: *Simón Bolívar, José Bonifacio de Andrada e Sylva, and José de San Martín.*

The Making of a Great Nation

In Latin America the first half-century of independence was marred by constant revolutions and by wars between the newly formed states. In North America the United States spent its first half-century of independence in extending its boundaries and paving the way to power.

The map we saw on page 121 shows the area of the United States in 1783, just after the American Revolution. This area was already about double that of the original thirteen colonies as they existed at the time of the French and Indian War. Only later had Americans received the vast territory stretching westward from the old colonial boundaries to the Mississippi. Part of that territory had been allocated to Virginia, Massachusetts, and Connecticut, and part had been included within the boundaries of North Carolina, South Carolina, and Georgia.

Almost all this vast new land was inhabited only by a comparatively small population of American Indians, who had to be either pacified or conquered. Its many millions of acres had never yet been brought under the plough. Yet almost at once thousands of Americans set out in covered wagons and by horse train, determined to make new homes, new ranches, new plantations, new farmlands there. The great trek westward, which was to go on until late in the nineteenth century, had already begun. By 1820 the new territory had given rise to, several states—new stars to join the thirteen stripes of the American flag: Kentucky in 1792, Tennessee in 1796, Ohio in 1803, Indiana in 1816, Mississippi in 1817, Illinois in 1818, Alabama in 1819. Meanwhile, in the original territory of the old colonies, other areas had come to statehood: Vermont in 1791 and Maine in 1820.

The settlement of the territories to the east of the Mississippi moved rapidly under the United States' first two Presidents, George Washington (1789-97) and John Adams (1797-1801); and during the presidency of Thomas Jefferson (1801-09) America was ready to embark on its next great expansion. In 1803, at a moment when France was in no position to exploit or even defend its distant overseas territories, Jefferson purchased the gigantic area of French Louisiana for 15 million dollars, a sum that would now buy only a small plot of land in New York City. It was here that the states of Louisiana, Missouri, Arkansas, Iowa, Minnesota, Nebraska, Oklahoma, Kansas, Montana, South Dakota, and part of North Dakota were later to take shape. (What is now the eastern part of North Dakota was ceded to the United States in 1818.

In 1819, during the presidency of James Monroe, later famous as the founder of the Monroe Doctrine, America purchased Florida from Spain. In 1845, nine years after General Sam Houston had led Texas in a successful revolt against Mexican rule and made it an independent republic, Texas was annexed by the United States under the presidency of James Polk. This action led to war with Mexico, and three years later, when the war ended, the United States had gained the area that now makes up the states of California, Nevada, Utah, Arizona, and parts of Colorado and New Mexico. Meanwhile, in 1846, the northwest frontier of the United States had been defined in an agreement with Britain; the area now comprising the states of Washington, Oregon, and Idaho was included within the United States.

Seven years later, when Mexico ceded a small area northeast of the Gulf of California, the United States' frontiers, with the exception of Alaska and Hawaii, had taken their present shape. A people who only eighty years before were hemmed in between the Atlantic and the Appalachians were now masters of a territory stretching from the Atlantic to the Pacific, from the Canadian border to the Gulf of Mexico.

Map showing dates of admission to the United States, and Jackson, top left, Monroe, top right, and Sam Houston, center. BOTTOM LEFT: *The Alamo mission.* BOTTOM RIGHT: *Covered wagon en route to the West.*

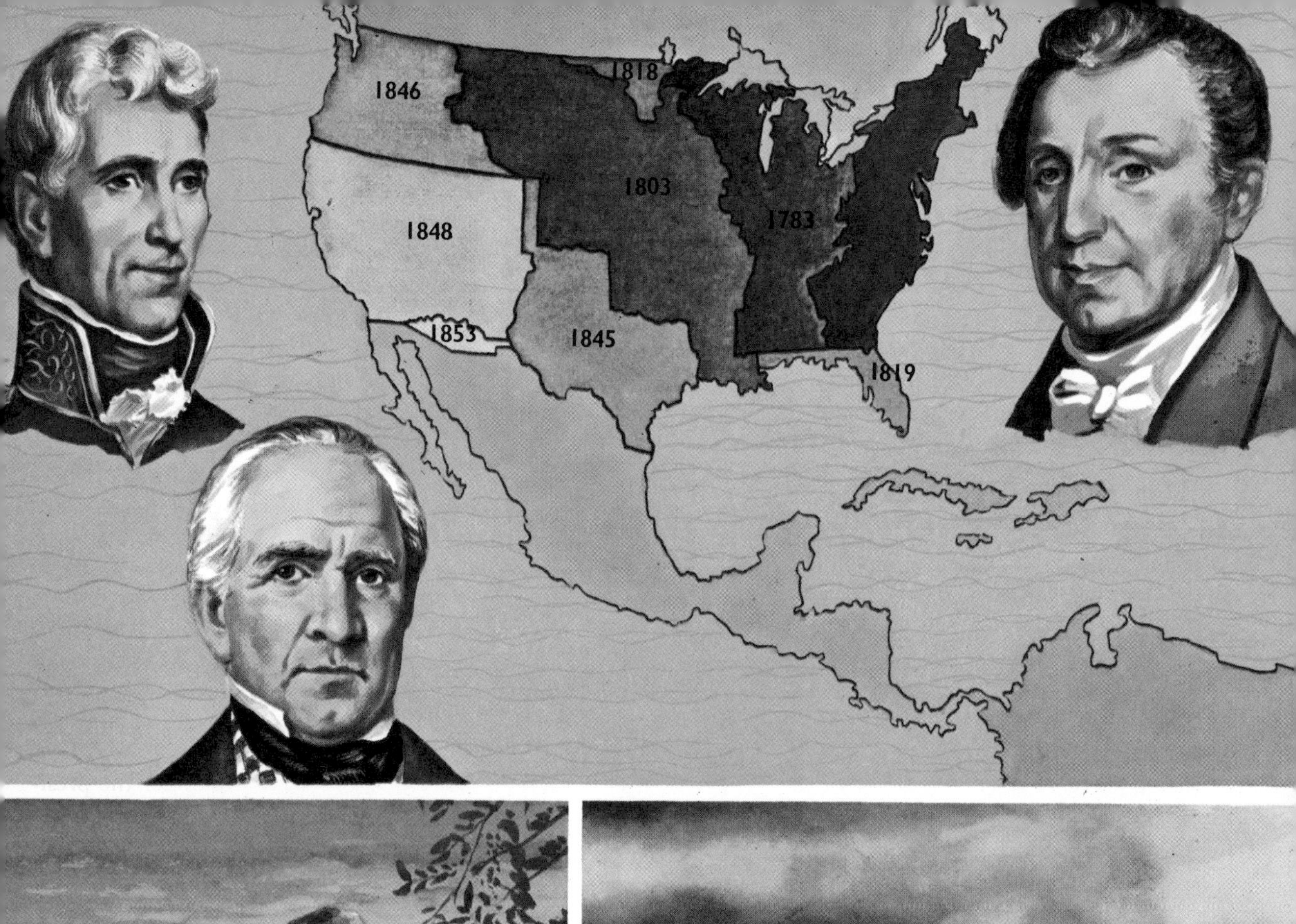
1846
1818
1803
1848
1783
1853
1845
1819

The War between the States

ABROAD, the United States had to establish a sound foreign policy. During the Napoleonic Wars, especially, this was not easy. In 1807, for instance, the United States had decreed that none of her ships should load or unload in French or British ports. To Britain, which badly needed trade, this was a severe blow, and it helped to bring about war between Britain and the United States from 1812 to 1815. It was during that war that British troops burned the city of Washington and put an end to American hopes of conquering Canada.

At home, the United States' problems were even more acute. There had long been strong differences of opinion about just how united the United States should be. Some people, such as Jefferson, held that the Union was a free Confederation, from which any state could break away if it wished; others, including Washington, held that it was a strong Federal Union from which no state could secede without the consent of all the rest. So long as no state actually wanted to secede this was merely a debating point. But as time went on big differences developed between the interests of the North and those of the South.

The northern states became highly industrialized and wanted to tax imported goods to protect their industries. The southern states had little industry and wanted to buy goods as cheaply as possible from Europe. The North had no use for slave labor and was uneasy that slavery existed in the South. When Harriet Beecher Stowe's book, *Uncle Tom's Cabin*, was published in 1852, its account of the horrors of slavery increased this uneasiness enormously. On the other hand, the southern states could see no way of harvesting and picking their cotton crops without the help of Negro slaves; they little realized that Eli Whitney's cotton gin would soon do the work of fifty slaves.

Over and above these differences, the southern states believed in the Confederation idea while the northern states held the Federal Union view. Further, the South supported the Democratic Party which voiced little objection to slavery, while most Northerners supported the Republican Party, which favored abolition.

After Abraham Lincoln, a staunch Republican and abolitionist, was elected as President in 1860, the situation came to a head. In 1861 eleven southern states banded together as the Confederate States and decided to secede from the Union. They elected their own president, Jefferson Davis, and chose Richmond as their capital.

In the war that followed, the Confederate States with their smaller population, were at first successful, for they threw every ounce of energy into the struggle. In April, 1861, they captured Fort Sumter, near Charleston; In May, 1862, they were victorious at Williamsburg; at Bull Run they successfully resisted the northerners' attacks on Virginia. For a time it looked as if the Confederate armies, under Robert E. Lee, would win the day.

But gradually the two great assets of the northern states began to tell: they had a far bigger reserve of manpower to call on and they had a far more powerful fleet with which to blockade the South. In 1862 the Northern forces, under General Grant, occupied Tennessee and much of Mississippi. In 1863 the Northern armies stopped Lee's offensive on Maryland and Pennsylvania at Gettysburg, and won another major victory at Chattanooga. Following victories at Atlanta and near Savannah, they compelled Lee to surrender in 1865.

When peace was restored, slavery was abolished in the United States. But Abraham Lincoln, chief architect of Negro freedom, was assassinated in the same year.

TOP: *Map showing northern states blue, southern grey. (W — Washington,* R — *Richmond,* FS — *Fort Sumter,* G — *Gettysburg,* A — *Atlanta,* S — *Savannah.) Left is General Grant, center Robert E. Lee, right Abraham Lincoln and a famous book against slavery.*
BOTTOM: *Historic naval battle between the Northern "Monitor" and the Southern "Merrimac."*

UNCLE TOM'S CABIN;
LIFE AMONG THE LOWLY.
HARRIET BEECHER STOWE
VOL. I.
G
W
R
A
F.S
S

Fifty Years of Change in France

IF the United States, the pioneer republic of the New World, saw many changes, so did France, the pioneer republic of the Old World.

The First Republic in France, proclaimed a few years after the Revolution, was soon followed by the First Empire, under Napoleon. Then, after Napoleon's defeat, France became a monarchy once more, Louis XVIII, the first of the restored kings, steered a middle course between being too royalist and too liberal. But Charles X, the brother who succeeded him in 1824, was a very different kind of man. He installed as minister a fanatical reactionary, Jules de Polignac, and in July, 1830, he made decrees changing the electoral laws and curtailing the freedom of the press. For the citizens of Paris this was the last straw. Once more they went to the barricades, and in a few days Charles X was compelled to flee the country.

Then a kind of liberal constitutional monarchy was set up with Louis Philippe, who had once fought with the Revolutionary armies, as king. For ten years Louis Philippe was popular enough, and gave France a breathing space of peace and quiet. During that time Algiers, which France had captured during the reign of Charles X, was steadily consolidated as a French possession. But two forces were building up in opposition to Louis. Many people thought that if only a Bonaparte could take control of France, everything would improve at once. At the same time, among many poorer citizens, as well as among many French philosophers, there was a growing demand for some form of government—perhaps socialist or communist—that would abolish poverty.

All these ideas boiled to the surface when, in 1847, Louis Philippe refused to dismiss his reactionary minister, Guizot, and resisted demands for the vote to be extended. In February, 1848, rioting broke out, and the king, finding the National Guard as well as many of the people against him, abdicated and went to England. For a few months France was a republic again, with a provisional government. Then in December, 1848, Louis Napoleon, a nephew of the great Napoleon, was elected President of this Second Republic. By 1852 he had made himself Emperor of the Second Empire, under the title of Napoleon III.

In home affairs his reign brought many benefits to France. Industry was encouraged, agricultural banks were set up, and great schemes of reforestation were put in hand. Several cities, including Lyons, Marseilles, and Bordeaux, were largely rebuilt, and in Paris itself fine new parks were laid out and many broad boulevards were driven through old and congested districts.

In foreign affairs Napoleon III was less successful, though he was on the winning side during the Crimean War. In 1859 he sided with the Italian patriots against Austria, and antagonized both powers by weak diplomacy.

A few years later, Benito Juarez, determined to curtail Catholic power, became President of Mexico. He refused to repay European debts contracted by his former enemies, and Napoleon III seized this excuse to make war on him. While the United States was torn by Civil War and unable to enforce the Monroe Doctrine, he sent troops to Mexico to help Maximilian of Austria to found a Catholic kingdom there. But the moment the Civil War ended, the Americans threatened France with war unless her troops were withdrawn. They were withdrawn, and in 1867 the unfortunate Maximilian was executed.

Then in 1870, Napoleon III allowed himself to be drawn into a Franco-Prussian War. France, heavily defeated, lost Alsace-Lorraine and was forced to pay a huge indemnity. Napoleon III, like Louis Philippe before him, fled to England, and the Third Republic was proclaimed.

TOP LEFT: *Map of Paris on which red shows boulevards built by Napoleon III.* TOP RIGHT: *Map of Mexico, with Juarez (top) and Maximilian (bottom).* BOTTOM: *Scene in Strasbourg during the Franco-Prussian War.*

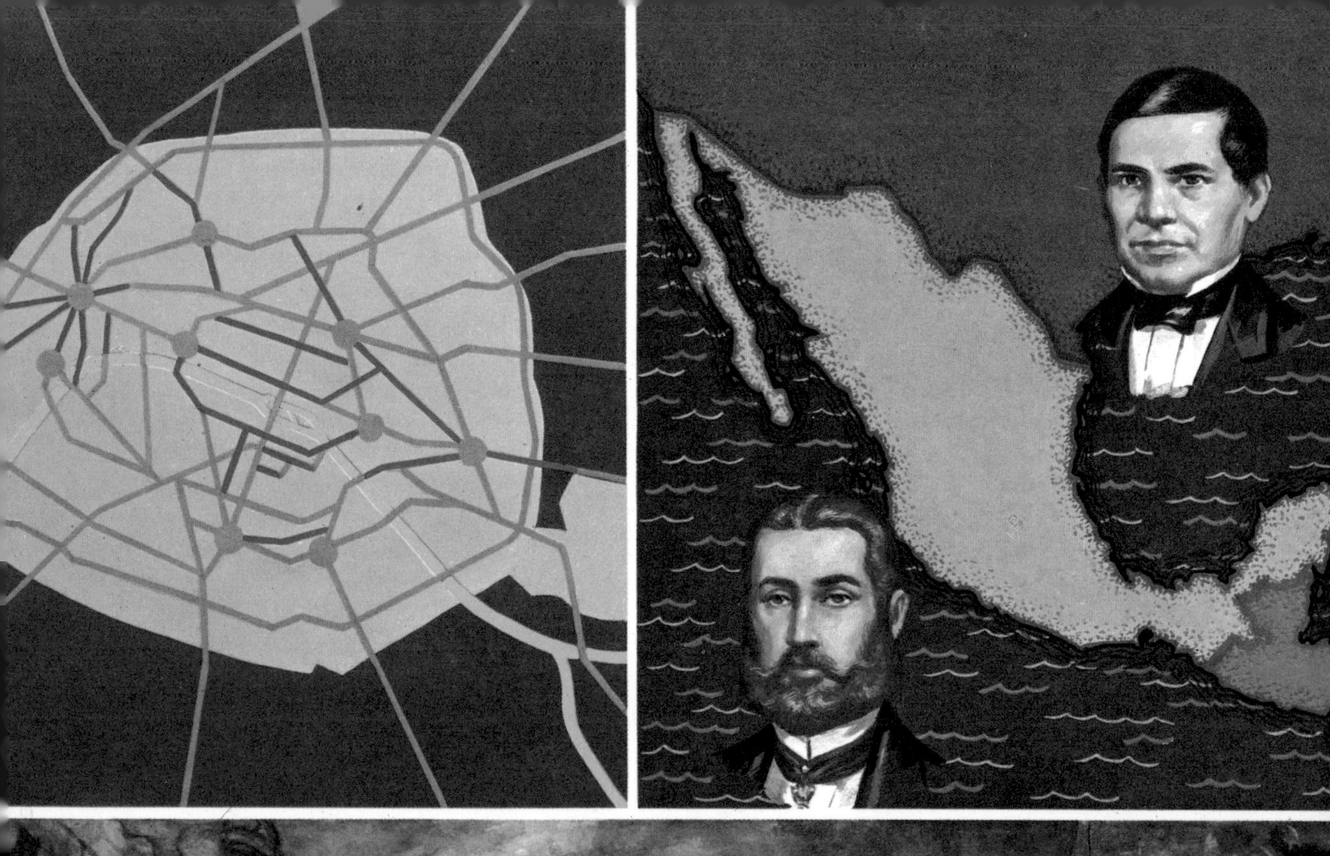

Britain's Century of Dominance

In many parts of Europe the first two-thirds of the nineteenth century were marked by violent political changes. In Britain the changes came about by a process of natural growth.

There was, indeed, a revolution in England, and a tremendously important one, but it was not political. It was the Industrial Revolution, which had its beginnings in the 1770s when James Watt's improved steam engines were first used. By the early years of the nineteenth century hundreds of steam engines, already far more efficient than Watt's early models, were driving all kinds of new machines. William Murdoch had already found how to extract gas economically from coal, and from 1805 onwards more and more factories were lit by gaslight. In 1825 Britain opened the world's first passenger railroad, and by 1850 Britain's railroad network was almost complete.

All this progress was not brought about without a great deal of hardship. In the old cottage industries, the weaver, the cobbler, the blacksmith, and the carpenter had all owned their own tools and been their own masters. The new factory system, however, demanded expensive engines and machines which only the wealthy factory-owners could afford to buy. Factory workers, including even young children, became mere "hands," toiling for incredibly long hours under appalling conditions for miserably low wages. Most of them, too, lived in towns that had grown up like mushrooms, with little sanitation and few amenities.

Britain's army of depressed industrial workers saw two ways of improving things: by forming trade unions to negotiate better wages and working conditions, and by getting better representation of the new industrial towns in Parliament. In the years immediately following the French Revolution their efforts in both directions were thwarted. Britain's rulers feared that any call for reform was merely the thin end of the wedge of revolution, and in 1799 and 1800 Combination Acts were passed making trade unions illegal. In 1824, however, these acts were repealed owing largely to the efforts of the reformer Francis Place, and from then on trade unionism, which the Combination Acts had never wholly destroyed, gained ground and won many grudging concessions from factory-owners.

The first big step towards better Parliamentary representation came with the Great Reform Act of 1832. This act, pioneered mainly by two Whig statesmen, Lord John Russell and Earl Grey, took away representation from almost nonexistent boroughs such as Old Sarum (a green mound) and Gatton (a mere wall), and gave it to flourishing new towns. It also increased the number of people able to vote at Parliamentary elections by reducing the property qualification for voters.

The next step came in 1867, during Lord Derby's Conservative ministry, and it was largely the work of Benjamin Disraeli, soon to become Prime Minister. This act extended the vote to about a million additional working class and lower middle class people. Under the first two ministries of Gladstone, the great Liberal statesman, other reforms followed. In 1872 the secret ballot was introduced and in 1884 the franchise was again extended. Though no women and not all men yet had the vote, Britain could nevertheless then claim to be a real democracy.

Meanwhile Britain had become the world's main carrier of seaborne goods and the workshop of the world. She had added Australia, New Zealand, and large areas of Africa to her Empire, and had extended her control to almost the whole of India. Queen Victoria had reigned with such statesmanship and good sense that she restored to the British Crown a devotion it had not known since the days of Elizabeth I.

TOP LEFT: *Queen Victoria meets Napoleon III at Boulogne.* BOTTOM LEFT: *The British Empire near the close of the nineteenth century.* RIGHT: *Lord John Russell, Gladstone, and Disraeli.*

The Sick Man of Europe

WHILE Britain's power was growing, that of the Turkish Empire was steadily declining. The weakness began to show itself as early as 1804 when Serbia (now part of Yugoslavia) raised a successful rebellion against Turkish rule.

Encouraged by that success, the Greeks also fought for and won their independence during the 1820s. It was a terrible struggle, and there were atrocities on both sides. The Turks massacred the whole Greek population of Chios; the Greeks massacred Turks in Morea. It was also a struggle that involved other countries. Egypt threw the weight of its fleet in on Turkey's side. Britain, France, and Russia came to the aid of the Greeks, and their fleets destroyed the combined Turkish-Egyptian fleet at the Battle of Navarino in 1827.

Navarino ensured Greek independence, and also exposed Turkey's weakness to the world. Formerly Turkey's position astride the Bosporus and the Dardanelles had prevented Russian ships from having any outlet from the Black Sea to the Mediterranean. Russia now used Turkey's weakness to gain that outlet. After the War of Greek Independence she obtained from Turkey the free passage of the Bosporus and the Dardanelles for her merchant shipping. A few years later the Sultan made a secret treaty with the Tsar by which he agreed to open the Straits to Russian warships but to close them to the navies of all other nationalities. This decision was amended by international agreement in 1841, when the Straits were closed to warships of all nations.

By the middle of the 1840s the Tsar Nicholas I referred to Turkey as "the sick man of Europe," and suggested to Britain that the Turkish Empire should be divided between Russia and Britain. But British and Russian interests were by no means identical, and furthermore other European powers had conflicting interests in the matter. Britain feared that a stronger Russia might threaten India; Napoleon III felt that only some outstanding success in French foreign policy could strengthen his own position; Austria wanted to take advantage of Turkey's weakness to extend her own dominions.

In 1854 these interests boiled up into war over a quarrel about whether the Greek Church (supported by Russia) or the Latin Church (supported by France) should have custody of certain Holy Places within the Turkish Empire. In this war, fought mainly in the Crimea, Britain, and France fought on the side of Turkey against Russia. Their declared aim was "to preserve the integrity of the Turkish Empire." But the efforts which their forces made, under the French General, MacMahon, to seize the Russian naval base of Sebastopol, showed that their main aim was to destroy Russia's Black Sea Fleet. In 1855 Russia's new Tsar, Alexander II, was compelled to sue for peace, and for the time being the crumbling Turkish Empire was shored up.

But in 1877 Russia was again at war with Turkey, this time with greater success. The ultimate results of the war were decided not by the treaty that the two countries made themselves, but by the international Congress of Berlin, held in 1878. Rumania, Serbia, and Montenegro gained independence from Turkey; Russia obtained a large territory north of the Danube; Austria was given a protectorate over former Turkish possessions in the northwest of the Balkan Peninsula; and Britain received Cyprus.

After the First World War Turkey, as an ally of defeated Germany, lost still more territory by the Treaty of Sèvres (1920). Today it holds only a tiny strip of Europe. But during the 1930s the statesman and patriot, Mustapha Kemal, embarked on a program of modernization and reform which made Turkey, though small, a power still to be reckoned with.

TOP LEFT: *General MacMahon and Tsar Alexander II.* TOP RIGHT: *Map showing Turkish territory before and after the Treaty of Sèvres. The figure is Mustapha Kemal.* BOTTOM: *The massacre at Chios, after the painting by Delacroix in the Louvre.*

Italy Becomes a Single Kingdom

UP to the middle of the nineteenth century Italy played little part in the power politics of Europe. From the Middle Ages onward it had consisted of many petty states, most of which were under the control of foreign monarchs.

At the Congress of Vienna (1814-15) Metternich had declared that it must remain so. But the Napoleonic Wars had given the people of Italy a taste of liberty, and they were never again prepared to accept foreign rule unquestioningly.

Between the signing of the Treaty of Vienna and 1848 there were many risings, but they failed to achieve any lasting result. Perhaps the only notable Italian patriot of that period who had any clear aim was Mazzini. He wanted to make Italy a united republic, and he wanted to do so without outside help. But in Venetia alone the Austrians had an army of 75,000 men, and the task of throwing such armies out of Italy was quite beyond the powers of poorly-organized rebels.

At one time it looked as if Pope Pius IX might help in the task of liberating Italy. Soon after his election, in 1846, he had liberalized the government of the Papal States and had freed all Italians formerly imprisoned there for political offenses; he had also protested to the Austrians against their occupation of Ferrara. But to liberate Italy meant war with Austria, and no Pope could risk encouraging war against the strongest Catholic country in Europe. Thus Italian patriots were forced to look elsewhere for help.

In the 1850s only the small Kingdom of Piedmont (shown dark green opposite) offered any hope. There an enlightened constitutional monarch, Victor Emmanuel II, and his brilliant Prime Minister, Count Cavour, were building up a go-ahead liberal state. Cavour realized that a united Italy could be brought about only with the help of powerful allies. As a step toward obtaining the goodwill of France and Britain, he sent Piedmontese troops to fight on their side in the Crimean War. Later he made an agreement with Napoleon III that if Piedmont were ever attacked by Austria, France would come to her defense. If France and Piedmont won the war, Piedmont could take Venetia and Lombardy from Austria, but France would have to be given Savoy and Nice (marked S and N opposite).

In 1859 Austria and Piedmont did go to war, and France came to Piedmont's assistance as agreed. The French and Piedmontese were successful, but Napoleon III made peace with Austria before Piedmont's ambitions were fully satisfied. Austria gave up Lombardy (adjoining Piedmont) but kept Venetia (around the V on the map).

Within a year the states of Parma (P), Modena (M_1), Lucca (Lu), Tuscany (south of F, Florence), and the Marches (west of Tuscany) had all declared themselves by plebiscite to be in favor of incorporation into Piedmont.

Meanwhile a republican conspirator, Crispi, was stirring Sicily to rebel against the King of Sicily and Naples, whose domains included the entire southern half of peninsular Italy. In May, 1860, Garibaldi, the great Italian patriot, set sail for Sicily with a body of Red Shirt volunteers, and turned the Sicilian revolt into a vital part of the struggle for Italian unity. Within a few months Garibaldi won the whole of Sicily and Naples for Italy and the King of Piedmont. In 1861 the first Italian parliament proclaimed Victor Emmanuel II King of Italy.

A few years later, during the Prusso-Austrian War, Italy seized Venetia, the last considerable province that the Emperor Francis Joseph of Austria held on Italian soil. Finally, in 1870, when Napoleon III withdrew his troops from Rome during the Franco-Prussian War, Italian troops occupied Rome itself.

TOP LEFT: *Cavour and Pope Pius IX.* TOP CENTER: *Map of Italy.* TOP RIGHT: *Francis Joseph and Victor Emmanuel II.* BOTTOM: *Garibaldi's triumphal entry into Naples.*

S
V
P
Mi
N
F

Germany Becomes a United Empire

THE Congress of Vienna, which left Germany as a loose confederation of 39 states with Austria as presiding power, came nowhere near to meeting German aspirations towards national unity.

Between 1815 and 1819 there were strong liberal and nationalist movements in the German universities, but Metternich sternly repressed them. Then in the early 1830s there were risings in several states, aimed at establishing "the sovereignty of the people." The rulers of Saxony, Brunswick, and Hesse-Cassel were compelled to abdicate, and in several other states more liberal constitutions were adopted. Meanwhile, a customs union between various states, which Prussia initiated in 1819, steadily increased its membership until by 1844 it included almost all of non-Austrian Germany. Prussia, as leading member, now exercised more influence over Germany than Austria did.

In 1848, following more uprisings, many states were granted new constitutions, and they elected representatives to form a National Assembly which met at Frankfurt. Some members of this assembly, the Big-German Party, wanted to unite the whole of Germany, including Austria and Bohemia; others, the Little-German Party, wanted to exclude the Austrian provinces. The Little-German Party gained control and offered the imperial crown to Frederick William IV of Prussia. But he refused to accept it from the hands of the people.

Eventually, unity was brought about only by blood and iron, and it was mainly the work of two men: William I of Prussia (brother and successor of Frederick William IV), and Otto von Bismarck, the astute Prussian Chancellor. Under their guidance, von Roon, minister of war, and von Moltke, chief of the general staff, built up an army of nearly half a million men, so that Bismarck could use war as an instrument of policy.

In 1863, before embarking on his first war, he gained the friendly neutrality of Russia by sending Prussian troops to the Polish frontier to overawe the Polish rebels. The next year, as the ally of Austria, he made war on Denmark over the disputed provinces of Schleswig and Holstein. The Danes were defeated. Schleswig was ceded to Prussia and Holstein to Austria.

Austria found it difficult to administer distant Holstein, and when the Austrian governor wanted to reconsider the whole future of the province, Bismarck made this the occasion for war. In 1866 Bavaria, Saxony, and Hanover allied themselves with Austria, so that Prussia had to fight on two fronts. But Italy declared war on Austria in an effort to complete her own unification; thus Austria also had to fight on two fronts. Von Moltke's Prussian troops concentrated first on defeating Hanover and Bavaria, then they rushed to Bohemia, where they crushed the Austrians at the Battle of Sadowa. In making peace, Prussia proved generous. Bismarck intended war on France and he did not then want Austria as an enemy.

Meanwhile the German states had formed two main blocs, those of the south under the direction of Bavaria, and those of the north under the direction of Prussia. Bismarck now made an alliance with the leading southern states by which they would support Prussia if France attacked her. Using a quarrel about whether a Hohenzollern prince should claim the throne of Spain, Bismarck then provoked Napoleon III to declare war (July, 1870). Prussia, now fighting in unison with all the German states, defeated the French at Metz and Sedan. France had to surrender Alsace and part of Lorraine, and Napoleon III himself was compelled to abdicate.

In Germany public opinion now demanded unity under Prussian leadership. In 1871 the imperial crown was offered to William I, and he became the first Emperor of Germany.

TOP LEFT: *Map of Central Europe between 1860 and 1870.* TOP RIGHT: *German imperial arms.* BOTTOM: *Germania Monument at Rudesheim with William I and von Moltke at the left, Bismarck and von Roon at the right.*

France Since 1870

THE capitulation of Napoleon III at Sedan ended the Second Empire. The defeated Emperor had to flee and in September, 1870, France declared itself for the third time to be a republic. Early in the following year a National Assembly was formed and Adolphe Thiers, who became Chief of the Executive Power, announced the terms of a proposed peace treaty with Germany.

The people of Paris now felt that the proposed treaty, offering Germany a huge indemnity and allowing German troops to stay in France until it was paid, was an unendurable humiliation. On March 18th, 1871, they revolted against the government of the largely right wing National Assembly and formed the Paris Commune, flying the red flag and introducing the Republican Calendar. But during Bloody Week (May 21st-28th, 1871), the troops of the National Assembly reconquered Paris and thousands of Communards were killed, deported, or imprisoned.

A few months later Thiers became President of the Third Republic. But this republic rested on shaky foundations. There was a strong faction anxious to make France a monarchy once more, and it included the great French soldier, MacMahon, who succeeded Thiers as President. In 1873 MacMahon paved the way for the Count of Chambord, a grandson of Charles X, to receive the crown. It was only the Count's refusal to accept the tricolor instead of the old royalist white flag that brought the scheme to nought.

The strong royalist element in France, however, persisted for many years. It showed itself especially during the Dreyfus Affair. In 1894 Dreyfus, a French army officer, was tried for treason involving giving information to Germany, and was sent to Devil's Island. For years France split into two camps. The Dreyfusards, interested in preserving the republic, believed in Dreyfus's innocence; the anti-Dreyfusards, anxious to restore the monarchy, believed him guilty. Not until 1906 was Dreyfus's innocence finally and completely established.

Up to and even after the outbreak of the First World War there remained a sharp cleavage between right and left in French politics. Among reactionaries were men like Raymond Poincaré, President from 1913 to 1920, and one of the architects of victory over Germany. On the left were men like Jean Jaurès, an outstanding figure of French socialism who was murdered on the eve of the war. For several years after the war Aristide Briand, a man of advanced views, campaigned for world peace. In 1936 Léon Blum formed a Popular Front Government which embarked on an ambitious but not wholly successful campaign of social reform.

The event that really brought about the end of the Third Republic was the over-running of most of France by Hitler's troops in 1940. Marshal Pétain, the aged hero of the First World War, formed a government of the partially-occupied area (striped in bottom map) at Vichy, while General De Gaulle organized the Free French Movement from London.

In 1946, after its liberation, France proclaimed the Fourth Republic, which lasted only until 1958. During this period there was a marvelous recovery from the devastating effects of the war, but there were also many bewilderingly quick changes of government. Perhaps the most outstanding political figure was M. Mendes-France, who in 1954 grappled successfully with the problems of French Indo-China.

The Fourth Republic ended in 1958 following a nationalist insurrection in Algeria, and General De Gaulle became a strong first President of the Fifth Republic. For three years the future of Algeria constituted one of his main problems.

Light areas on maps show extent of German penetration during successive wars. Top map (1871) also shows Thiers and Jaurès; center map (1914-18), Poincaré and Briand; bottom map (1940), Blum and Pétain. On the right are Dreyfus and Devil's Island; M. Mendes-France and a scene in French Indo-China; President De Gaulle and a scene in Algeria.

The Scramble for Colonies

IN nineteenth-century Europe pressure of population and the desire to find new markets produced a new wave of colonialism.

Britain, which had lost most of its North American possessions in 1783, was not slow to gain new ones. Within a century these included about two-thirds of what is now the Dominion of Canada. In India, following the Indian Mutiny against British rule (1857-58), the British East India Company was abolished and its territories placed under the Crown. Eighteen years later, in 1876, Queen Victoria was proclaimed Empress of India. Meanwhile, in the 1850s, Britain conquered Burma.

In Australia the first British settlers did not arrive until about 1790; by 1890, New South Wales, Victoria, Queensland, South Australia, and Western Australia were all flourishing states with their own representative governments. New Zealand, ceded to Britain by Maori chiefs as late as 1840, became a self-governing Dominion by 1907.

In East Asia, European rivalry was so intense that only three countries there managed to retain their independence—Japan, Siam, and China. The Boxer Rising of 1900 was a clear warning that the Chinese resented foreign interference.

Between 1862 and 1867 the French occupied Cochin-China and instituted a protectorate over Cambodia. After 1883 they extended this protectorate to cover Tonkin, Annam, and Laos. Meanwhile the Dutch steadily extended their dominions in the East Indies, until by 1914 they controlled the whole archipelago except for British North Borneo and Portuguese Timor. In 1898 even the U.S.A. gained a foothold in East Asia, by purchasing the Philippine Islands from Spain. The first American administrator there was Judge W. H. Taft, later United States President.

The purchase of the Philippines arose out of an event on the other side of the world. Early in 1898 Cuba had risen against Spanish rule, and the U.S.A., under President McKinley, had backed her. After the defeat of Spain, the peace treaty provided for the American purchase of the Philippines. From 1898 to 1901 and in 1906, during the presidency of Theodore Roosevelt, the United States formed provisional governments in Cuba.

Before about 1880 European countries held only a few coastal areas in Africa. The French had Algeria; the Portuguese had Angola and Mozambique; the Boers, ousted from the tip of South Africa by the British in 1814, had later trekked northward to found the Orange Free State and the Transvaal. For the rest, Africa was still the Dark Continent. Then came a wave of exploration in which Livingstone and Stanley took part.

Suddenly Europe saw and seized the chance of expansion. In 1884 and 1885 Germany seized Togoland, the Cameroons, South West Africa, and German East Africa. In 1888 the Congo became a free state under King Leopold II of the Belgians, and in 1908 it became Belgian territory. In 1889 Italy gained a large area of Somaliland. Between 1880 and 1900 Britain pushed northward from South Africa, largely by the efforts of Cecil Rhodes. This northward push was consolidated by war with Kruger's Boer forces at the close of the century. In the northeastern sector of Africa Britain gained control of an area stretching from Lake Victoria to the southern frontier of Egypt.

Meanwhile France, with the help of the Foreign Legion, built up a vast empire in the Sahara and Equatorial Africa. In 1896 Madagascar was proclaimed a French colony, and in the next few years its first French Governor, Joseph Gallieni, gave the island many schools and new roads. In 1912 much of Morocco, under the administration of Louis Lyautey, became a French possession.

TOP: *Great figures in African history.* LEFT: *A Legionnaire, Stanley, and Kruger.* RIGHT: *The top figure is T. E. Lawrence, the Englishman who persuaded Arabia to fight against Turkey in World War I.* BELOW: *Rhodes and Gallieni.* BOTTOM LEFT: *Lyautey, a Boxer, and W. H. Taft.* BOTTOM RIGHT: *President Theodore Roosevelt and President William McKinley.*

Preparing for Conflict

EUROPEAN countries had been scrambling for colonies since the late fifteenth century, but in the nineteenth century competition was especially fierce, for two reasons. First, many of the best "prizes" had already been won; only Africa and parts of East Asia remained to be colonized. Next, there were two new competitors in the field, Germany and Italy. Both had only just completed their unification and both felt entitled to begin building up overseas empires. Both of them did win colonies in Africa, and Germany also obtained part of New Guinea. But neither Germany nor Italy gained African possessions to compare with those of France and Britain.

Germany in particular felt this to be a tremendous grievance, and one that could be remedied only by building up a powerful fighting fleet. Under the direction of Admiral von Tirpitz, Secretary of the Navy, the German fleet grew rapidly, and Britain saw it as a weapon intended essentially for use against her. British fears were increased by the fact that between 1909 and 1914 the Germans deepened the Kiel Canal, connecting the Baltic and the North Sea, so that even the largest battleships could use it.

Meanwhile there were many other sources of international friction. First, Frenchmen long remained bitter about the German annexation of Alsace-Lorraine in 1871; and this feeling was aggravated in 1911, when Germany sent the gunboat *Panther* to Agadir to support anti-French Moroccan chiefs. Next, the unification of Germany under Prussian leadership had left the Empire of Austria-Hungary considerably weakened. The Hapsburgs now had only one way left of increasing their territories—by expanding eastward at the expense of the crumbling Turkish Empire. But Russia also had designs on Turkish territories in the Balkans, and her interests were therefore in sharp contrast with Austria's. Furthermore, in 1905 Russia suffered severe defeats, both on land and on sea, in a war with Japan concerning their rival interests in Korea. After that, Russia was doubly determined to preserve her prestige and power.

These and many other sources of international tension were intensified by the overbearing and provocative attitude of Germany's second emperor, Kaiser William II. He had compelled Bismarck, the real architect of German unification, to resign. Without Bismarck's advice, he pursued policies that antagonized Britain and Russia.

The great powers formed rival alliances to strengthen their own positions. The Triple Alliance, between Germany, Austria-Hungary, and Italy, had already been made in 1882, under Bismarck's influence. In 1891 France and Russia replied by forming the Dual Alliance. The Anglo-French Entente of 1904 was followed in 1907 by an Anglo-Russian agreement on colonial issues. Thus the Triple Entente was formed.

From then on, almost any incident could have led to a colossal war. Yet several major incidents passed without producing that result. In 1908 Austria annexed Bosnia and Herzegovina, in the Balkans; in 1911 Germany intervened in French-Moroccan affairs; in the same year Italy seized Tripoli; in 1912 and 1913 there were two minor wars in the Balkans. But world peace was preserved.

Then on June 28th, 1914, the Archduke Francis Ferdinand, heir to the Austro-Hungarian throne, was assassinated at Sarajevo, in Bosnia, by a member of a Serbian terrorist organization. That incident precipitated a world war.

For the next four years almost the only news that counted was news from the world's battlefronts. Names of military commanders became household words everywhere.

TOP: *The Archduke Francis Ferdinand about to enter his carriage, on June 28th, 1914. A moment later he was assassinated.* BOTTOM LEFT: *German war lords: von Hindenburg, William II, and Ludendorff.* RIGHT: *The French Marshals Foch and Joffre* (TOP), *Albert I, King of the Belgians* (CENTER), *Lord Kitchener and the American General Pershing* (BOTTOM).

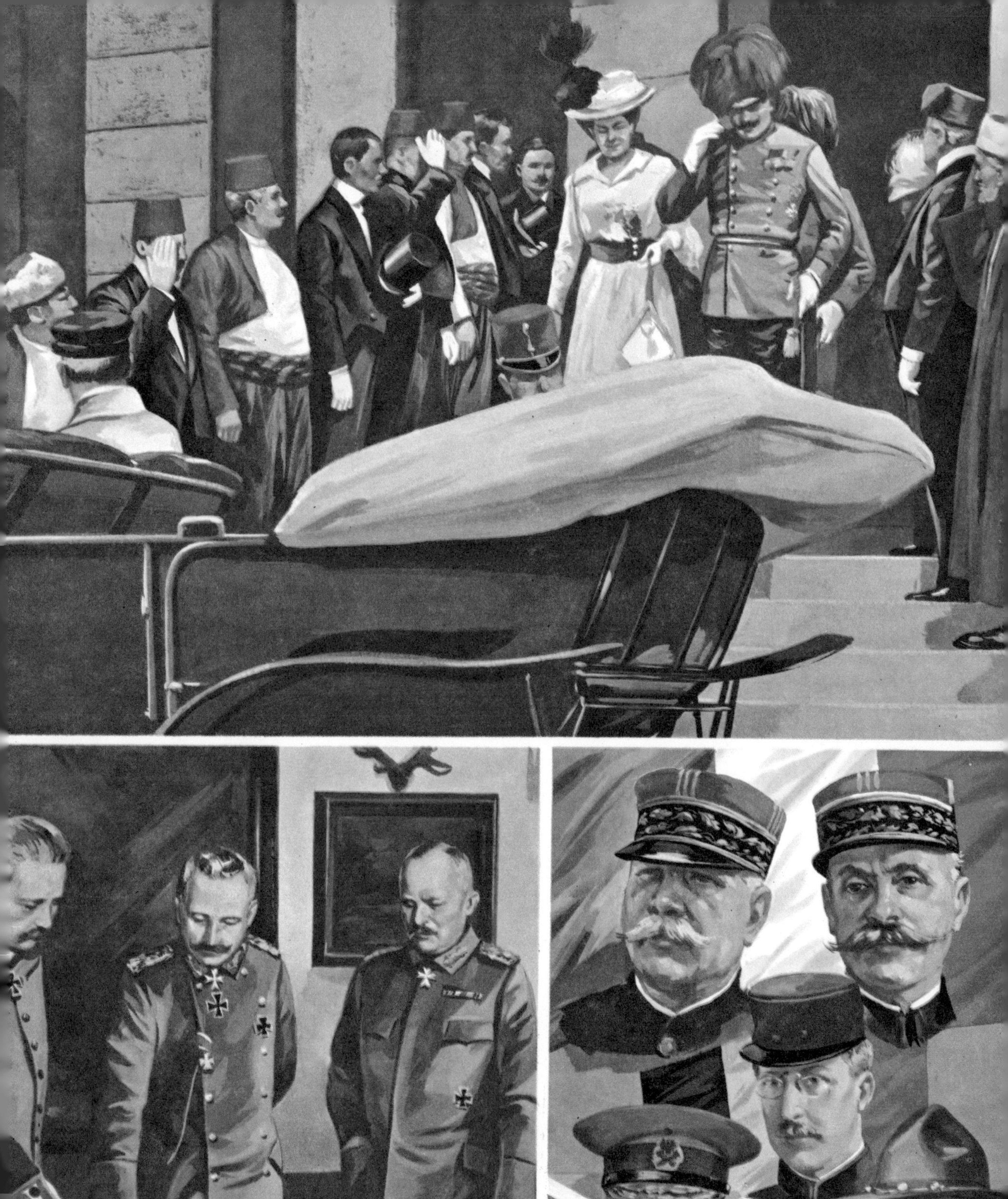

The First World War

AUSTRIA demanded that its own police should take part in the Serbian inquiries concerning Francis Ferdinand's assassination. Serbia refused. On July 28th, 1914, Austria-Hungary declared war.

Other declarations of war followed with the swiftness of a chain reaction. Russia proclaimed general mobilization, and on August 1st Germany declared war on her as a result. French mobilization began at once. Two days later Germany declared war on France and three days later on Belgium. In 1839 Britain and certain German states had signed a treaty guaranteeing not to violate Belgian neutrality; now, on August 4th, 1914, Britain declared war on Germany for breaking that treaty. Before 1914 ended there were thirteen further declarations of war; in the following two years more than a score of others followed.

The map opposite shows the hostile groups in Europe and the Near East. Brown indicates the Central Powers, green the Allied Powers, and grey the neutral countries. Here we can catch only the barest glimpse of a titanic struggle that lasted more than four years, involved some 40,000,000 armed men and cost close to 10,000,000 lives.

At the outset Germany was better prepared for war than her adversaries. Her best chance was to race through Belgium and Luxembourg and deliver a quick knock-out blow to France. This would leave her free to concentrate against the Russians, whose movements over vast distances would inevitably take time. The German armies did indeed push deep into northwest France in the first month of the war; but the Allies put up fierce resistance at the Battle of the Marne (September 5th to 12th), and in October and November German progress towards the Channel ports was halted at the Battle of the Yser, where the Belgians flooded much of the region. Germany's hope of a knockout blow had vanished. For four years war on the western front was to be an almost static test of endurance and resources.

Meanwhile, on the eastern front the Central Powers gained many early successes against Russia. At the Battle of Tannenberg, in August 1914, they took more than 100,000 prisoners; at the Masurian Lakes, a few weeks later, they captured even more. In 1915 the Russians were forced to retreat from Galicia, Poland, and Lithuania, and in the same year the Central Powers gained notable successes in the Balkans. They occupied Serbia and Rumania and brought about the failure of the Allied operations against the Dardanelles and Gallipoli. The only comparable early success by the Allies was the capture of all German overseas colonies in the early months of the war.

But as time went on the scene slowly changed. Britain's naval blockade began to produce serious shortages in central Europe. It is true that Germany's submarine attacks had similar effects on Britain, but the German sinking of the *Lusitania* played an important part in bringing America into the war on the Allied side. In 1916, after the Battle of Jutland, supremacy at sea passed more and more into Allied hands. In the air, Germany's zeppelins had given her an early advantage, but the Allies gained an advantage on land by being the first to use tanks.

From 1917 onwards, war shortages were producing unrest in several countries, especially in Russia which had so little success to show for its war effort. In November the Russian Revolution broke out, and in the following March the Bolshevik leader Lenin signed the Peace Treaty of Brest-Litovsk. This released a large number of German troops, and almost at once Germany began a great offensive in the west.

But under the command of Marchal Foch, the Allied forces, now augmented by a considerable American army, launched a counter-offensive. The Germans were forced to retreat, and German morale suddenly collapsed. Kaiser William II abdicated, and on November 11th, 1918, an Armistice was concluded.

TOP: *Europe during World War I. Brown shows Central Powers, green shows the Allies, grey shows neutrals.*
BOTTOM: *Trench warfare near the Yser, in 1914.*

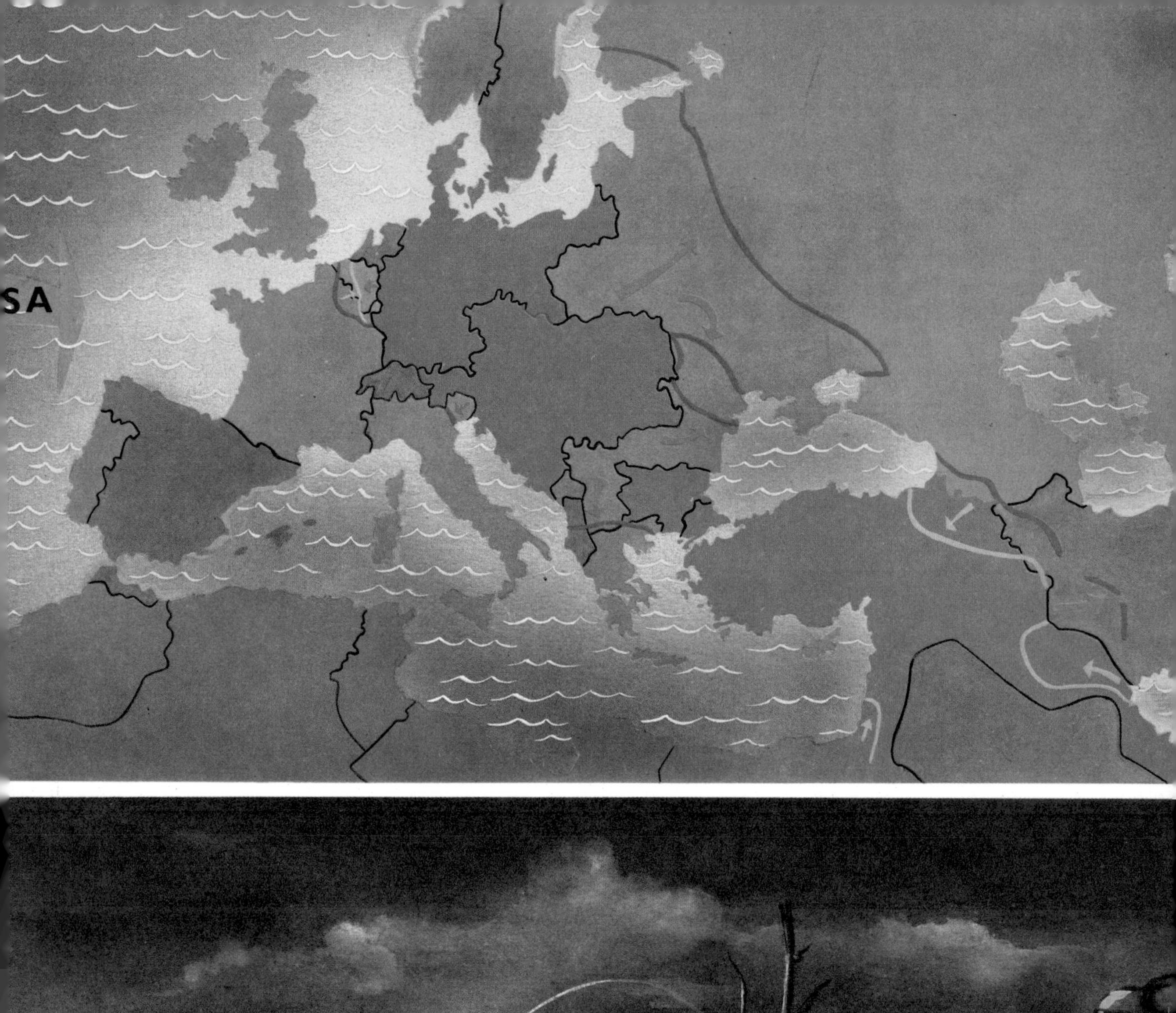
SA

Versailles, Geneva, and The Hague

THE armistice agreement, signed in a railroad coach near Compiègne, was simply an agreement for a cease-fire subject to certain conditions. And the conditions which the Allies imposed were intended to weaken Germany so that she could not later refuse to accept the peace terms offered her. Germany had to surrender vast quantities of munitions, hand over her submarines and other war vessels, and withdraw her troops east of the Rhine.

Then in January, 1919, delegates from twenty-seven victorious nations met in Paris to work out a resettlement of Europe. The countries which carried the greatest weight were France, Britain, the United States, Italy, and Japan. Germany was excluded until the Allies had agreed on terms. Russia was unrepresented, mainly because she had signed a separate treaty with Germany. The most influential delegates were Georges Clemenceau of France, openly intent on revenge, Lloyd George of Britain, committed by election promises to make Germany pay for the war, and President Woodrow Wilson of the United States, whose main concern was to set up a League of Nations.

Slowly, over many months, peace treaties were drawn up and signed: first the Treaty of Versailles with Germany, next the Treaty of St. Germain with Austria, next the Treaty of Neuilly with Bulgaria, then the Treaty of Trianon with Hungary, and finally the Treaty of Sèvres with Turkey. No doubt the treatymakers tried to mete out justice, and no doubt they aimed at putting peoples before princes. But justice sometimes involved reparations that could not be made, and peoples were rarely settled in such compact geographical areas that tidy frontiers could be drawn around them. The treaties contained germs of future discontent.

Here we can but glance at the main outlines of the peace settlement. Germany had to return Alsace-Lorraine to France and give up Eupen and Malmédy to Belgium. Large parts of Posen, West Prussia, and Silesia had to go to a resurrected Poland. Poland also received land forming a narrow outlet to the sea—the Polish Corridor. The rich industrial Saar area was to be administered for fifteen years by the League of Nations. All German overseas colonies went, as mandated territories, to the Allies, the African colonies going to Britain, France, and Belgium while the Pacific possessions went to Australia, New Zealand, and Japan. In addition, Germany was asked for colossal reparations which she could not possibly pay.

Out of the ruins of the Austro-Hungarian empire were created four smaller states, Austria, Hungary, Czechoslovakia, and Yugoslavia. Trieste and the Trentino (north of Venetia) went to Italy. Both Germany and Austria were permitted to keep only small armies and were forbidden to unite. The Hohenzollern dynasty was ended in Germany and the Hapsburg dynasty in Austria.

Turkey was shorn of all but a fragment of its European territories. Iraq and Palestine went as mandated territories to Britain, while Syria and Lebanon went to France. Much of Arabia became independent.

Perhaps the most significant event of 1919 was the setting up of the League of Nations, aimed at settling international conflicts by peaceful means. Working toward the same end was the International Court of Justice at The Hague, whose function was to settle disputes involving questions of international law. In a few years the League settled over thirty disputes between small states. But several great powers, including the U.S.A., were never League members, and it was some years before the defeated Central Powers were even allowed to join. Then, too, the League had no armies to enforce its decisions, and Japan, Italy, and the U.S.S.R. chose to ignore them when they proved inconvenient. Thus, slowly, the League lost much of its influence and prestige.

TOP LEFT: *Clemenceau, Wilson, and Lloyd George.* TOP RIGHT: *The Armistice railroad coach and the Palace of Justice at The Hague.* BOTTOM: *The Palace of the League of Nations at Geneva.*

From Tsars to Soviets

THE revolution which led to Russia's making a separate peace with Germany was not an unpremeditated rising. It was the result of grievances that had been building up over many years.

For centuries almost all the Tsars had ruled in completely autocratic fashion. Then in 1855 a more enlightened monarch, Alexander II, came to the throne. At that time a large proportion of Russia's population were serfs—people who worked the land and could be bought and sold with it like cattle. In 1861 Alexander II decided to free them.

But freedom was useless unless they could earn a livelihood, and at that time almost the only way of doing so in Russia was by working on the land. So the state bought land from the landowners and handed it over to village communes which parcelled it out among the newly-freed serfs. They, in turn, were given 49 years in which to pay off the cost of their allotments.

The village communes represented a new and widespread, even if limited, form of local government, and in 1864 local government was greatly extended. Zemstvos, or local boards consisting of nobility, townsmen, and peasants, were empowered to raise taxes for the building of roads, schools, hospitals, and the like. These tastes of political power whetted people's appetite for more, and several revolutionary movements sprang up aimed at liberalizing the constitution of Russia.

The next two Tsars, Alexander III (1881-94) and Nicholas II (1894-1917), tried to reverse the liberal trend and rule autocratically once more. But Russia was then beginning its first phase of industrial expansion. Coal and iron fields were being opened up, factories were being built, railroads were rapidly developing, and a new depressed class of industrial workers was coming into being. Then in 1891-92 there was a great famine which caused tremendous distress among the peasants. All these people thought of a more representative government as their only hope of betterment. Thus liberal and revolutionary ideas increased.

In 1905, when Russia suffered defeat by Japan, people lost their remaining faith in the government. In January working people assembled before the Imperial Palace at St. Petersburg to ask the Tsar for reforms. They were met by charging Cossacks, and several hundred were killed or wounded. In the late summer mutinies broke out in the army and in the Black Sea fleet. When crowds tried to view the body of one of the mutineers at Odessa, Cossacks again opened fire. Only after all these disorders did the Tsar allow an almost powerless national assembly, the Duma, to meet.

Utterly dissatisfied, many revolutionaries, including Lenin and Trotzky, now went into exile and began to organize more serious risings. Their aim was to set up a government based on the communist teachings of Karl Marx. The opportunity came in 1917, when the people of Russia were sick of defeat and shortages and disgusted with the Tsarist government's conduct of the war. In March, following a series of strikes and mutinies, Nicholas II abdicated. Later he and his entire family were assassinated. At first a socialist, Kerensky, made himself leader of the provisional government that was set up. But in the autumn Lenin seized power, and Trotzky, at the head of the new Red Army, crushed all opposition.

In 1922 the Union of Soviet Socialist Republics was formed, and before Lenin died, in 1924, other European powers, however reluctantly, had to face the fact that the new regime was firmly established. Lenin's successor, Stalin, supplanted Trotzky, made himself the strong man of the U.S.S.R., and concentrated on industrializing Russia. It was under his leadership that the U.S.S.R. withstood the onslaughts of Hitler's troops and finally drove them back to Berlin. It was also under his leadership that Russia seized the moment of victory to extend its frontiers westward, and to use several states of eastern Europe as mere Soviet satellites.

TOP: *To the left of the Soviet flag are Karl Marx and Nicholas II. To the right are Lenin and Trotzky.* BELOW: *Cossacks firing on crowds on the Richelieu Staircase in Odessa in 1905.*

Democracy and Commonwealth

In Britain in the present century political power has moved from the few to the many.

By 1884 most men in Britain were entitled to vote, but it was still difficult for a working man to enter Parliament, for members of Parliament still had no salaries. Trade unions did support a handful of Members, but it was only after 1911, when the payment of members was introduced, that the way was open for any man, irrespective of wealth, to sit in the House of Commons. In 1918 women over thirty were given the vote and were able to sit in Parliament. Ten years later the vote was extended to all women over twenty-one.

During the nineteenth century the House of Commons had consisted almost exclusively of the high-born and the wealthy. By 1935 it included 40 mineworkers, 18 metalworkers, 30 clerks and draughtsmen, 10 printers, 6 builders, 2 painters, a warehouseman, and a locomotive engineer. And as the Commons began to become more representative of the people, they claimed wider powers. In 1911, after the House of Lords had rejected several Bills passed by the Commons, its powers were drastically curtailed. It could no longer veto finance bills at all, and it could not veto other bills for more than two years.

All this did not mean that the conditions of ordinary people were improved in a twinkling. Indeed, during the depression of the 1920s and 1930s, widespread unemployment caused great distress throughout Britain. But when hunger marchers from Jarrow and other hard-hit towns marched to Westminster, they could at least be sure that Parliament included many men who really understood their problems. Today the emphasis of economic policy is on promoting full employment. This is part of the significance of Britain's pioneer atomic power stations.

The trend towards a more democratic Britain was reflected in Britain's attitude to her overseas "possessions." Until late in the nineteenth century Britain was still building an Empire. Since then she has been a partner in the more difficult task of creating a Commonwealth.

In 1875, when Disraeli bought over 40% of the Suez Canal shares from the Khedive of Egypt, thus giving Britain a controlling interest in it, his main aims were to safeguard British power in India and to extend British influence in Egypt. The interests of India and Egypt were secondary to those of Britain. That was Empire-building.

But already a different idea had begun to take shape. As long ago as 1839 Lord Durham had recommended that the provinces of Canada should unite under a single government. Britain, he said, should control virtually no aspect of Canada's affairs except her foreign policy. In 1867 Ontario, Quebec, New Brunswick, and Nova Scotia did indeed form the Dominion of Canada with just such a government, and other provinces later joined them. Then, shortly after the Boer War, Lord Milner who had formerly been British High Commissioner for South Africa, and Field Marshal Smuts, who had formerly been in command of Boer forces in Cape Colony, worked together for the interests of both British and Boers in South Africa. This was true Commonwealth-building.

Today the British Empire has given place to the British Commonwealth of Nations: a society in which each member-state runs its own affairs and in which all members have an equal voice in discussing matters of mutual interest. Member states are free to leave the association, as the Republic of Ireland did in 1949 and as South Africa did in 1961. Equally, countries having newly gained their independence, such as Ghana, Cyprus, and Nigeria, are welcome to join.

TOP LEFT: *Canada and Lord Durham.* TOP RIGHT: *Suez Canal and statue of its builder, de Lesseps.* CENTER LEFT: *South Africa, Lord Milner, and Field Marshal Smuts.* CENTER RIGHT: *Jarrow hunger marchers.* BOTTOM LEFT: *Calder Hall atomic power station.* BOTTOM RIGHT: *Commonwealth leaders of 1961 grouped around Her Majesty, Elizabeth II.*

JARROW
CRUSADE

America's Growth in Ninety Years

If we try to sum up the United States' recent history in a few words, as we have done Britain's, we can pick out only three main trends: the incorporation of new states into the Union, the tremendous increase in population, and America's rise to the leadership of the Western World.

The maps and pictures opposite highlight some important stages in these developments. The top three squares cover roughly the three decades between 1870 and 1900; the center three cover the decades between 1900 and 1930; the bottom three cover the period from 1930 to the present.

Up to 1880, the War between the States was still a recent memory. Nevertheless, the settlement of the western territories went rapidly ahead, and already the first transcontinental railroad was completed. But much of the West (the pale area on the first map) was still sparsely populated, and had not reached the stage where new states could be formed. Indeed, the total population was still little more than 40 million people.

Between 1880 and 1889 the United States' population increased by twenty-five per cent, but no new states came into being. On the initiative of W. H. Seward, America had bought Alaska from Russia in 1867, but it did not become a state. From 1884 until 1903 it was governed according to the laws of the state of Oregon. It was only between 1889 and 1900, the period we associate with the Klondike Gold Rush, that Washington, Montana, Idaho, the Dakotas, Utah, and Wyoming were admitted to the Union. By then the population was over 60 million.

During the first ten years of this century (the period when the United States began constructing the Panama Canal, under the direction of Lieutenant-Colonel George Goethals) only a smallish area near the Mexican border had not yet joined the Union. In 1912 this area gave rise to Arizona and New Mexico. No further states were added until Alaska and Hawaii achieved statehood in 1959.

In the little groups of human silhouettes opposite, each figure represents 10 million people. They show that at the time of building the Panama Canal, the United States' population was about 90 million. Today it is over 180 million.

The last two pictures in the middle row and the first two in the bottom row remind us that the United States, like Britain, has had severe ups and downs of fortune during the twentieth century. Partly as a result of the sinking of the *Lusitania*, America came into the World War I against Germany in 1917. During the War, a prominent American critizen, Herbert Hoover, became head of the relief organization for occupied Belgium. Later, in 1929, he was to become U.S. President. In 1919 America took a step that Britain had taken a year earlier by giving votes to women. In the same year, on the initiative of Senator Andrew Volstead, it also prohibited the sale of alcoholic liquor. This led to illegal manufacture and smuggling of liquor, conducted largely by rival criminal elements.

Prohibition was not repealed until 1933, by which time Franklin Delano Roosevelt had succeeded Hoover as President. It was under Roosevelt that the United States embarked on the New Deal Legislation which established many great public works and which included the famous National Recovery Act, aimed at pulling the country out of a severe economic slump. In the 1940s America emerged as the leading military and industrial power of the Western World, the first country to use atomic power in war, and among the first to exploit it for peaceful purposes. At the close of the Second World War, Secretary of State General George Marshall produced a plan by which America placed a generous share of her resources at the disposal of other countries impoverished by years of fighting.

Nine squares showing outstanding events and outstanding people in the last nine decades of the United States' history. The people are (top row) W. H. Seward; (center row) Goethals, Hoover, and Volstead; (bottom row) General Marshall and an astronaut.

NRA
MEMBER
U.S.
WE DO OUR PART
US

Lands of the Future

IN Central and South America it is not easy to pinpoint outstanding tendencies of recent history. To the outsider, the history of Latin America since the Wars of Liberation seems to consist mainly of a long succession of revolutions.

It was not until nearly the end of last century that this vast region of the New World broke the last of its connections with the monarchies of Europe. We saw on page 136 that in the 1860s Napoleon III set up the Archduke Maximilian of Austria as a Catholic Emperor of Mexico. It was not until 1867 that the Mexican people were able to rid themselves of this foreign emperor and to put the native Liberal leader, Benito Juarez, in power as President once more. In Brazil ties with one of the royal houses of Europe remained unbroken until 1889. When Brazil broke away from Portugal in 1822, the elder son of the Portuguese king became its emperor, under the title of Pedro I. Pedro I reigned until 1831, when he abdicated in favor of his infant son, Pedro II. After 1870 Pedro II became increasingly unpopular among the clergy, the landed aristocracy, and the army, and in 1889, after a short revolt led by General Manoel Deodoro da Fonseca, he was deposed. Only then did Brazil become a republic.

Yet from first to last, the mere breaking of ties with Europe did little to improve conditions in Latin America, for the causes of bad conditions were too deep-seated to be cured by any such simple means. The wide racial differences between different classes of the population, which we noted on page 130, still remained, and the gulf between rich and poor was still very wide. The great majority of people lived by agriculture, yet about half the land belonged to less than two per cent of the population—wealthy landowners with estates of fifteen thousand acres or more.

Throughout the nineteenth century powerful movements based on a mixture of American-Indian nationalism and socialist doctrines sprang up in several South American countries. So, too, did Liberal movements, aimed at weakening the influence of the great landowners. Movements of this kind were heralded in Cuba by José Martí, in Colombia by Miguel Caro, and in Argentina by Bartolomé Mitre, Juan Bautista Alberdi, and Don Parrafos de Sarmiento.

This, then, was one cause of frequent revolutions. Another was that Latin America, while primarily a producer of food and raw materials, was harder hit by fluctuations in world prices than most regions are. Yet another cause was the fact that the United States has sometimes openly favored one political faction against another. In recent years the situation is further complicated because the Soviet Union and other communist countries are apt to support any strong left-wing movement that gains power while America is apt to support any anti-communist rising, as happened in Cuba in 1961. Thus it is no wonder that in the 1930s Ecuador had eleven presidents in eight years, Chile eight in eighteen months, and Cuba six in less than two years.

But constant revolutions are by no means the whole story. There is a far brighter side. During the present century most Latin American countries, in common with the United States, have sent representatives to Pan-American Conferences aimed at fostering economic cooperation, furthering mutual interests, and preserving peace in the Western Hemisphere. While much remains to be done to improve agricultural methods and the lot of agricultural workers, industries are rapidly growing and city dwellers enjoy conditions that compare not unfavorably with those in far older industrial countries. Mineral resources, especially oil and iron ore, are being exploited on an unprecedented scale.

The lands of South America are not so much lands of the past as lands of the future.

TOP LEFT: *Mexico, with Benito Juarez.* TOP RIGHT: *Cuba, with José Martí.* CENTER LEFT: *Colombia, with Miguel Antonio Caro.* CENTER RIGHT: *Brazil with General Manoel Deodoro da Fonseca.* BOTTOM: *Argentina, with Bartolomé Mitre, Juan Bautista Alberdi, and Don Parrafos de Sarmiento.*

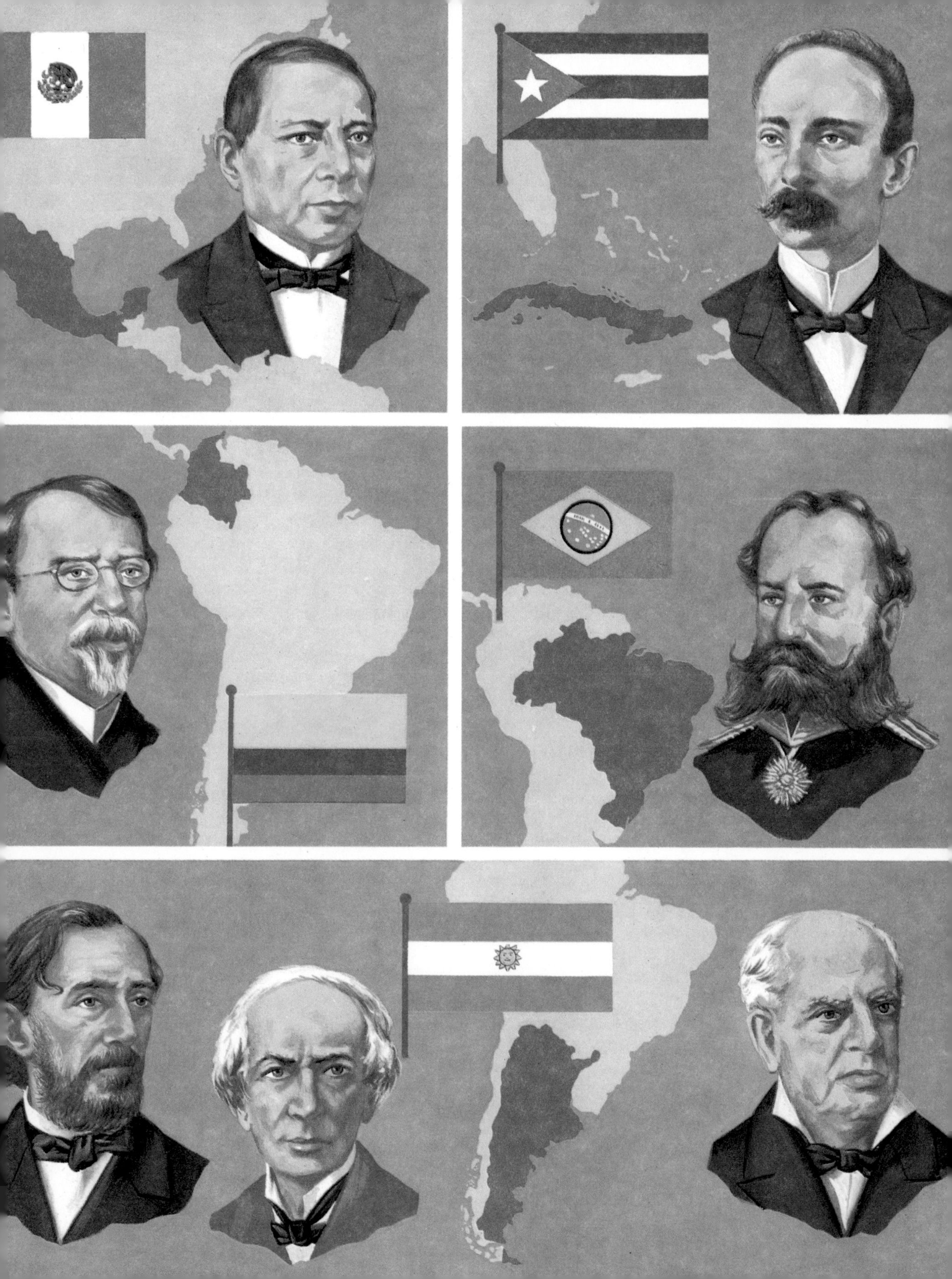

Japan Since 1844

JAPAN was slow in forging ties with Europe. As late as 1844 the shogun Iesyoshi gave orders that all foreign vessels approaching Japan must be fired on. But the time had come when no country could remain in utter isolation. Sailing ships were giving place to steamers, which simply had to visit foreign ports to refuel; whaling was increasing, and when whalers were wrecked their survivors needed to be sure of proper treatment wherever they landed. So from 1844 onwards several countries pleaded with Japan to open her ports.

Success came in 1853 when the Japanese Emperor himself studied an appeal from the United States president, brought by Commodore Perry. In 1854 Japan and America signed the Treaty of Kanagawa, which opened two ports to American ships and provided for better treatment of American castaways. Within a few years Japan made similar treaties with Britain, Russia, Holland, and France. But there was still a powerful anti-foreign party in Japan until 1867.

Then a new Emperor, Mutsuhito, or Meiji, came to the throne and inaugurated an entirely new regime. He brought the office of shogun to an end, gave Japan a constitution, embarked on a great scheme of industrialization, introduced compulsory education, and ordered the construction of railroads. Japan built up a modern army and a formidable fleet.

Quickly Japan learned many of the leading ideas of Western civilization. Unfortunately two of those ideas were militarism and imperialism.

During 1894-95 Japan was at war with China, and wrested from her the control of Korea and Formosa. The intervention of Russia prevented a complete Japanese occupation of Korea, and this fact gave rise to the Russo-Japanese War of 1904-05. Besides winning many land victories, the Japanese seized Port Arthur, thus bottling up the Russian Pacific fleet. When Russia's Baltic fleet reached the Far East, it was annihilated by Japanese vessels under the command of Admiral Togo. When the war ended, Japan gained control of Korea, which it later annexed, in 1910. Russia was compelled to evacuate Manchuria and to hand over part of the island of Sakhalin.

For her part in World War I, Japan received several former German possessions in the Pacific. But still her expansionist aims were not satisfied. In 1931-32 her armies seized control of Manchuria and set up the former Chinese Emperor, P'u-i, as a puppet ruler. Then in 1937 Japan began a campaign of conquest against China, capturing Peking, Nanking, Shanghai, and Canton. Fighting was still going on when World War II began.

In 1940 Japan signed a three-power pact with Germany and Italy, and in 1941 a treaty of neutrality with Russia. Then on December 7th, 1941, without warning, Japanese planes destroyed a large part of America's Pacific fleet at Pearl Harbor, in Hawaii. Almost simultaneous attacks were launched on the Philippines, Malaya, Hong Kong, and Singapore. Japan later seized Indo-China, Thailand, Indonesia, and part of Burma. It took over three years of fighting to regain even part of these territories. Only by the Battle of Iwo Jima, in the spring of 1945, did the Americans gain an airbase from which they could bomb Japan.

In August, 1945, following the dropping of atomic bombs on Hiroshima and Nagasaki, Japan surrendered, and American forces under General MacArthur began the occupation of the country. Several Japanese war leaders, including General Tojo, were sentenced to death for war crimes.

Today Japan has a constitution modeled on that of the United States, and its Emperor, Hirohito, reigns as a constitutional monarch.

On the map J shows Japan, F Formosa, S Sakhalin, K Korea, T Thailand, I Indonesia, MA Manchuria, IC Indo-China, C China, B Burma, M Malaya, C_1 Carolines, and H Hawaii. Dark arrows show Japanese expansion in the Second World War; light arrows illustrate the Allied counter-offensive. On the right are the Emperor Meiji, Admiral Togo, General Tojo, and the Emperor Hirohito. Inset is General MacArthur. Below U.S. Marines raise American flag after victory at Iwo Jima.

S 1905
MA
1934
C
1940
K
1910
J
F
1895
B
1942
T
1937
IC
P
1942
M
1941
I 1942
CI
1920
H
12/7/41.

The Rise of Fascism

After 1870, relations between the Pope and the newly-unified Italian state were strained and the Pope forbade Catholics to take any active part in Italian politics. This helped to produce an unstable parliamentary regime in which power was frequently in the hands of anti-clericals. Italy's economy was unsound, financial crises were frequent, and millions of Italians emigrated.

Yet abroad, Italy embarked on a campaign of colonial expansion. By 1890 she had seized Eritrea and much of Somaliland, but an attempt at the conquest of Ethiopia six years later ended disastrously, with Italy being compelled to sue for peace. Then during 1911 and 1912 Italy wrested control of Tripoli from Turkey.

Although she had signed the Triple Alliance with Germany and Austria, Italy "sat on the fence" when the First World War broke out, waiting to determine from which side she could reap the greatest territorial rewards. Eventually in May, 1915, she cast in her lot with the Allies and declared war on Austria-Hungary. Among those who advocated this course was Benito Mussolini, a young statesman who had recently broken with the Italian socialist party.

As it happened, the Italian front provided a series of disasters for the Allies, and when peace was restored Italy's territorial gains fell far short of expectations. Further, Italy, which had lost more than half a million men, was left deeply in debt. Discontent was therefore rife, and for three years there were lockouts, strikes, riots, and frequent changes of government. From 1919 onwards, many malcontents rallied to the new Fascist movement, led by Mussolini, Generals Balbo and de Bono, and Dino Grandi. In 1922 the Fascists marched on Rome and seized power.

Within a few years, by banning other political parties and exercising strict control over press and public meetings, Mussolini made himself dictator. During the hey-day of "Il Duce," as his Black-Shirt followers called him, strikes and lockouts were forbidden, and workers and masters in each industry were organized into corporations. The state carried out many worth while public works, including the draining of the Pontine Marshes near Rome, the building of hydroelectric power stations, the electrification of railroads, and the construction of Europe's first modern highways.

But Mussolini also sought territorial aggrandizement at whatever cost. In 1935-36 Italian forces under Marshal Badoglio conquered Ethiopia, driving out the Emperor Haile Selassie, and proclaiming the King of Italy as Emperor of Ethiopia. Later, in April, 1939, Italy invaded and conquered Albania. This expansionist policy, carried out largely by Mussolini's son-in-law, Count Ciano, ultimately weakened Italy's bargaining power with Germany. So widespread were her military commitments, that when, in 1938, Hitlerite Germany seized Austria, on Italy's very doorstep, Italy simply accepted the fact without protest.

Throughout the 1930s it did seem, for a time, that military dictatorships could gain advantages while the peaceful democracies slumbered. Thus it is not altogether surprising that men like Mussolini had their imitators. In 1936, a group of right-wing officers, under the leadership of General Franco, began a civil war to seize power in Spain. This three-year war, in which one of the most notable events was the siege of the Alcázar in Toledo, in fact became a rehearsal for World War II. Germany and Italy came to Franco's aid with troops and supplies; Russia, France, and an International Brigade from many lands rallied to the side of his left-wing opponents. In May, 1939, Madrid fell and from then on Franco was master of Spain. Unlike Mussolini he avoided following Germany into World War II and, mainly for that reason, he was able to retain power.

On the map S *marks Somaliland,* T *Tripoli,* E *Eritrea,* E_1 *Ethiopia, and* A *Albania. On Ethiopia is a portrait of Haile Selassie. Top pictures show fascist leaders in the March on Rome, and portraits of Mussolini, Ciano, and Badoglio. Below is the Alcázar of Toledo and, inset, General Franco.*

I
A
T
E
E1
S

Germany under the Nazis

IN Germany, as in Italy, unrest and economic distress following the First World War produced ideal conditions for the emergence of a dictator.

When the Kaiser abdicated in 1918, Germany became a republic, and early in 1919 a national assembly met at Weimar to draw up a new constitution. This gave executive power to a president and legislative power to a diet or parliament. The president was to choose a chancellor commanding a majority of votes in the diet, and the chancellor, in turn, was to choose a cabinet.

But to govern a defeated and disgruntled Germany was no easy task. During the next few years unemployment was rife, the value of the mark plunged steeply and Germany was quite unable to pay the reparations the Allies demanded. For this reason French and Belgian troops occupied the Ruhr in 1923. These troubles led to frequent changes of government and several risings.

One rising, in Munich in 1923, was led by General Ludendorff and Adolf Hitler, leader of the new but growing National Socialist Party—the Nazis, whose emblem was the swastika, or crooked cross. The rising was poorly organized and easily suppressed, and Hitler, a former corporal in the German army, was sent to prison.

The economic outlook in Germany now began to brighten. Under a plan organized by the American Charles G. Dawes, Germany received a colossal loan. A sound currency was soon restored and Germany's economy began to recover. The government pursued a peaceful policy, and in 1926 Germany was admitted to the League of Nations.

But the world had not heard the last of Hitler. While in prison he began writing a book, *Mein Kampf* ("My Struggle"), outlining his career and stating his political views. The German people, he declared, were a master race, destined to rule the world; it was not they but the Jews who had caused Germany's recent defeat; the Slav peoples, and especially the Russians, were an inferior race, worthy only of extermination.

Released from prison after less than a year, Hitler continued to build up his Party. Soon it possessed many semi-military shock troops, the Brown Shirts. It also had a personal bodyguard, the notorious S.S., led by Heinrich Himmler. Assisted by men like Joseph Goebbels, a genius at distorting truth, the Nazis also began to fight and win elections. By 1932 they had 230 members in the Reichstag and in 1933 Germany's President von Hindenburg proclaimed Hitler Chancellor.

Within a few years, with von Hindenburg now dead, Hitler became absolute master. The cry of the German people was "Ein Volk, ein Reich, ein Führer"—"One people, one state, one leader." And the leader was soon to lead state and people along the most disastrous path in history. All political parties other than the Nazis were banned, and dissension within the party itself was ruthlessly stamped out. In 1934 over seventy Nazis who favored a more left-wing policy than Hitler was prepared to follow were summarily executed. They included Roehm, former leader of the Brown Shirts, and Strasser, one of the earliest Nazi leaders.

With all opposition gone, Hitler ruled with a rod of iron. By inaugurating the building of *autobahnen* (later used as military roads) and by spending vast sums on rearmament he reduced unemployment by ninety per cent, and vastly increased Germany's industrial output. But the price was a course of aggression—in the Rhineland, in Austria, in Czechoslovakia, and in Poland—that led inevitably to war. Germany also witnessed an upsurge of inhuman cruelty. By the early 1940s extermination camps were set up at Auschwitz and elsewhere, and all told some six million Jews were brutally murdered. After World War II ended the men responsible for these and other horrors were tried at Nuremberg as war criminals.

TOP: *Himmler, Hitler, and Goebbels.* CENTER: *A concentration camp and a map of Hitler's* autobahnen, *or highways.* BOTTOM: *A scene at the trial of war criminals at Nuremberg after World War II.*

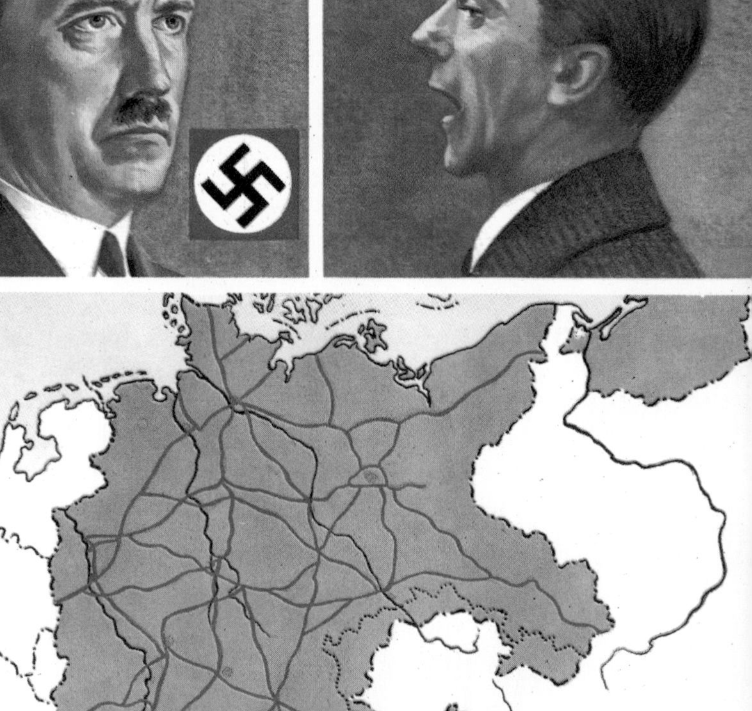

Night Falls Over Europe

WE have seen that during the early and middle 1930s Japan, Italy, and Germany all had reason to think that aggression paid.

Then in 1939 Hitler tested the patience of the western democracies too far. Up to that time it was just possible to believe that his acts of aggression were aimed only at unifying all people of German origin within one state. But early in March, 1939, Germany annihilated Czechoslovakia. Bohemia and Moravia became a German protectorate and Slovakia a mere puppet. A few days later Germany forced Lithuania to give up the port of Memel. It was now clear that no part of Europe was safe from Hitler's ambitions, and both Britain and France quickly pledged support to various potential victims, including Poland.

Before making his next move, Hitler secured the neutrality of his most powerful eastern neighbor by signing a non-aggression pact with Russia. Then on September 1st, 1939, he launched a massive land and air attack against Poland, which refused to give him part of the Polish Corridor and resisted his demands to incorporate the free city of Danzig into Greater Germany. Two days later both Britain and France honored their pledge to Poland by declaring war on Germany.

But the Allies were in no position to save Poland. So rapidly did German tanks, artillery, and motorized infantry move in from East Prussia, Silesia, and Slovakia, that within a week they were at the gates of Warsaw. On September 17th the Russians, doubtless alarmed by the speed of events, invaded Poland from the east; and by the end of the month the country was divided between Germany and Russia. Then, not having yet entered the main conflict, Russia effectively occupied the Baltic states and made war on Finland.

Meanwhile, throughout the winter of 1939-40, there was little action on the western front. The Germans behind the Siegfried Line and the Allies behind the Maginot Line, remained immobile. But at sea German submarines began to take toll of Allied shipping. Then in April, 1940, after Britain mined Norwegian waters to prevent the passage of German ships, Germany replied with a lightning conquest of both Norway and Denmark.

The following month action on the western front began with a vengeance. On May 10th, without declaring war, Germany invaded the Netherlands, Belgium, and Luxembourg. Pushing through to the coast, German armies surrounded a British expeditionary force, and only by an almost miraculous effort was it possible to evacuate over 300,000 men —two-thirds British and one third French—from Dunkirk. Next the Germans battered the Maginot Line and overran northern France. Meanwhile, on June 10th, Italy entered the war and invaded France from the southeast. Before the month ended Marshal Pétain sued for an armistice. France, except for the Free French under General de Gaulle, was out of the war.

During the next year Germany and Italy gained victory after victory, in Rumania, Crete, Greece, Albania, and Yugoslavia. Practically all Europe outside Russia, Spain, Portugal, Sweden, and Switzerland fell under German control. Only in North Africa did British and Free French troops make headway against the Italians. Even these gains vanished after Germany's General Rommel and his Africa Corps went into action in August, 1941. Thus, after the summer of 1940 Britain was fighting virtually alone and feeling the full weight of German air attacks on her great cities. Only the strength of the British navy and the unceasing efforts of the R.A.F. during the Battle of Britain prevented Hitler from accomplishing his "Sea Lion" plan for invading the British Isles.

The arrows on the map show German and Italian advances during the first two years of World War II. The three figures on the left are Admiral Raeder (German naval Commander-in-chief from 1935 until 1943), General von Rundstedt (Commander of German forces in the west), and General Rommel. On the right is General Guderian (Commander of German forces in the east).

The End of Hitler's Empire

By the end of 1940 Hitler's Germany had defeated every country it fought except Britain. Further, in September of that year Germany and Italy signed a three-power pact with powerful Japan.

But within a year the seeds of its downfall were already sown. The German air bombardment of Britain had failed. Already, in 1941, Britain under Churchill's leadership was rapidly rebuilding and re-equipping its army; military planes were already pouring off the production lines; and from March, 1941, the United States began to provide Britain with goods under the new Lend-Lease Act.

Then on June 22nd Hitler made the mistake of invading Russia, intending to wipe her out as a major power. Into his surprise attack, Hitler threw 3,000,000 men, including Germans, Italians, Finns, and Rumanians, never doubting that he would win within a few weeks. And, indeed, by September Leningrad was surrounded, the suburbs of Moscow were under fire, White Russia and the Ukraine were occupied.

But as the Russians retreated they burned and destroyed everything. The Germans won little except scorched earth. Their lines of communication became longer and more vulnerable, and they were faced with a bitter winter campaign for which they were quite unprepared. Yet despite heavy losses they weathered the winter, and in 1942 fought on as far as Stalingrad, on the Volga. It was then that Stalin gave the order not to yield another inch. Russia, backed now with military supplies from America and Britain, passed to the attack. In February, 1943, an army under General von Paulus surrendered. Germany lost not only 300,000 men but also its reputation of invincibility. From then until May, 1945, the Germans were almost continuously pushed back, the Russians being aided in the Balkans by partisans under Marshal Tito.

Meanwhile, in December, 1941, following the Japanese attack on Pearl Harbor, the United States, under Franklin D. Roosevelt, was at war with Japan, Germany, and Italy. In October, 1942, Britain's Eighth Army under General Montgomery began to hurl Rommel's forces westward out of Egypt; in November, British and American forces under Eisenhower landed in Morocco and Algiers and drove eastward; and by May, 1943, Germany's career in North Africa had ended.

In July, Britain and America began the invasion of Sicily, and in September the invasion of the Italian mainland. Mussolini, arrested and forced to resign, was rescued from near Rome by German paratroops, and later became head of a puppet government in northern Italy. But his successor, Marshal Badoglio, dissolved the Fascist party in southern Italy and signed an armistice with the Allies. German forces in Italy fought on until the last few days of the war, but this placed yet another drain on Germany's dwindling resources. Mussolini himself was shot and killed in April, 1945.

The greatest single blow to Hitler's tottering empire came on June 6th, 1944, when a vast Allied force under General Eisenhower began landing in Normandy and quickly opened up a great western front. By September, aided by a landing in southern France under General de Lattre de Tassigny, the Allies had liberated almost the whole of France and Belgium. On April 28th, 1945, with Berlin in flames, Hitler committed suicide, and on May 8th his successor, Admiral Doenitz, surrendered unconditionally to the Allies.

TOP: *Churchill, Roosevelt, and Stalin, and flags of some Allied nations.* BOTTOM: *Map on which arrows show Allied advances. Dotted line shows limit of German advance in Russia. The portraits on the map are of Eisenhower (top left), de Lattre de Tassigny (center left), Montgomery (bottom), Tito (center right), and Zhukov (top right). Green: Western Allies; maroon: Russia; grey: neutrals; blue: areas recaptured by end of 1944; beige: areas recaptured by May, 1945; green-and-blue: territory which joined Allies after recapture; brown-ochre: territory in German hands at capitulation.*

The UN and the Post-War World

PERHAPS the most terrifying thing about World War II was that naked aggression came so very near to succeeding. Long before the war ended, statesmen of countries fighting against Germany, Italy, and Japan sought ways and means of preventing future aggression.

As early as January, 1942, fifty-one of the Allied nations signed a United Nations declaration, pledging themselves to act together when war ended. Two years later representatives of Britain, the U.S.A., Russia, and China met at Dumbarton Oaks, near Washington, D.C., and drafted a plan for a World Peace Organization. The new organization, intended to continue and improve on the work of the old League of Nations, came into being in 1945 and was named the United Nations Organization. At first its membership was limited to the fifty-one nations that had signed the 1942 declaration, but as time passed other countries were admitted, and today there are more than ninety members, including several which fought against the Allies during World War II.

The main aims of the UN are to promote security and welfare, to uphold international justice, and to champion human rights everywhere. Its members are pledged not to resort to force or the threat of force, not to support aggression, and to assist in carrying out the United Nations Charter.

The work of the UN is carried out by six main organs: a General Assembly, a Security Council, an International Court of Justice, an Economic and Social Council, a Trusteeship Council, and a General Secretariat. The General Assembly, which consists of representatives of all the member nations, is a kind of world parliament which meets periodically to elect members of the other UN organs and to discuss all questions of peace and security brought before it. But the actual action to be taken is referred to the Security Council, which is much more like a world cabinet, and remains in permanent session. The Security Council consists of five permanent members (the U.S.A., Britain, France, the U.S.S.R., and Nationalist China) and six others, each elected for two years by the General Assembly. The day-to-day work of the UN is carried out by the Secretariat. The first two secretaries-general were Trygve Lie, a Norwegian, and Dag Hammarskjold, a Swede. After Hammarskjold's tragic death, U Thant of Burma became acting secretary-general.

Decisions of the Security Council must be carried by seven out of eleven votes, and five of those seven votes must be cast by the permanent members. If only one of the permanent members refuses to agree to an action, then that action cannot be taken.

The Trusteeship Council is broadly responsible for the welfare of people in colonies taken from defeated countries, and the International Court of Justice, which meets at The Hague, is responsible for settling dangerous disputes which arise out of problems of international law. Much more complex and varied is the work of the Economic and Social Council, which aims to eliminate such possible causes of war as poverty, ignorance, lack of economic progress, and epidemic diseases. Much of the work of the Council is carried out by regional economic commissions, and by commissions dealing with particular problems, such as transport and communications, human rights, the status of women, and technical assistance. There are also about a dozen specialized agencies, including the World Health Organization (WHO), United Nations Educational, Scientific, and Cultural Organization (UNESCO), the Food and Agriculture Organization (FAO), and the International Labor Organization (ILO).

The specialized agencies of the UN have made a valuable contribution to peace, by raising living standards, promoting literacy, preventing epidemics, and caring for homeless refugees.

TOP: *Flag, map, and headquarters of the UN, together with portraits of the first two secretaries-general, Trygve Lie and Dag Hammarskjold.* BOTTOM: *A refugee camp in Germany (left) and an Arab refugee camp (right).*

Trouble Spots of Recent Years

Among the first places where danger threatened after World War II was Indo-China. While the Japanese occupied former French possessions there, the native peoples were naturally fired with the desire to run their own affairs. In 1946, little more than a year after the Japanese surrender, this independence movement showed itself in a revolt against French sovereignty, but later it developed into a struggle between communist and anti-communist forces. Fighting continued for nearly eight years, and at almost any stage it could have developed into a major war between the communist and the anti-communist powers; but largely owing to world opinion as expressed through the UN this tragedy was averted. Eventually, in 1954, the region was divided into four sovereign states: North Vietnam, South Vietnam, Laos, and Cambodia.

Similar causes gave rise to conflict in Korea. Russia had declared war on Japan only a few days before the Japanese surrender, and Korea, wrested from Japan, was then occupied by both Russian and American troops. A provisional frontier, drawn at the thirty-eighth parallel of latitude, divided communist-dominated North Korea from American-influenced South Korea. Then in June, 1950, North Korean troops crossed the frontier. At a moment when the Russian representative was absent and could not therefore apply the veto, the Security Council appealed to the United Nations to come to South Korea's aid.

Armed forces of many nations, with Americans most numerous, did so, but thousands of "volunteers" from communist China fought on the side of North Korea. Hundreds of thousands of men were killed and wounded before an armistice was signed at Panmunjom on July 27th, 1953, and then the frontier was scarcely changed.

In the Arab countries, too, there have been numerous troubles. In 1956, when Egypt, Syria, and Jordan placed their troops under a centralized command, the Jewish State of Israel feared an attack. Israel seized the initiative and invaded the Sinai Peninsula of Egypt, east of the Suez Canal. Britain and France, already angered by Egyptian threats to nationalize the Canal, attacked Egypt and seized Port Said. Whether or not Britain's action could be justified is still a source of heated argument, but the UN and much of world opinion was against it. The UN police occupied the Gaza strip, and British, French, and Israeli troops were quickly withdrawn. In 1958, when pro-Western King Feisal of Iraq was assassinated, there were fears that Iraq would become communist, but the revolution proved to be a Pan-Arab victory.

Perhaps the UN's greatest failure came in 1956, when the Russians used overwhelming military strength to crush a popular rising in Hungary, and to re-establish the control of the communist party there. In spite of pleas from Budapest, the UN did virtually nothing to prevent Russian intervention. But this event coincided with the French and British landings in Egypt. The UN's power was thereby undermined, since the western nations were divided among themselves.

More recently the UN has had the task of limiting troubles in the Congo. After Belgium granted Congolese independence in July, 1960, there was an army revolt followed by attacks on Belgian civilians. Fierce fighting followed between forces of Prime Minister Lumumba, backed by communist powers, and those of President Kasavubu, backed by the west. In February, 1961, Lumumba was assassinated. The conflict could have spread, but the presence of UN troops enabled a calmer atmosphere to prevail. In September, on a peace mission to Katanga, Secretary-General Hammarskjold's plane crashed, killing him and his aides.

Sketch maps of some of the world's recent trouble spots. The portraits, from top to bottom, are Syngman Rhee (former President of South Korea), King Feisal of Iraq, and a Congo citizen.

HUNGARY
N. KOREA
S. KOREA
CHINA
N. VIETNAM
BURMA
LAOS
THAILAND
CAMBODIA
S. VIETNAM
SYRIA
ISRAEL
IRAQ
JORDAN
EGYPT

CONGO

The Return to the Promised Land

THE Suez crisis of 1956 was precipitated partly by the Israeli invasion of Egypt. Yet only eight years earlier the State of Israel had not been born.

We saw earlier how Moses led the exodus of Jews from Egypt to the Promised Land, and how, after several centuries of prosperity, the Jewish kingdoms of Israel and Judah were destroyed by the Assyrians and the Babylonians. After that the Jews were without a homeland, a people scattered over the face of the earth. Yet they always preserved a strong sense of nationhood, and from time to time dreamed of return to the Promised Land.

In 1896 Dr. Theodor Herzl, a journalist and playwright working in Vienna, expressed this national aspiration in a pamphlet entitled "The Jewish State." Such was the enthusiasm he aroused that in the following year he found himself at the head of a Zionist movement whose aim was to establish a Jewish state in Palestine. A Zionist congress met at Basle, drew up a plan of action, and formed branches among Jews in many lands.

The movement met with no sudden success, but after 1907, under the leadership of Chaim Weizmann, Zionism steadily gained strength, and more and more Jews began to settle in Palestine.

Towards the end of the First World War, when Britain conquered Palestine from the Turks, the rapidly-growing Jewish population in a mainly Arab country presented a difficult political problem. In November, 1917, the British government tried to steer a course that would satisfy both Jews and Arabs. It declared that it favored "the establishment in Palestine of a national home for the Jewish people," but at the same time insisted that nothing should be done to prejudice the rights of existing non-Jewish communities.

Although this policy was later endorsed by the League of Nations, it never worked well. As still more Jews entered Palestine, often buying Arab land, tension between Arabs and Jews increased. In 1921 and again in 1929 there were serious Arab attacks on the Jews. In 1930 and in 1933, when Britain attempted to limit Jewish immigration, the Jews retaliated first by striking, then by rioting. In May, 1939, the British government published a plan which envisaged a future independent Palestine governed jointly by Jews and Arabs, but this plan was flatly rejected by both sides.

Hitler's persecution of the Jews rendered their need for a homeland even more urgent, but when World War II ended the Arabs still resisted further Jewish immigration into Palestine. And Britain, responsible for the administration of the country as a whole, tried to limit immigration to a level that the Arabs would tolerate. But this satisfied nobody, and it was intolerable that Britain, impoverished by years of war, should not only carry the burden of keeping the peace but also incur the hatred of both sides to the dispute. So in 1947 the Palestine problem was referred to the UN, and early in 1948, with the problem still unsolved, Britain withdrew her forces.

On May 14th, 1948, the very day on which the British mandate in Palestine ended, David Ben Gurion proclaimed the Jewish state of Israel. Its first president was Chaim Weizmann, the man who had so long led the Zionist movement. The new state was immediately recognized both by the U.S.A. and the U.S.S.R. But the problem of hostility between Arabs and Jews was still not settled. There was war between Israel and the Arab League before 1948 ended, and after a number of uneasy truces hostility again flared into war at the time of the Suez crisis.

Yet, at last, after many centuries, the Jews again have a homeland of their own, and there has been a second exodus of Jews from many parts of the world to the Promised Land.

TOP LEFT: *Theodor Herzl and David Ben Gurion.* TOP RIGHT: *Palestine before 1946 and after 1948.* (H — *Haifa,* T — *Tel Aviv,* J — *Jerusalem,* J_1 — *Jaffa.*) BOTTOM: *Israeli flag and map showing places from which the second exodus to the Promised Land began in 1948. Brown figures represent immigration after independence, blue, before 1948.*

H
T
J1
J
Jo
W. GERMANY
AUSTRIA
POLAND
TURKEY
U.S.S.R.
CZECHO-SLOVAKIA
RUMANIA
IRAQ
BULGARIA
HUNGARY
AUSTRALIA
N. AFRICA
YEMEN

The Growth of Arab Unity

WHILE Turkey remained strong, Arab affairs had not greatly troubled western Europe, for the Turkish Empire embraced most of the Arab world and shouldered most of its problems. But when Turkey became the Sick Man of Europe two changes began to take place. First, certain Arab lands set up their own rulers who paid only lip-service to the Sultan; indeed, as early as 1832 Mohammed of Egypt made open war on him. Next, the great powers of Europe, fearing that changes in the Near East might threaten their colonial interests in India and East Asia, began to intervene more in Arab affairs.

By the time the First World War ended and Turkey was defeated, the Arab world was largely under European domination. Syria and Lebanon were under the tutelage of France; Palestine and Transjordan were British mandates. Egypt was a British protectorate until 1922, when she was granted her independence. But it was not until 1936, when the young King Farouk came to the Egyptian throne, that Britain confined her forces in Egypt to the Suez Canal Zone. Iraq, too, became a British mandate and Britain did not recognize her independence until 1928.

In fact the only Arab area which enjoyed real independence between the two World Wars was Saudi Arabia. This was a vast but mainly desert area of the Arabian Peninsula which King Ibn Saud had conquered and welded into a single kingdom between 1902 and 1926.

Most of the Arab world remained subordinate to western Europe until World War II. Then, quite suddenly, one country after another gained its independence. In Syria and Lebanon, French tutelage ended during the war; in Jordan, British control ended in 1946; Libya became independent in 1951, the Sudan in 1955, Morocco and Tunis in 1956. There are several reasons for these changes. First, Britain and France, which had both played a large part in Arab affairs, were weakened by war; next, world opinion was tending to condemn colonialism everywhere; and above all the sense of nationalism among the Arabs was increasing, fostered by their common language and religion.

In 1945 the kings of Egypt, Jordan, Yemen, Saudi Arabia, and Iraq, together with the presidents of Syria and Lebanon, formed the Arab League, a body powerful enough to make its voice heard in the councils of the world. From the beginning the League set itself against Zionist ambitions. It also worked strongly for the recognition of Algeria as a non-French Arab state.

Egypt, the most densely populated and most centrally situated of Arab lands, has played a leading part in the Pan-Arab movement, especially since 1954, when President Nasser seized power from General Naguib. After the Suez crisis of 1956 Nasser's prestige in the Arab world stood especially high, and in 1958 Egypt was able to persuade Syria to join her in forming the United Arab Republic, with the Yemen as an associated member. However, in 1961, Syria revolted against the domination of Nasser.

One great need of Arab lands, especially Egypt, is for irrigation schemes. For this reason Nasser wanted to erect a vast dam at Aswan. When the western powers refused to support the financing of this scheme (because it appeared that Nasser was using it to play off the U.S.S.R. against the West) Egypt threatened to nationalize the Suez Canal, and so precipitated the 1956 crisis.

One of the great assets of the Arab lands is their vast reserves of oil. Kuwait, Saudi Arabia, and Bahrain, as well as Iran, all reap a rich income from this source. This income takes the form of royalties on profits made by the foreign companies which extract and market the oil.

TOP: *King Farouk, General Naguib, President Nasser, Ibn Saud.* CENTER: *Map showing* A — *Algeria,* E — *Egypt,* I — *Iraq,* I_1 — *Iran,* K — *Kuwait,* M — *Morocco,* S — *Sudan,* L — *Lebanon,* S_1 — *Syria,* T — *Tunisia,* J — *Jordan,* L_1 — *Libya,* SA — *Saudi Arabia.* BOTTOM: *Site of Aswan* (A), *and scene a desert oilfield.*

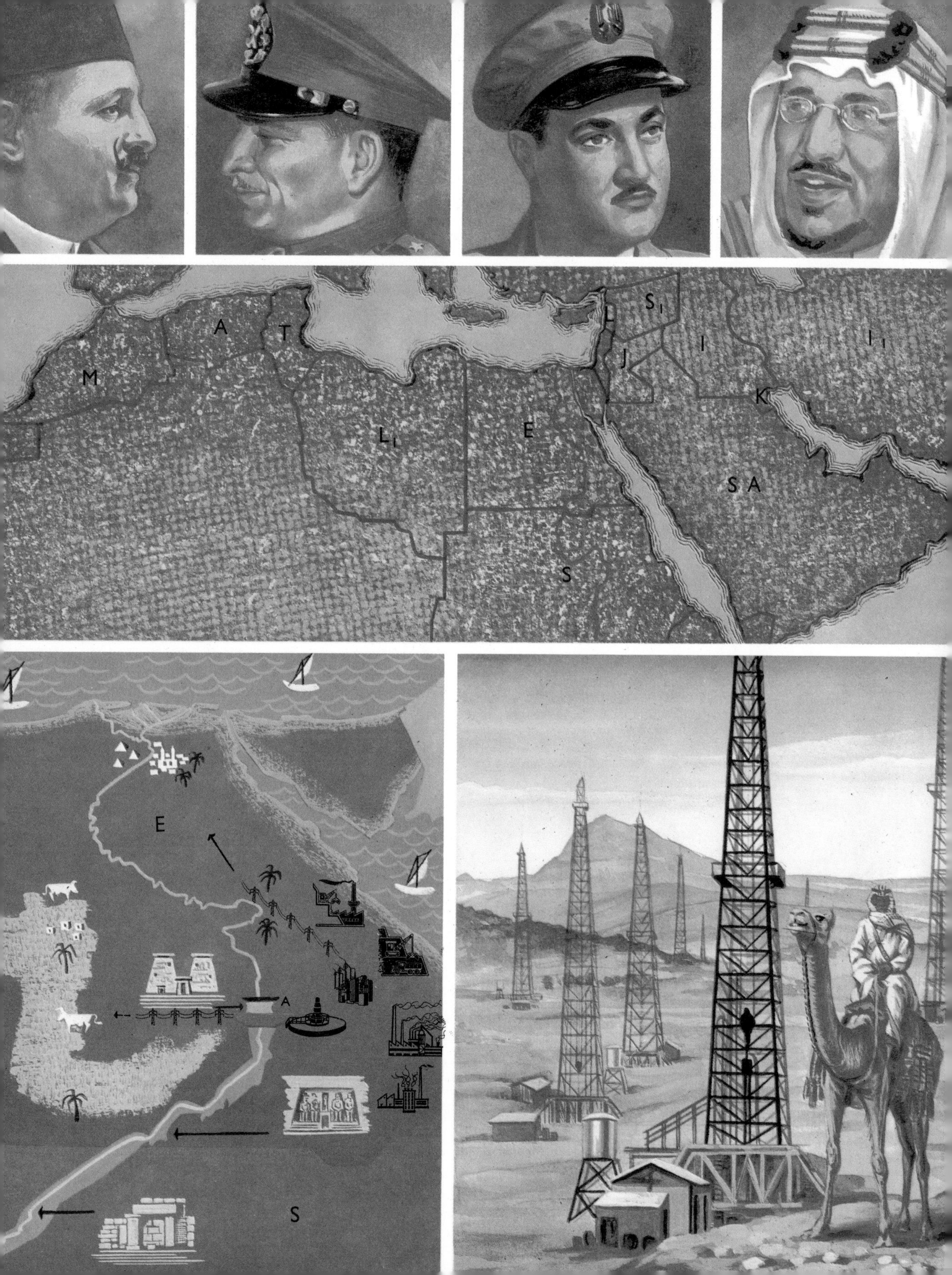

A
T
M
L
S_1
I
I_1
J
K
L_1
E
SA
S
E
A
S

The Shaping of Modern China

UNLIKE many other Asian countries, China was never submerged by nineteenth-century European imperialism. But she was under heavy pressure from the western powers, and the Manchu dynasty was also steadily declining.

In 1841 Britain was at war with China and China was forced to cede Hong Kong and to open Shanghai, Canton, and other ports to British trade. Then in 1851 natural calamities, high taxation, and the greed of landlords brought about a rebellion which lasted for thirteen years. During that time the rebel leader, Hung Hsiu-ch'uan, set up his own capital at Nanking and at one time advanced almost to Peking.

Then towards the end of the century China was involved in more wars. In 1883 she had to accept a French protectorate over Annam; in 1895 the Japanese forced her to give up Formosa and recognize the independence of Korea; and in 1896 the Russians occupied Manchuria.

By the close of the century the country was in turmoil. The Emperor, Kuang Hsu, wanted to embark on a program of reform and westernization, while the Dowager Empress led a movement to resist reform and to drive out foreigners. It was this movement, culminating in the anti-foreign Boxer Rebellion of 1900, that brought an international expedition post-haste from Europe to enforce an "open-door" policy. But though it was not clear at the time, there was one man in China more important than any royal personage. He was Sun Yat-Sen, who had already organized several secret revolutionary societies, and who had already made attempts to overthrow the Manchu dynasty.

In 1911 the revolutionary movement was successful. In the following February the boy-emperor, P'u-i, abdicated and China became a republic. After a time Sun Yat-Sen's Kuomintang party, pledged to a parliamentary system of government, became the main force in the land.

In the early 1920s the Kuomintang party, led by Sun Yat-Sen's successor, Chiang Kai-shek, admitted communists to its ranks, but within a few years it not only reversed this decision but also found itself in violent conflict with communism. This was between 1927 and 1934, when landless workers seized a great area of land in southern China, and, under the leadership of Mao Tse-tung, organized themselves on communist lines. For years China was torn by civil war between communists and anti-communists, but war with Japan, which broke out in 1937, brought about a period of national unity under Chiang Kai-shek. And when World War II ended, it was Chiang's Nationalist China that became a member of the UN with a permanent seat on the Security Council.

But real power did not long remain in Chiang's hands. In 1945 the Chinese communists took advantage of Japan's sudden collapse to seize control of most of China's northern provinces, and in 1946 civil war again swept the country. By October, 1949, the communists had gained control of all the Chinese mainland, together with the large island of Hainan. The Communist People's Republic was proclaimed at Peking, with Mao Tse-tung as Chairman and Chou En-lai as Premier. Together they were masters of a nation of 600 million people. All that remained of Nationalist China was the island of Formosa, with some ten million people, and a few small off-shore islands.

Yet Communist China is still unrepresented in the UN while Nationalist China holds a key position there. To change the representation might be construed as making a concession to superior force; and such a change would certainly weaken the voice of the western nations in the UN. But to resist the change can be construed as an attempt to ignore facts and to live in the past. The problem is one of the most difficult that the UN faces.

TOP LEFT: *Chiang Kai-shek and Madame Chiang Kai-shek.* TOP CENTER: *Sun Yat-Sen and Mao Tse-tung.* TOP RIGHT: *Map showing Peking* (P), *Nanking* (N), *Shanghai* (S), *Canton* (C), *and Hainan* (H). BOTTOM: *A youth rally in Communist China.*

P
N
S
C
H

East and West

In most major political debates today the nations of the east generally take one view and the nations of the west another.

Russia, the leading power of the eastern bloc, relies on the communist political and economic system, in which ownership and control of industry, agriculture, and transport are largely in the hands of the state, the U.S.A. operates on a different system, by which all these things are run mainly by private enterprise. The Russian system brings tremendous concentration of power into government hands, while the American system leaves more power, including the power to change the government, in the hands of ordinary citizens.

Karl Marx, father of communism, taught that the "capitalist" system was doomed to ultimate failure and that communism would eventually embrace the whole world. Many communists still hold that view, and regard it as a duty to encourage communism wherever it appears in non-communist countries. In recent years some non-communist countries have been equally ready to encourage anti-communist movements in communist countries.

During World War II, the U.S.A. and Russia fought together against the same enemy, Nazi Germany, and for a short time afterwards it seemed that they might continue to work amicably together in peacetime. But in the early postwar years many countries of eastern Europe, as well as of east Asia, turned to communist forms of government, and in the U.S.A. distaste for communism grew to new heights. On the other hand, the U.S.A. was then the only power armed with atomic weapons, and this, coupled with the American program of economic aid to nations threatened with communism, caused fear and distrust in eastern countries.

In 1948 this mutual distrust came to a crisis over the question of Berlin. Soviet troops occupied the eastern zone of Germany and the troops of America, Britain, and France the western zone. Berlin, the former capital of all Germany, lay deep in the eastern zone, but the western allies occupied a large sector of it. Following a quarrel about a proposed change of currency in west Germany, the Russian authorities attempted to blockade the city. Only by means of a great airlift, was west Berlin supplied with food and materials. After the blockade was lifted, in May, 1949, West Germany became a federal republic, with its capital at Bonn and with Dr. Konrad Adenauer as Federal Chancellor. East Germany became a "people's republic", with the eastern sector of Berlin as its capital and Otto Grotewohl as Premier. A second crisis arose over Berlin in 1961, when the Russians threatened to make a separate peace treaty with East Germany.

Since 1949 both the communist-led eastern world and the democracy-bent western world have formed their own powerful alliances. On the western side there is the North Atlantic Treaty Organization (NATO) which includes the U.S.A., Canada, Britain, Turkey, Greece, West Germany, and most countries of western Europe; there is the Baghdad Pact (now called the Central Treaty Organization), which includes Iran, Pakistan, and Turkey; there is also the South East Asia Treaty Organization (SEATO) which includes the U.S.A., Britain, France, Australia, New Zealand, Pakistan, Thailand, and the Philippines. On the eastern side, the Warsaw Pact countries include the U.S.S.R., Poland, East Germany, Czechoslovakia, Hungary, Rumania, Bulgaria, Albania, and Communist China.

Leaders of many African and Asian states have attempted to highlight a neutral viewpoint. Prominent among them were President Sukarno of Indonesia and the Indian Prime Minister, Jawaharlal Nehru.

TOP LEFT: *Communist leaders Khrushchev and Mao Tse-tung.* TOP CENTER: *Nehru and Sukarno.* TOP RIGHT: *Two architects of American and British foreign policies in postwar years, John Foster Dulles and Ernest Bevin.* CENTER: *Map showing alliances.* BOTTOM LEFT: *Adenauer and Ulbricht.* BOTTOM CENTER: *Map of the two Germanys (B – Berlin, B1 – Bonn).* BOTTOM RIGHT: *Memorial to the Berlin airlift.*

NATO
EATO
ON-MEMBERS
AGHDAD PACT
ARSAW PACT

B
B

Mankind in the Modern Age

WHEN we come to the end of a book on political history it is hard to avoid a feeling of disappointment. In the early pages we read about wars and battles of thousands of years ago. In the last few pages we read about wars and battles that our own fathers, or even we ourselves, fought in. And at the very end, when we look at our world as it is today, we find it split into two hostile groups, glowering at each other across the invisible barrier of the Iron Curtain. Are we to conclude, then, that mankind has made no real progress throughout its long history?

If that really were so, history would indeed be a dismal study, but fortunately it is not so. On the opposite page are illustrated many happenings of the past on a long scroll. It begins at the bottom of the page with events of 4000 B.C. and earlier; it ends at the top of the page with some of the outstanding happenings since A.D. 1900. We have only to compare some of the earlier pictures with some of the later ones to convince ourselves that mankind has made very real progress in many directions.

The men in the bottom picture—primitive hunters and food-gatherers—were never sure where their next meal was coming from. One night they might be lucky enough to eat and sleep in the comparative safety of a cave; the next night, after a long and unsuccessful day's hunting, they might have to sleep cold, hungry, and unprotected under the open sky.

The man in the next fold of the scroll, the farmer of about 3800 B.C., was already far better off. By day he worked with his oxen and plough or with his stone sickle in the cultivated fields, and at night he had a permanent dwelling to sleep in. Stored in his simple barn were vegetables and grain from last year's harvest. Only when drought ruined the harvest was he faced with famine. Today, although there are still large areas of the world where people are undernourished, there is rarely any actual danger of death from starvation, and some people are actually in danger of eating more than is good for them.

Again, we may look at the Viking ship in the fourth fold of the scroll and remind ourselves what fine seafaring men the Norsemen were; but even the greatest of their voyages cannot compare with the voyages of the full-rigged sailing ships and early steamships of the nineteenth century. When we look at the monk of A.D. 1000, laboring to make a single copy of one book, we have only to remember the great printing presses of today to realize what progress mankind has made in disseminating knowledge. Indeed, it needs little thought to find a score of examples of material progress.

If, however, we return to the main theme of this book—the relations between nation and nation—we have to admit that progress is less obvious. On almost every fold of our scroll are pictures of men of one country fighting men of another. And as time has passed wars have become more devastating, for a medieval knight armed with sword and shield could do nowhere near the damage of a khaki-clad soldier of 1914, armed with a machine gun; and even a regiment of 1914 machine guns had nothing like the destructive power of a single hydrogen bomb of today.

But even in the quest for peace there has been real progress. First the League of Nations and now, with more success, the UN, have encouraged nations to negotiate rather than resort to force. Next, the weapons of destruction are now so powerful that no responsible statesmen would use them except as a last resort. Third, when conflicts do arise, there is always a strong body of world opinion which seeks to limit their scope.

A scroll of history from before 4000 B.C. to the present day. Though marked at every stage with violence, it reveals real progress and offers hope of a more peaceful future for mankind.

1800
1400
1000
300
-500
-4000

In this book we have been able to look back over the thousands of years of man's recorded history and follow each stage in his progress to material prosperity. Now we stand at the end of past history and at the beginning of the future. Yet, in this age of atomic power we see the hydrogen bomb, and in an age that could mean plenty for all we see the world divided into hostile camps, a problem that must be solved, for without its solution man cannot live peacefully with man and so fully enjoy the new leisure that economic prosperity can give him. It all hangs on the cloud of emotions that fills men's minds, and that is why the greatest philosophers and prophets of all ages have concerned themselves with teaching the fundamental values essential to the well-being of humanity—love, tolerance, and goodwill between peoples.

The dignity of the individual soul and the freedom of the individual mind are ideals which all men must learn to value and respect before world-wide co-operation and understanding can become realities.

Index